ONE
MAN'S
WAR

ONE
MAN'S
WAR

THE WWII SAGA OF
TOMMY LAMORE

Tommy LaMore
and
Dan A. Baker

TAYLOR TRADE PUBLISHING

Lanham • New York • Oxford

Published by Taylor Trade Publishing
An Imprint of the Rowman & Littlefield Publishing Group
4720 Boston Way
Lanham, MD 20706
Distributed by National Book Network

Book design and composition: Barbara Werden Design. Set in Adobe Meridien.

Library of Congress Cataloging-in-Publication Data Available
0-87833-269-3

∞ The paper used in this publication meets the minimum requirements of American National Standard for Information Sciences—Permanence of Paper for Printed Library Materials, ANSI/NISO Z39.48–1992.
Manufactured in the United States of America.

To Rosa

And in the dust they raise, the combatants are lost.
HENRY FIELDING

CONTENTS

ONE

"You're a Runner, Tommy"

1

TWO

Off to War

36

THREE

Missions

54

FOUR

The Freedom Fighters

92

FIVE

Into the Arms of the Gestapo

126

SIX

Stalag Luft 4

149

SEVEN
Küstrin
178

EIGHT
The Enemy's Enemy
196

NINE
The Last Miles
227

TEN
Damgarten
239

ELEVEN
The Way Back
254

TWELVE
Homeward Bound
278

THIRTEEN
The Weariness
293

CODA
305

TOMMY'S DECORATIONS
309

ONE
MAN'S
WAR

"YOU'RE A RUNNER, TOMMY"

"You're a runner, Tommy. Remember that. You are a runner. My father was a runner in our tribe, and so was his father. It was an honor then, to run from village to village with news and messages from the chiefs. Remember that you, too, are a runner and that you should be proud."

WHEN I was a small boy my Cherokee grandmother, LaBell, told me this on the porch of our house in Waco, Texas, in 1927. It was one of the first things I heard that made an impression on me. Grandma LaBell was a very quiet person, with a big round face and a warm smile. When she said something, everyone listened, because when she spoke it was important. And she was right. I did love to run as a boy. To run made me feel proud.

My mother's family was descended from a Cherokee tribe who had survived the "Trail of Tears," the forced march of 1838 that killed thousands of Cherokees. My father's family was French Canadians who settled in the bayou country of Louisiana, where I was born in 1920. I never knew my father. He left our family when I was small, and my mother remarried. That's when we moved to Waco, Texas, where we lived in a small white house. I remember the wind in the gnarled oak tree in the front yard and the lightning storms. I asked everyone what lightning was, but no one seemed to know. It bothered me that grown-ups didn't know what lightning was.

My home life was very unhappy. There were a lot of problems and arguments. Sometimes my stepfather would come home late and shout at my mother. I knew this hurt her, and it made me feel afraid and angry, but there was nothing I could do. I did everything I could to stay away from home, and I became independent very early.

WHEN I was about ten, there was a big change in everyone around me. People became very worried. They talked about jobs all the time. I heard, "How am I going to feed my family?" over and over. It was as though a big dark cloud had settled over the country, soaking everyone in worry and despair. The Great Depression was settling in.

My family was as bad off as everyone else. Although we didn't like the idea of taking charity, there just wasn't enough food in the house. On Saturday mornings, I was sent out to the Cotton Palace Fairgrounds to pick up government relief food. I walked four miles to stand in a long line of sullen people. I hated every minute of it. Everyone felt embarrassed to be seen there. It was either hot and dusty or cold and wet. You could see people squirming with the indignation of it all, and the defeat and helplessness I felt standing in that line really affected me. I didn't feel like I belonged there. I swore then that I would never stand in any damn dusty line of hungry people again. Never.

I finally found a job selling magazines door to door in Waco. I sold *Liberty* and *The Saturday Evening Post* for ten cents a copy. As tight as money was, people still needed some diversion, and magazines were just about the cheapest thing around. It was a lot of hours and endless walking to make a few cents, but it was my first money, and it kept me out of the house. After a while the walking seemed longer, and the money seemed smaller. I started looking and listening for another way to make money—and sure enough, there it was, bright as a dime, and only ninety-three million miles away.

The Spanish called Texas the "land of many lands" and said that the scorching sun was unlike anything in Spain. They said the Texas heat in summer punished men and animals until they were withered, brown bags of skin. They cautioned Spanish soldiers and men of God alike to "seek shelter and relief from the harsh heat." Earl's Dairy and Ice Cream Company in Waco agreed with the Spanish and saw a market there.

I bought ice cream bars from Earl's at forty cents a dozen and sold them around Waco all day at five cents a bar. I walked to the pool halls and domino parlors that were very popular then, and I made sure I showed up at about the same time every day. The men who were winning bought my ice cream bars. I sometimes made as much as $3.00 a day. At a time when construction workers were making about $2.50 a day, that was big money for a ten-year-old kid.

It made me feel ten feet tall to be able to give my family money. "Thank you so much, Tommy. You're such a big help now in all this trouble." Mom always said the same thing when I gave her my money. She always kissed my forehead and held me for a minute. I felt proud.

I had a paper route, too. I found I could cover it best by running with my papers, kind of loping along easy so I wouldn't get winded. People would say to me, "Where's your bicycle, son? You're gonna wear out your legs that way!" I guess I did look a little funny, but I just loved to run.

I USED to run out to Rich Field, a municipal and Army flying field about a mile outside of town. I loved to watch the planes come in and take off. You could see the flames coming out of the exhaust pipes when they took off, and the sound of those motors would stay in my mind for days. Flying was still very new then, even after World War I, and certain planes and aviators were as famous then as the astronauts and moon landings were in the sixties. I knew every plane type, and I watched every move of the pilots. I admired their cocksure confidence, their upbeat "can-do" attitude. I tried to understand what they were saying when they talked about airplanes. I read everything I could to learn what words like "ailerons" and "nacelles" meant.

I carved my own balsa wood model airplanes, a whole squadron, and carefully hung them on strings in front of our big fan and got them to fly straight. I read every *Tailspin Tommy* comic strip in the papers. Tommy was a barnstormer who rescued damsels in distress with his roaring biplane.

I made sure everyone knew I loved airplanes, too, including my Uncle Jim. Uncle Jim was a big, soft-spoken man who was nice to everyone and would spend a lot of time talking to me when he didn't have to. I wished he was my dad.

One sunny spring morning when I was about twelve, Uncle Jim walked into the house and said, "Get your coat, Tommy! We're going to go flying in a big Ford Tri-Motor." Flying? Me? I was so excited I could hardly breathe. The new Ford Tri-Motor was the greatest thing airborne. It was in all the newsreels, and to actually go flying . . . I don't think I got more than one arm in my coat until we got to the airfield.

There was a big crowd there, and people were all dressed up in their best clothes. It was clear and windy, and from the road we could see the big new airplane glistening in the sun. The Ford Tri-Motor was one of the first all-metal monoplanes, and the single wing was really big. It was built with corrugated aluminum, which was a new metal then, and people had trouble saying the word. Uncle Jim called it "aliminum." Henry Ford had built the Tri-Motor, and some people were saying that everyone would have one in a few years. I couldn't wait.

I finally worked my way through the crowd and got right up to the plane. It was beautiful. I couldn't move my head fast enough to see every little part of the plane. I walked all around it and told people what they called the tail and the parts that moved on the wing. "You sure know them airplanes, son. Sounds like you're selling 'em," one man said, and everyone laughed. Not many people in 1930 knew that a plane's tail was really a "horizontal stabilizer."

It cost a lot of money in those days to go flying. When we stepped into the group that was boarding the plane, I just about burst with pride. We tried not to look at the other folks. We all knew they wanted to go, too. Uncle Jim buttonholed a man in a business suit on the plane and asked him if I could sit by the window. I wished so hard and clenched my fists so tight that my knuckles turned white. It must have showed, because he stood up a little reluctantly and gave me the window seat. I slipped into his seat about one whole second after he left it and glued my face to the big square window. I could see the ailerons moving on the wing and the pilot moving the tail. We were going to fly.

When the big motors started up, the vibration and noise surprised everyone. All the excited talking stopped, and all the women looked around nervously. Even I wondered if the motors were supposed to be so loud. "Cotton balls for your ears, cotton balls for your ears. . . ." The young stewardess walked down the aisle, earplugs in her hands.

"Oh, no ma'am, I like the noise just fine," I said.

When the pilot opened up the throttles and the roaring power pushed us back into our seats, it took my breath away. The power was so exhilarating I could hardly stay quiet. I felt a long scream of joy taking shape in my throat, but I stayed quiet.

When the chattering of the wheels on the runway gave way to the whistling smoothness of the air, I changed as a person. I was in love. Every movement of the plane filled me with excitement. To see the ground slipping away below, to see big buildings and long roads suddenly become small, to see the brown hills fall into the land around them and to look straight at a cloud . . . that feeling of wonder and lightness has never left me.

The pilot banked the plane around in a steep turn after takeoff, which surprised us passengers. Everyone *oohed* when we winged over. I couldn't stay quiet any longer. "Uncle Jim, Uncle Jim . . ." was all I could say. When we leveled off at about five thousand feet, the passengers relaxed a little and took turns at all the windows—except mine.

I could see Lake Waco. I could see the hills and the outline of the land and the clouds miles away. The sunlight on the tops of the clouds looked like the pictures of heaven in the Sunday school books. Everyone seemed carefree and excited and started talking away, even to people they didn't know.

I could see the pilot moving the controls, and I could feel the plane respond. Everything came together for me then. How my balsa planes worked and how the big plane worked was clear to me now. But I still squeezed the seat cushion flat every time the pilot winged over. I could never have imagined before how it must feel to fly, no matter how hard I tried. Now I knew. I knew right then that this was for me. I didn't really know how I would do it, but I knew flying was what I wanted to do.

I inhaled everything that day—the power of the engines; the unfathomable complexity of the cockpit; the exhilaration of lifting off; the heady, almost arrogant, feeling of being above it all; and the clutching fear of landing.

The pilot actually talked to me after we landed, and he was like a god to me. He was tall, with dark, wavy hair and a big smile for everyone. "What do you think of the Tri-Motor, sonny?" he said.

"Well, I think it flies just grand, and those motors sure have a lot of power!" I said.

All the passengers thanked him, and you could tell everyone looked up to this man. He was a pilot. A man of the future.

That's the day I became a flyer.

It was hard to get back to work after that. There wasn't much excitement in those hardscrabble days, and you really had to make the special times last. Every time I heard an airplane motor, my heart jumped and I could see myself up there, flying along on an important mission in my leather coat and goggles. When I flew my model planes, I knew how it felt to take off and to wing over. I could feel the floor beneath my feet fall away when I pulled up, and I even felt a little knot of fear when I landed my planes on the couch.

THERE WAS a bit of local excitement during that time. A couple of weeks after my Tri-Motor flight, my stepfather took us to get a hamburger at a little roadside place on Speight Street in Waco. Going out to eat was a big occasion during the depression. While we were waiting for our food, I saw the waitress bus a messy table. There was a half of a piece of peach cobbler left on a plate. Everyone noticed that.

We had just gotten our food when my stepfather leaned over to us and said quietly, nodding his head slightly toward another table, "There's Bonnie and Clyde, Clyde Barrow and Bonnie Parker." We all stretched our necks and looked and looked. Clyde was kind of funny looking, but Bonnie was very pretty and wore an expensive pink sweater. I wanted to go over and meet them, but we knew you weren't supposed to notice them. I made up an excuse of needing a glass of water and walked by their table. To my surprise, both Bonnie and Clyde smiled broadly and said hello. I had never seen anyone famous before, and the excitement around them was a new thrill for me. When I looked at them, I wondered what would happen to them, and I felt a strange, far-away feeling.

Several years later at the Texas State Fair, I would spend hours looking at the new V-8 Ford they were killed in. It was heart-breaking to see such a beautiful car all shot up like that. The interior was still bloodstained, and when the women would stick their heads in the window they would jump right back and hold their hands over their mouths. Seeing the blood really got to me. I felt sorry for Bonnie, especially—she seemed like a nice person to me.

WHEN I was about thirteen, my home life became unbearable. I had saved about $1.50, and I decided to leave and go to West Texas, because there were supposed to be lots of cowboys and action out there. I just walked out of the house one day and left. I hitchhiked all night and was let off in the little town of Cisco, Texas, about ninety-five miles west of Fort Worth on the way to Abilene.

Just before eight o'clock in the morning I walked into the Red Front Drugstore, which looked like the nerve center of the town. I ordered coffee and tried to sit up real straight and look as old as I could. A man named Joe Lee Moore, the owner, noticed me right away and knew I was from out of town. He was a soft-spoken, kind man who treated me like a grown-up. When I told him I was traveling west, he knew I had run away. I tried to present myself as an honest, clean-living person who just wanted a job and a place to call home. When I asked about work in the area, he paused, then said, "Well, one of my drugstore assistants just left here to join the Army. Might be a job right here for you. Can't never tell." I must have looked like a puppy when the dishes are scraped, because Joe just handed me an apron the next minute.

I worked hard in the drugstore. I helped out behind the soda counter, stocked shelves, and did a lot of the cleaning. I rented a nice little room in the attic of the high school principal's house the next day, then enrolled in Cisco High School. Everyone in Cisco just automatically helped me in those first few days, and it seemed like I belonged there.

I enjoyed being right in the center of small-town life, and I rapidly got to know just about everyone in town. I read the papers every day, all I wanted. I followed the career of Wiley Post, the famous one-eyed aviator who was born in Texas. It seemed like he was setting a new record every week, and his planes were really special—and fast looking. Wiley's Lockheed Vega looked like a rocket to me. The *Winnie Mae* was in the newsreels all the time, especially after Wiley set a record for flying around the world in eight days in 1931. That feat really impressed the customers.

"I just can't hardly believe a man can fly the whole way 'round the world in a week's time," they'd say. "Can't hardly be so. Joe here says you know a lot about this flying business. Just how fast do them airplanes fly, son?"

I tried hard not to seem excited when I answered the questions. "Well, Wiley Post's Lockheed Vega will cruise real easy at about two hundred knots; that's faster than miles per hour by a little bit, you know, so she'll fly along at around two hundred and fifty miles per hour."

"Two hundred fifty miles per? Man, that's agoin', that is." They'd shake their heads in disbelief. I liked being an expert.

One of the benefits of working at the drugstore was access to the magazine and newspaper racks. I read all I could and learned a lot. I found myself becoming interested in the political life of the nation, and I began to form opinions. I listened to the discussions at the lunch counter and found that people could look at something a lot of different ways. There were some people who seemed to get very excited, and they would say some stupid things. I learned that these people generally knew the least about the issues they were talking about.

People felt like they were a part of the government then, like it belonged to them, and they cared about what was happening. As heated as some of these discussions got, you never heard people run the government down. We respected our government, and everyone wanted President Roosevelt to succeed. I thought Roosevelt's NRA and WPA programs were good. They offered us a chance to work our way out of the depression instead of borrowing our way out.

I started high school that fall. Cisco High seemed to be a good school. We studied civics and American history, along with everything else, but somehow they seemed to mean something special. We learned how the philosophical principles that led to the Constitution were formed as a response to generations of leaders abusing power and riding roughshod over people in Europe. We learned how tough it was for the early Americans to stand up to King George and beat the British army with a bunch of untrained farmers in 1776, when no one, but no one, beat the British at anything. We learned that, no matter how poor or uneducated you were, in our country you had rights, and the government had to respect those rights.

We learned that you could make anything you wanted to out of your life, and you could keep what was yours. Above all, we learned that this was our country, and the government was ours. We felt involved, and we felt proud.

One source of national pride came from an unexpected quarter for most Americans that year.

I began to notice the career of Jesse Owens, the runner, around 1934. I followed his success with great interest, because I was just starting track at school. Sometimes I thought I was the only person in the country interested in running. When Jesse Owens made the 1936 American Olympic track team and then won four gold medals in Berlin, the whole country cheered. For a runner to become an international celebrity was just unheard of. Boxers and baseball players, sure, but for a runner, this was new. That inspired me to develop my running.

Jesse Owens inadvertently brought something else to the world's attention in 1936—the evil ideology that the Nazis were bringing to Europe. When Hitler publicly refused to acknowledge or even shake hands with Jesse Owens after he won his gold medals, I think all Americans felt like they had been slapped in the face. Everyone saw the newsreels and even people who didn't think much of blacks felt the insult. I was enraged. I knew how hard you had to work to excel as a runner, and to see the leader of a modern country insult a man like that in front of all those people, well, it got to me.

People began to pay attention to the Nazis after that, and it seemed like there was an endless river of news stories about Hitler and his march to power. The Nazis looked arrogant and just plain mean from the very beginning. Their uniforms made them look like they wanted to be superior to the rest of the world. You could tell they were a bad bunch just by looking at them.

The rest of Europe was terrified of the Nazis and what was coming, but many Americans were sure it would never involve us. The American neutrality movement was very powerful then, and many Americans were still disgusted about all our men killed in World War I. There was a widespread feeling that we would stay out of any future wars in Europe, and Roosevelt couldn't get anything out of Congress to prepare us for a war, even if it came. "If the damned Europeans want to blow each other all to hell for nothin' again, I say let 'em. But they can sure as hell do it without killin' our boys." I heard a lot of comments like that at the counter. Unfortunately, that distaste for war played right into Hitler's hands.

The national radio networks would broadcast Hitler's speeches on the radio once in a while and translate what he said as he ranted. You could walk down the street and hear the broadcast from houses as you passed by, that shrill, relentless voice screaming out into the streets. He kept telling the Germans they were a chosen people and that they deserved to run the world. Hitler was always angry, always yelling, but in a lovely little town like Cisco, it all seemed so far away.

I loved Cisco. There was a beautiful lake, a roller-skating rink, and a city-owned country club where we school kids danced to a big jukebox with colored lights. That was my scene when I was in high school, and I felt included. I caddied at the golf course for extra money, and I worked on my running. I won some events and set several school records in track. I was a runner. I sometimes heard my Grandma LaBell's words when I ran.

We had a beautiful hotel in Cisco called the Laguna. I started there as a bellhop and was promoted to the night clerk's job. At night I had time to listen to the radio, which was throbbing with the new big band sound. It was a larger-than-life, brassy, confident sound that people couldn't get enough of. The music was so vibrant and new and happy. You were sure the depression was coming to an end and better days were ahead when you heard those bands.

In the newsreels and in magazine pictures we saw many of the farmers leaving the dust bowl. Decades of agriculture on the plains had worn out the soil and created dust storms that billowed into Cisco like giant tidal waves of hot dirt and air. They were huge, reddish-brown clouds that changed color as they approached. When they passed over, the sun would look like a red moon, and it would get so dark the chickens would go to roost.

This was a new experience, and no one knew if it would ever stop. When you stood there and watched those towering clouds bearing down on you, you realized life could be pretty frightening sometimes. A lot of danger can come out of the sky.

I was a senior at Cisco High School in 1938 when President Roosevelt began to tell the country that a military draft might become necessary. We all spent a lot of time talking about the draft and how it would affect us. Like all teenagers, we were an independent-minded group, or thought we were. None of us wanted our decisions made for us.

I knew one thing for sure: I didn't want someone deciding that I was going to be a soldier in the cold mud and rain and hand-to-hand combat. I had seen several Hollywood movies about World War I, and the misery of trench warfare terrified me. If there was a war coming, I wanted to do my fighting in the air, in a clean uniform. None of us really knew what war was, but a little preview wasn't far off.

■ ■ ■

THE RED Front Drugstore was busy as usual on the evening of June 17, 1938. I was getting ready to close the store and thinking about going home to study. Earlier, we had heard a very distant low rumble, but we thought maybe it was blasting for road building. Just past nine o'clock the phone rang. Joe Lee Moore started talking very loudly and rapidly. I heard, "Yes, yes we can," and "We'll bring all we have." Then he hung up and hollered over to me. "We've got to close the store real quick, Tommy. A big tornado just hit Clyde, and we have to get over there right away!"

We packed bandages and tape and antiseptics into Joe's old blue Ford and drove off to Clyde. When we got close to Clyde, the air turned very still, and there were dark clouds that seemed like they were solid black. "Do you think many people are hurt?" I asked. Joe just shook his head and tried to get a little more speed out of the Ford. As we drove into what was left of Clyde, everything changed. The air was heavy and wet like an invisible fog, and the ground was covered with hail and long wood splinters. The light seemed strangely subdued and sounds were muted.

People were standing in small groups, shivering and looking from side to side. They stared at us with a look I had never seen before. Their eyes were open wide, but it was like they were not seeing, like they were looking past us. Their faces were twisted and hollow. They were sobbing so loudly it seemed amplified, and small groups of women were holding each other and crying. As we drove in, I saw white sheets everywhere, on both sides of the road and for blocks around. They covered bodies of the dead. There were people sitting beside many of the bodies, rocking back and forth on the rain-soaked ground. I looked at Joe, who just shook his head. "That's bad," he said, so softly I barely heard him.

The county highway department set up floodlights for us to work, and we bandaged and treated as many people as we could.

The injured formed ragged lines and moaned as they waited. There were a lot of deep cuts that were full of dirt and pieces of wood and glass. I held the tape and bandages for Joe and tried to clean the cuts with a towel soaked in alcohol. I thought the sting of the alcohol would hurt them, but it didn't. They were just numb.

It took me a long time to realize that everyone was soaking wet and shivering from the cold. This made it hard to treat the wounds, because the children were shivering violently. When they were handed to us, there were small slender bruises on their arms from being held so tightly. Their mothers could hardly let go of them for treatment, but these were the lucky ones.

I saw two women wandering in the debris, looking every-where, sobbing loudly and shaking their heads slowly from side to side. They were shoeless and bloody and completely devastated by the loss of their babies. They called in weak, hoarse voices that drifted all around us. "Katie . . . Katie . . . where are you, Katie?" The other women gently tried to stop them from stumbling through the smashed houses in the darkness, but they went on looking.

We worked all through the night. The loud piercing sirens of the ambulances never stopped once. There was a shortage of doctors in West Texas then, and for a lot of people we were it. I felt utterly helpless. People were crying out loudly for help, grabbing at me and holding on to me, but all I knew how to do was unload bandages, treat small wounds, and get water.

"Water, water, water. . . ." The word came out of the darkness all around me in croaks and shaking whispers. The little white paper cups we had were held so tightly by many of the people that all the water spilled out of them as they shivered.

I helped move bodies later that night. I never thought I would see so many people broken and mangled in my life. You can't help but look into the faces of the dead, even though you try not to. I wondered then about life and what it really is, because when it ends, when it goes out of a person, the change is so complete.

That night I changed. The world became larger, and I became smaller.

Joe Moore was everywhere at once, giving people just what they needed. He knew what shock was, and he knew which patients should be lying down with their feet elevated and, with his big hands in the dim light, he quickly closed and sutured cuts that were spurting blood. I desperately wanted to help, but all I could do was bring supplies to Joe and try to keep blankets on the moaning people all around me.

When we finally drove out of Clyde about seven the next morning, I wanted to feel good about what I had done, but all I thought about were the people I couldn't help. It seemed like it took forever to get back to Cisco. I wanted to say something to Joe, about how I wished I could have done more, but neither of us said anything.

When people at the drugstore asked about the tornado, I found I just couldn't say much. The emotion I felt that night welled up in me, and all I could say was, "It was bad." Joe was right.

A FEW days later, the tornado experience hit me like a double whammy. That inadequate, helpless feeling washed over me again. I wanted to be there for people like that in the future, to somehow get what it takes to help people. I decided to become a doctor.

In those years only rich kids could go to college, and even thinking about medical school for someone without a wealthy family was just unheard of. But I'd learned one thing on the streets of Waco. I learned that there are always ways to get what you want—if you have the desire and the guts to ignore everyone who says no.

Baylor University and Medical School gave everyone in the Waco area a lot of pride. The school had an excellent reputation, and more importantly, a winning football team. About all I had to offer Baylor was a high school degree and several documented seasons as a Baylor Bears football fan. But I figured it couldn't hurt to ask. I hoped maybe my track records would interest the athletic department.

That fall, on a windy, cold Monday, I caught a ride to Baylor with a friend of Joe Moore's. The president of Baylor was Mr. Pat Neff, a former governor of Texas and a man larger than life. I didn't quite know where to start, so I just went to his office and asked to see him. The secretaries told me that you didn't just walk in and ask the president of the university if you could attend the school without funds, but I just refused to leave. I kept standing there and sitting there all day, and the two days after that. I became a low-intensity nuisance, because I couldn't think of anything else to do. I was desperate.

When Pat Neff finally walked in on the third day, you could tell he was the man in charge. He had poise and a warm manner that brought a smile to everyone. I asked him if I could speak with him. He looked at me, smiled, and led me into his office. Those typewriters all stopped at the same time.

I told him how much I wanted to go to Baylor, and I pleaded more than asked if there wasn't some way I could work my way through. I tried not to blurt out my experiences in Clyde, but it came out anyway, with more emotion than I wanted. I felt kind of dumb, but I said what I had come to say.

Mr. Neff was a compassionate man who seemed to be impressed with my drive and sincerity. He tapped his thumb on the desk for a long time and looked out the window.

"Maybe we could get you started by having you attend some first-year classes on an audit basis and see how you do." All I heard was "get you started." Mr. Neff worked out an informal plan for me, where I could attend classes at Baylor and also work for the university in the grounds department. He sent me to the YMCA to attend classes in first-aid treatment and public health. He seemed to be a man who would bend over backwards to help someone, and I think what I told him about the Clyde tornado meant something to him. I floated out of that office past those startled secretaries and swore to give my opportunity at Baylor everything I had.

My Aunt Florence gave me a room in her house in Waco. The other kids in my classes didn't know what to think of me. I wasn't enrolled, but I was a student. They were all from well-off families, and they sure knew I wasn't, but they didn't snub me too badly. I had three shirts, and I pressed one every morning before class, which helped some.

The YMCA classes in first aid were excellent. We learned a lot about diseases like typhoid and diphtheria and how modern medicine had conquered them. I was able to contribute a lot to the classes because of my work at the drugstore. I knew a little about medicines and what problems they were made for.

My days and weeks were full. Every day was packed with work, classes, potting plants, setting up the football field, and digging through books. I had a small dictionary that I almost wore out that year. Man, were there ever a lot of words I didn't know.

Finding the money to formally attend Baylor slowly came to occupy my every waking moment. There were very few scholar-

ships in those days and almost no aid to education. There wasn't a
chance for any support from my family, and in the last years of
the depression it seemed like all the money in the world had been
sucked into some big hole.

I WAS just completing my first informal year at Baylor in 1939
when the war news reached a new intensity. The first stories
about Nazi atrocities were coming out of Poland, and there was
a lot of discussion about what America would do if the Nazis
invaded England. About all we could do was wave good-bye. The
news from Asia was bad, too. The Japanese were rolling over
Manchuria, and they had the biggest fleet of warships in the
world.

Poland was the first country to really fight the Germans. Their
antiquated army was quickly chewed up by the Wehrmacht, but
the people of Warsaw held out for three weeks. Everyone followed the story, mostly on the radio. The Germans had these big
240mm siege guns that pounded Warsaw night and day for three
weeks. We saw some pictures and newsreels of the terrified, battered people of Warsaw. I saw some footage of a young Polish
woman, very pretty, sitting on a street in Warsaw, bleeding badly
and shaking her head from side to side as the dust and fires
swirled around her. The memories of Clyde slammed back to me,
and I got my first glimpse of the true nature of war. It was just like
Clyde. Darkness, crying, bewildered people, blood, broken glass,
fear, and crushed bodies that would never be people again. I had
to leave the theater.

My nightmare of ending up as an infantry soldier became
unbearable. The draft was coming for sure now. There were long
war stories every day in the papers. I wasn't enrolled in Baylor as
an official student, and I was slowly coming to grips with the fact

that I just wouldn't be able to get the tuition. I made a halfhearted run at joining the Navy, but I couldn't make the minimum weight requirement, even after stuffing myself with bananas and water. I was just small for my age. I was well muscled and kind of wiry, but I was just short, and I didn't weigh much.

For a while I had been seeing a girl in Cisco named Mary Helen Whitfield. She was interested in joining the newly formed Women's Air Force Service Pilots Corps. We'd met when I was a junior at Cisco High. We shared a love of flying, and she was very excited about joining the WASPs. This got me to thinking about my future, and my boyhood love of airplanes suddenly filled me with excitement. I could fly! I could join the Army Air Corps and become a pilot.

Roosevelt announced plans to train fifty thousand pilots in May of 1940, and the programs were open to everyone. In the early summer I took a bus to Randolph Field just outside San Antonio and took the test for the Army Air Corps Cadet program. They were a lot more interested in my educational level than my weight, and I passed. I was on my way to becoming an Army Air Corps pilot! Getting accepted into the Air Cadet program was a big deal. Many young men didn't pass the tests, which were tough. My classes at Baylor helped me.

When they posted the test results on the bulletin board, all the guys who passed immediately formed a group and started talking.

"I'm going to get my wings chromed so they knock the eyes outta the girls."

"Do we get uniforms right away?"

"Man, I can't wait to crank up that Wright and fly, baby, fly!"

"I'm gettin' a white scarf. I want a white scarf."

Everyone had a big statement to make, but I didn't say much, I just looked at my name on the list.

We didn't want to waste any time seeing if our new status as

Air Cadets would impress the local ladies, so we all got together about seven o'clock that night and headed into San Antonio. Daryl was a tall, rough-looking guy from Abilene. He had his own car, an old black Ford touring car with no top and bald tires. He screeched up to the curb and picked us up without stopping. I made a headlong dive into the back seat, and we were off. Bobby, a tall, lanky kid from Odessa, was sitting next to me shouting, "I'm goin' straight for the fighter program, right from the start. Fighters! I'm gonna learn everything there is to know about them new fighters. Man, are those instructors gonna be impressed!" We were all really pumped up. We were Air Cadets!

We had driven about ten minutes when Daryl swerved to miss something on the road and rolled the car. We slammed into the embankment so hard I was knocked out for a few minutes. When I came to, I was pinned under the car. I could just hear the boys yelling, "Tommy! Tommy!" over the buzz in my ears. They lifted the car off me, and I sat with my back to the car for a long time, trying to breathe.

"Take a deep breath and hold it!" The doctor shouted at me as he taped my rib cage. It felt like knives were being pushed into me every time I breathed. Sharp, long knives. My face and hands were badly skinned up where I had slid along the pavement. I felt like I had been dragged through a hedge backwards, but the worst was yet to come.

"The Flight Surgeon has advised me that your injuries will preclude you from the Air Cadet training program for at least six months. He also advises that your injuries may affect your piloting ability for a period of one year. We'll have to wash you out of this class, Cadet." The next morning the CO (commanding officer) said this while looking directly at me, like a stern father. You need breath to argue, and I was still in pain, so I just nodded my head.

Washed out before the first day of class. Six months to a year as a civilian when the draft started. I was so low all I could do was sit down and hope the roof didn't collapse on me. I walked into the recruiter's office next door and found an empty, padded office chair. I was devastated, broke, injured, and jobless.

"You're lookin' like you already done went a few rounds with ol' Mr. Hitler," the sergeant said in a thick Mississippi drawl.

I was sitting in his chair. "I sure feel like I did, and I feel like he won. I suppose now I'll get drafted," I said in a whisper.

"Well, son, you ain't gonna make pilot school here for some while, but them boys over yonder at Brooks Field, they're doin' their damnedest to recruit men for ground crews. You go over and talk to Sergeant Fryer, and you tell him Ernie done sent ya," he said. "And get outta my damn chair."

Fortunately for me, Brooks Field was right next door, and Ernie was right. They looked at my files and signed me up on the spot. "You can fix airplanes with broken ribs," the recruiter said. In thirty minutes I was in the U.S. Army Air Corps.

Colonel Stanton T. Smith, the base commander, looked like a Hollywood movie star. He was tall, with silver hair; dark, bushy eyebrows; and flinty blue eyes. He told me there were several possibilities for me at Brooks Field. They were opening an armament school, and they needed men who could think for themselves to help set up the school. That sounded good enough to me. I was sure I could get back into pilot training the following year.

I went to Lowry Field in Colorado for three months of training in small arms, machine guns, and explosives. We learned how to fabricate explosives from rifle ammunition powder and how to fuse and detonate all types of charges, including booby traps. I didn't think I would ever need this kind of training in the Air Corps, but I learned all I could anyway.

Our instructor was a grizzled veteran of WWI who had also

chased Pancho Villa around Mexico with General Pershing. Master Sergeant Jenkins was a tall, wiry old bird. He walked kind of crooked and wore a constant white stubble that he seemed proud of. He had a strange way of talking to some of the men and not talking to others.

"Explosives want to go off, and they want to kill you and the men around you. You either pay good attention to what you are doing every time you handle the materials or you, and the men with you, will be blown up and killed." He started every session with the exact same words. Some listened, some didn't. In our last week, three men were killed on the range. It wasn't really a very big explosion, but it was big enough.

I went back to Brooks Field and helped set up the armament department. I taught small arms and machine gun maintenance to the Air Cadets. The new Browning machine guns were beautifully designed and very simple to strip and clean. The Cadets needed to know the range and fire rate of the guns on their planes, but it went in one ear and out the other.

It was hard for me to hear them talking about the flying and the planes. I just swallowed hard and figured I would be there next year. At least I was in the Air Corps and around planes.

I looked forward to the flying time and flew in anything I could. I flew in the North American BC-1, a snappy fixed-landing-gear combat trainer that was the forerunner to the AT-6 and the graceful top-wing North American O-46 observation plane. If it was going up and I could get in it, I did. The thrill of flying hadn't left me. I absorbed every moment of flying, from the wild washing machine vibration of takeoff to the tense floating mo-ments before landing.

I was really excited when Colonel Smith sent me to Eagle Pass, Texas, to set up a target towing operation for the advanced Cadet program. The importance of gunnery skills for fighter pilots was becoming clear, and they wanted the Cadets to have as much real shooting experience as possible. We jury-rigged an electric reel in an AT-6 trainer to tow targets. I sat in the back seat and operated the target reel. The target had to be reeled in for takeoffs and landings, and the towing distance had to be right, so we marked the cable with bright red paint at 150 yards.

We towed a white banner about five feet wide and about fifteen feet long behind the plane at a distance of 150 yards. The pilots were supposed to fly in at a designated angle, about ninety degrees, and shoot at the target. We scored their runs by counting the holes in the target. They painted the bullets of each plane a different color, which stayed on the cloth when the rounds punched through. It seemed easy. One hundred fifty yards seemed safe.

We learned quickly that the shooting scores were very important to the Cadet pilots. They learned quickly that if they flew on a more parallel track to the tow plane, they got a longer firing pass. This put the tow plane at considerable risk as these pilots were green and often began firing too soon, which peppered the tow plane with machine gun fire. I knew someone was going to get hurt if they didn't clamp down on the Cadets, and I raised all the hell I could over this, but no one seemed to listen.

THE BIG excitement in those months was the arrival of the first of the new Boeing B-17s. Everyone knew that aerial bombardment was going to be a big part of modern wars, and there was a race in the late thirties to produce long-range bombers. The British were developing the huge four-engine Lancaster, and the Germans had settled on the fast twin-engine Heinkel HE-111. When people first saw the American response, the Boeing B-17, there was world-wide excitement. It was the biggest plane in the world, and it could fly faster, higher, and farther than anything in the air. And the pilots loved it. It was great to fly, tough and very reliable. It was an American plane in every way.

The big debate concerned how airpower would be used. Most people said that the bombers would have to be escorted to the targets by fighters, or opposing enemy fighters would simply shoot them out of the air. But the Army Air Corps believed that you could build a plane with enough firepower and build it tough enough to literally fight its way to the target and back. This was a revolutionary idea, and there were many skeptics, not the least of which was the Luftwaffe.

When they called the B-17 the "Flying Fortress," it was an idea that fired people's imagination. To think you could build an airplane so tough and rigged up with so many guns that it could fight off fighter planes really amazed the whole world. The B-17 was a statement airplane from the Americans, and it talked big.

Colonel Smith sent for me on a blustery November morning and casually asked me if I wanted to go on a B-17 ferry mission to the Philippines. I couldn't talk at first. Fly in the new B-17? To the Pacific? Me? I just smiled, tried not to drool, and said, "Why, yes, I would, sir. Very much indeed, sir. I would that like much very, sir."

I caught an early morning flight out to California. The B-17 sitting on the concrete tarmac at Hamilton Field in California looked bigger and tougher than its pictures. It was as advertised: a Flying Fortress.

The pilots were all talking about its revolutionary new electrical system, which made it a dream to fly and was supposed to be tough to knock out. They had just begun fitting .50-caliber Browning machine guns to the B-17, which gave it tremendous punch and range. We had shot up some oil drums with a water-cooled version of these new guns in Colorado, and they were impressive. The new "high-tech" Pratt and Whitney radial engines gave the B-17 an operational ceiling of 35,000 feet, which seemed halfway to outer space and which required oxygen masks for the crew.

I helped with the installation of the bomb bay fuel tanks and sat in on the navigation briefings at Hamilton Field. The fuel was very carefully calculated, and there were lots of discussions of factors such as headwinds and the loss of an engine or a turbocharger.

We finally lifted off from Hamilton Field on a perfectly clear, windless day in November 1941. The B-17 was a powerful plane that climbed easily, almost effortlessly. When we crossed the California coastline headed for Hickam Field, Hawaii, I realized we were going to fly over the largest body of water in the world without any islands or land. Twenty-five hundred miles of open ocean. Just fly over it. One shot. No sweat.

I had never seen ships at sea from the air before. There were several beneath us, their long white wakes trailing behind them. They quickly disappeared as we worked up to our cruising altitude. I figured we would see them all the way across, but we saw no more. The ocean was so big I just couldn't believe it. There were hundreds of ships out there somewhere, but it was a big, big somewhere.

It was a long flight to Hickam. We all felt like we were doing something really important. I hung out in the radio room and tried to figure out how the navigation was worked out. Somehow it went in one ear and out the other.

I was beginning to believe that familiar fact about three-quarters of the world being water when we saw the dark outlines of the Hawaiian Islands. We landed late in the afternoon, and after we taxied to the tarmac, the reception was surprising. A large crowd of people gathered around and everyone wanted to see the plane and hear all about it. You would have thought we were bringing in Rita Hayworth.

"She sure looks good. Does she fly good, too?" we were asked.

"The Japs had better damn well mind their manners from now on. How far will those Browning fifties shoot, anyway?" The questions never stopped.

We left the next day for Clark Air Base in the Philippines, island hopping across the big, blue Pacific. That was the first time I really got an idea of how big the world was. That ocean seemed like it went on forever.

The B-17 was a great ship, and you felt like it would always get you home, sort of like a car that runs way after empty on the gas gauge.

I never really knew what the expression "to smile from ear to ear" meant until we got to the Philippines. The Filipinos were the warmest, kindest people I had ever met. They couldn't quite believe that we had flown across the ocean. They kept saying, "You mean you flew this plane across the Pacific, the whole way? But it is not a seaplane, like the Clipper."

Life was very different in the Philippines. Everyone was fearful of the Japanese and what they might do. They all knew it was coming, and the Filipinos liked seeing these big new American warplanes.

"They are coming, you know. The Japanese. They are bad. They want everything only for themselves, the Japanese. Big trouble. Big trouble coming from them, you know." The Filipinos all made a point to tell us how bad the Japanese were.

There were a lot of American ground troops arriving as well, and there were some artillery units from Texas and New Mexico. We talked with these men, and they all felt certain war was coming, but no one knew when.

"They're a-sayin' the Japs aim to gobble up this here little country, but when they hear there're some Texans here to help out MacArthur, they'll find another spot to light on."

"The Japs know better than to take on Uncle Sam. We're just here so they can't attack the place without they attack the U.S."

"Hell, this is the best duty we've had. These Filipino girls are lookin' to make us real comfortable. Not sure I care if the Japs do attack, least it would give us something to do."

The men were sure they would probably never have to fight the Japanese, and they were pretty cocky, but when the trucks came for them, I got the same feeling I did when I'd looked at Bonnie and Clyde.

We discovered a much rumored part of our flight bonus package was true. We shuffled off to the enlisted men's club on the base and found ourselves flanked on all sides by the prettiest, friendliest Filipino girls in the world. This caused a little grumbling in the club, as having an Air Corps uniform and wings was like having a license to steal. I met a lovely young girl named Lupe with a huge smile and beautiful big brown eyes. We danced and danced, and she showed me all around the Clark area. She cooked the most wonderful, exotic meals I had ever tasted. She introduced me to her family, and introduced me to her family, and introduced me to her family. I think there were about thirty of them altogether.

The smell of flowers was everywhere. The warm, soft tropical winds washed over me and made me feel peaceful. Lupe and I walked along the ocean in the evenings and talked. "America is like a brother country to us here in the Philippines. The Spanish, they were mean to us, and when they were forced to go, the old people were not sad. Nowadays we are lucky, because no other country around here has such a lot of Americans to keep the Japanese away. General MacArthur has made a good army for us, and we are strong now. Do you have a wife?" Lupe tended to string many sentences together.

"No, no wife," I said.

"But you need one, a good one, you know. Every man needs a good wife." Her eyes got larger as she talked.

A lot of nice things came with those aircrew wings.

When we departed a few days later, we reluctantly left the new B-17s at Clark and picked up some beat-up old Boeing B-10s and B-18s to take back. These planes had been design steps along the way to the B-17, and they were crude and ugly as a mud fence, but they flew. That was the first time I ever felt reluctant to go down a runway, but it wouldn't be the last.

I was promoted to a staff sergeant rating by Colonel Smith when I returned, then went on leave to Waco to visit my Aunt Florence. Everyone wanted to know about the trip and what was going on in Asia, and if the B-17 was as great a plane as they said it was. The range of the plane amazed people. It was hard to believe there was a plane that could fly that far and that high. "If there ain't no oxygen up there, how can the damn motors run?" That was just one of the endless questions.

I went out to dinner in Waco with friends that Saturday night and had a great time. I stayed out late, and I slept in for the first time in a long while.

The hand shaking my shoulder was insistent. "Tommy! Tommy! The radio is saying the Japanese are bombing Pearl Harbor in Hawaii! Hurry!" Aunt Florence had the radio in the living room turned up full blast. I stumbled out in my robe and listened. I couldn't believe it. It had to be a mistake, a hoax. No one thought the Japanese would attack Pearl Harbor. We thought that if war started, it would probably start in the Philippines, or somewhere else in Asia, but Pearl? Man, this was it! We were in this thing all the way.

I immediately thought about the people in the Philippines, and what this was going to mean for them. I thought about what they had been saying and how true it was. They felt war was imminent, and no one seemed to be listening. I thought about our shortcomings, about how our government had let us down and allowed the Japanese to sneak up on us. We deserved better than this. Now we had a job to do, but we were entering the game already behind by two years and two touchdowns.

NOTHING WAS the same after those first few hours. If you were in uniform, everyone wanted to shake your hand and talk to you. They wanted to tell us how great we were. They were thankful, too. Thankful that we were there to fight for the country. I'd never had the feeling of belonging so much before in my life.

I walked right out on the San Antonio highway to hitchhike to Matagorda Island, and there was a traffic jam of cars trying to stop to pick me up. I could have ridden in anything. When we stopped for lunch, I hadn't even sat down before people started offering to buy my lunch. A serviceman couldn't buy a beer, or a meal, or anything in those days. People really wanted to express their gratitude.

The news of the 2,000 deaths at Pearl was devastating, and it gave people an idea of how big and horrible the attack must have been. We were really afraid then, and most everyone thought the Japanese were going to invade Hawaii, and then the West Coast.

If you were in uniform, people would rush up to you with all kinds of questions. "Can the Japs shoot that B-17 down? Will the Philippines fall? Do you think they'll invade Hawaii? Can we really stop the Japs?"

America was weak militarily, and everyone knew it. The Japanese had the largest battleships, the largest carrier fleet, and the largest amphibious capability in the world by far. They had just rolled over Manchuria and China, and three days after Pearl Harbor, the Japanese sank both of the biggest battleships in the British fleet, the *Repulse* and the *Prince of Wales*. I was beginning to wonder myself if we could stop the Japs.

When I got to the base, it was a different world. Everything was in high gear, everything had to be done *now*, there was no tomorrow. All the waiting around and shoe shuffling was gone. They intensified our air-to-air target training right away. I suddenly had more operators and more planes to deal with. We were working daylight to dark at Matagorda Island, just off the Texas coast about seventy-five miles from Houston. We kept planes in the air all the time and kept new targets and new crews ready to go almost around the clock.

Unfortunately, enthusiasm can have a downside. The Air Cadets and new second lieutenants were rabid to make big scores on their gunnery training, and they quickly learned they could bend the rules and make their passes almost parallel to the tow plane. We had three operators killed right away in those first two weeks. When the first one taxied in and parked, I saw the blood dripping from the belly of the plane on the tarmac. I thought it was oil at first.

I had tried to call attention to this problem earlier, and now we were pulling dead crewmen out of the planes. Men I was responsible for. Suddenly, the mundane duty of towing targets was getting damned dangerous.

I charged into Colonel Smith's office and right into a lot of trouble. Enlisted men are not expected to suggest policy or change in the military, something I learned the hard way. It was like stuffing diamonds up a goat's ass—a waste of valuable resources, and no one seemed to appreciate the effort. I felt disgusted.

A few days later I was operating the tow mechanism in an AT-6 when the target release lever jammed. I tried everything I knew to break it free, but it wouldn't budge. We couldn't land towing a target, so the pilot decided to take the plane down to the water to try to dislodge the target. He got too low and somehow got seawater up into the engine. He tried to get back up, but the engine was damaged and started running rough. "You're going to have to bail out, Tommy," the pilot said and gently rolled the plane over. I just slipped out. He bailed out right behind me. My chute opened, and there I was, gently gliding down into the jade green of the Gulf of Mexico.

I always wondered what bailing out would be like, and I just assumed I would land, gather up my chute and start walking. For some reason, it took a long time for me to realize that I was going in the water, and there wasn't anyone there.

I looked everywhere for a rescue boat as I drifted down. There was nothing in sight for what seemed like hundreds of miles around. Slowly, I realized that just because there was nothing in sight didn't mean there was nothing there. When I hit the water and my chute finally settled, it became quiet. I began thinking about something that might be there. Sharks. I looked down into the jade green water and wondered how deep it was, then I began to wonder how fast boats can go in the water, then I started to calculate how far out I was. About five miles, I thought. Welcome to your new home. I never saw the pilot.

I tried to keep from splashing the water and crossed my arms in front of me to keep warm. I reached a point where I realized it was out of my hands, and I began thinking about life, my life. If it ended here, was I happy? Was I the best person I could have been?

You sure get tired of your own company after eight hours in the water. It was almost dark when they picked me up. "Didn't know there were any Jap fighters in Texas, buddy! Better luck next time." The boat crew thought the whole thing was very funny. I didn't. The pilot was picked up the next morning.

That experience and the unnecessary deaths of my tow operators got to me. The last sixteen months had gone by in a blur of eighteen-hour days, impossible flight schedules, and the numbing drone of the AT-6. It was even hard to keep up with the war news.

NINETEEN FORTY-TWO was a bad year for Americans, that much was for sure. The drumbeat of news was so bad for so long, I'd find myself avoiding the battered old radio in the hanger. The Japanese were rolling over Asia, capturing British bases, and sinking British ships at will. It seemed like every day there was another big story about a British or American defeat, and Americans were talking about what would happen to the thirty thousand American soldiers captured in the Philippines. President Roosevelt's Commission on Pearl Harbor reminded us how unprepared we were when it blamed Admiral Kimmell and General Short for not being ready for an attack.

The only good news we got was in early April when Doolittle's boys bombed Tokyo. Roosevelt even got in a little joke when they asked him where the bombers took off from. He said, "Shangri-La." That was a great lift for all Americans, and the President's little joke told the world the Japs would have to work a damn sight harder to get us down.

In June, the Navy sank a bunch of Jap carriers out near some flyspeck called Midway. When we learned some of the carriers had been in on the strike at Pearl Harbor, the cheers really went up. Two thousand Americans were killed in that attack at Pearl, and most of us knew of families who lost sons out there. It galled us to think that it was so one-sided, that we never laid a glove on them. Midway helped ease those feelings in a big way.

The Nazis were gaining unbelievable chunks of Russia. They used to print maps in the paper with a dark line that showed the advance across Russia. One day at lunch a mechanic measured the little map with a machinist's measure. The front stretched from Leningrad, right next to Finland, all the way to the Turkish border. Eleven hundred miles. When someone said, "That's all the way from Seattle to San Diego," we suddenly realized just how big that war was. We knew that our Army couldn't even begin to mount an attack that vast.

During the summer, the pattern changed in a subtle way. The reports of the imminent capture of a city called Stalingrad went on for a long time. Then it kind of dawned on people that the imminent capture of Moscow and Leningrad hadn't happened either. Hitler and his boys were saying they were just taking their sweet time, but if they were, they were taking a lot of it. Pretty soon, whenever we heard the word Stalingrad, we stopped and listened. About November, the Russians somehow surrounded the whole damn German Sixth Army and were starving them out. The whole world stood right up and cheered out loud for the Russians in those weeks. It looked like they had really knotted Herr Hitler's underwear, but good. There were even some newsreels of the fighting in Stalingrad. The pictures of the men fighting in piles of blasted rock and torn up streets just terrified me. I was glad I would never have to fight that way.

Even the battered British managed to hog-tie one of Hitler's pet monsters in North Africa. Montgomery finally stopped Rommel's rampage at some dusty craphole by the name of El Alamein. It was a rotten year, but things were looking up.

I overheard our base commander on the telephone just before Christmas saying that the boys in Washington were going full bore on getting a big outfit over to England now that they were sure they wouldn't be building airfields for Hitler. They were going to call it the Eighth Air Force. That's all I needed to hear.

I asked a colonel whom I had flown with if there was any way I could go overseas and fly as a gunner. I told him I was tired of being shot at when I couldn't shoot back. He laughed and told me they were forming a new part of the Air Corps, and they were calling it the Eighth Air Force. He pulled some strings for me, and a few weeks later I got orders to the aircrew training program at Rattlesnake Air Force Base in Pyote, Texas. I was going back to the big beautiful B-17s and away from those trigger-happy fighter pilots.

TWO

OFF TO WAR

WHEN MY orders finally came through in April 1943, I was asked to select men in my unit who would qualify as aerial gunners. It seemed like everyone wanted to get into the real war. I took twelve of my best men, which ticked off the brass at the base. Whenever people are forced to perform under pressure, it becomes very obvious who the achievers are and who the big talkers and stumblebums are; and when they saw my list, they realized that these were the men who got things done, and men like that were damn hard to replace. But these were the same officers who refused to listen to my warnings about the danger to my tow operators, so I wasn't too sympathetic. Their objections were overruled, as forming crews for the B-17s was a priority.

We left on the "short" train trip to Salt Lake City with our spirits high. After all, we were leaving the backwaters of training and heading for the real war. After three weeks of paper shuffling, we were finally sent to Pyote, Texas. Orders were being changed by the hour, and it seemed like the whole country was one big Chinese fire drill. One thing was obvious. Aircrews had some kind of priority, but we usually just had to hurry more to wait longer.

We rolled into Pyote on a warm, clear morning in early May. Pyote, Texas, is about fifty miles west of Odessa, and it was about the most forlorn place I had ever seen. What few buildings there were had never been painted, and most of them had dusty tar paper flapping in the relentless, dry wind. There was one small, rickety hotel and a filling station right in the middle of that flat, barren country. The few people around the station looked a lot like the buildings. "Won't take long to get to know the streets of Pyote," we kidded each other, but it was pretty grim.

When we got out to the base, about seven miles out of town, we all jumped out of the truck and looked around for buildings and barracks that would indicate a base. The Pyote, Texas, Eighth Air Force Base looked like a Boy Scout convention. There were rows and rows of tents. Big tents and small tents, green tents and white tents, flapping loudly in the hot, dry wind. But once we saw the familiar shapes of the B-17s, we felt better. We still got excited every time we saw one, and there were several flying over the base with that low, powerful hum.

The B-17 Es and Fs at Pyote were early, war-weary models that had been brought back from the Pacific with the 19th Bomb Group. We slowly walked up and down the flight line and looked at these planes. They were beat to hell. There were numerous patches where some pretty big holes had been fixed. The repairs were ragged and crude. A lot of the paint had been flown off the planes. "Whatever the hell these boys flew through was hard, hot, and metal," the ground crewman drawled, spitting tobacco. "You'd never know these planes are only a few years old. I've worked on planes twenty years old that looked better than these."

We got a few glimpses that morning of the vicious wear and

tear of war on airplanes. Soon we would see some of this wear and tear on men.

WE BEGAN our training by shooting at stacks of painted fifty-gallon oil drums on the ground as we flew by. The big Browning .50s hit the drums so hard they went spinning off across the desert, and the sand kicked up so high it was almost even with us. These new guns were very powerful, and they had the reach and punch to knock down fighters with just a few rounds. Seeing this stopping power gave us confidence.

"I'd say one, maybe two rounds would tear up a damn Zero fighter right good," Jack Everett, our gunnery instructor said. "Right good." None of us doubted him.

There was great emphasis placed on the proficiency of gunners in the B-17 program. Early missions flying against Japanese targets proved the effectiveness of the gunners in the B-17s, but the key seemed to be accurate firepower. The enemy fighter pilots saw which planes were putting out accurate fire and tended to stay away from them. The gunners took on a new importance, and we wanted to be as good as we possibly could. The rest of the crew was depending on us to keep the plane in the air by drilling holes in enemy airplanes and not the sky.

We received valuable experience with our guns at Pyote. We learned how to lead a target, how to control bursts, and how to hold on a target. The motorized upper and lower ball turrets were marvels of engineering, but they took a lot of practice to get used to. The real crunch was the lower ball turret. Every crew had to find a man small enough and crazy enough to get into that turret, then hope he could get the feel of it and make it work. The lower ball turret protected the belly of the plane, and it covered the favored attack direction of the enemy: from below.

Buzzy Walker was our lower ball turret gunner. He was a short, wiry guy with curly brown hair and a big smile. Buzzy was a natural for this important position. He had quick reflexes and learned fast. Reaction time was everything in that turret, and Buzzy was quick. He was a real spark plug for the crew. "Time to go to work now, darlin's," he would say every time we helped him into the turret.

We knew that Japanese fighter pilots were favoring attacks from the six o'clock low position, which is directly behind and below the plane. The early B-17s didn't have a tail gun position, so the men of the 19th Bomb Group actually sawed off the tail end of the fuselage and bolted in a pair of .30 caliber machine guns. The gunner lay on his belly on a mat or a rug and fired from a prone position. Several of our planes were still fitted with these cobbled-up mounts. They were half welded, half wired together and looked like they had come from a Mexican junkyard, but they worked. "These boys are just a hair short of being skilled surgeons," Buzzy said, looking at the installation.

I noticed that all these planes had a fine coating of red dust inside them, from the red earth in the South Pacific islands where they were based. It made me think of the Philippines and the warm, soft world of the Pacific.

The tail gunner position was just fine for me. I liked being by myself in the tail of the plane. This was my hangout. The tail position was a twin gun mount, which I liked. The rear mount was not motorized, but the guns swung and tilted very easily. I rehearsed moving the guns at the precise speed the veterans from the Pacific had shown me—fast.

They told me the hardest part was to listen to the intercom as the crew called out the enemy fighters' positions and quickly try to anticipate where they'd be coming from. We used an imaginary clock system to indicate direction. We were told to imagine that the plane was sitting on a clock, with the nose pointed at twelve o'clock and the tail at six o'clock. The wings pointed at three o'clock and nine o'clock. Anything flying above the center of the plane was high, and anything below the centerline was low. Therefore, if a plane were coming in from directly behind the plane and below, the indication would be "six o'clock low."

Anticipation was everything. The Pacific veterans showed us how to whip the guns around so we'd be pointing in the direction of the fighters as they flew past. They flung the guns around in violent, precise jerks. Their knuckles were white on the handles, and they broke into a sweat right away. They tried hard to teach us everything they could.

The blind spot was directly below the tail, which explained why the fighters favored coming in from that position. I made pads out of flight suits for my knees to get me up as high as possible so I could see down. The designers didn't spend much time on seating comfort for the tail gunner. There was a large bicycle-type wooden seat and two boards to kneel on. It took me quite a while to find the right points to brace myself when I swung the guns around.

I was assigned to Lieutenant Armour Bowen's crew. Lieutenant Bowen was a tall, soft-spoken man from a prominent family in Memphis, Tennessee. He was thoughtful and firm in his decisions and commands. "All right, gentlemen, let's go to work," he would say as we headed out to the plane. The whole crew liked and respected him. He was a natural leader and a big reason why there was little friction in the crew.

The waist gunners were Glenn Terry from California and Robert Fain from Texas. They manned single gun mounts in the middle of the fuselage and had to endure the icy air stream from their open gun ports.

Glenn was full of hell. He liked his beer at night, and he was always in the middle of things. Robert was a quiet guy who took his job very seriously. He asked question after question during our training and made notes in a leather notepad, which seemed a little formal for a door gunner.

Johnny Yergo, our radio operator, was just a kid of eighteen. He was a crackerjack radio operator, and he knew how important a resourceful radioman could be. He would single out the most experienced radiomen on the base and pump them for tips and tricks.

Our copilot was Julian O'Neal. He was from California, and he insisted on wearing cowboy boots with his uniform. I think he was the only American airman in Europe who flew all his missions in cowboy boots. Julian was Lieutenant Bowen's right-hand man, and they worked perfectly together. He had a dry sense of humor that kept everyone cracked up. "These Boeing boys would have been smart to just hire some saddle makers from Texas for this here cockpit. These damn seats are no good," he would say.

Jim Pilger, our navigator, was from New York. Jim was a short, slender guy, very quiet and extremely competent. We would find out later just how good Jim was.

Hank Matty was our bombardier. Hank was a happy-go-lucky guy who possessed that mystical quality that women went for. Hank was a great practical joker and a storyteller. Hank and Julian had a long-running argument on who helped who close down which bars and who was the best ladies' man.

"Now, I know you think the tall one was with you, Julian, but she was really just using you to get to me, that's all." Hank kidded Julian mercilessly.

WE BEGAN our training schedule immediately. We flew long training missions every day and slowly began to integrate the plane and the crew. There was a lot to do: planning the flights, checking the plane and the guns, navigating, fueling, and practicing the all-important bomb runs.

I taught all of the gunners how to fieldstrip the .50s, with a few shortcuts and tricks. I learned that the adjustment of the headspace on the gun's receiver was important, and I made a small tool to speed up this adjustment. I found a lot of the guns had been overlubed, which caused them to jam in the cold air at high altitude. The cold would make the oil gel up, which seized the gun's receiver. I got some small cotton pads from the nurse in the infirmary and used these to wipe down the guns.

The training officers wanted to get us used to flying long missions, up to ten hours. We would get up at five A.M., hit the mess hall, and go directly to the plane. We took a sack lunch and were usually in the air by dawn. We didn't fly much above 10,000 feet, but we made several flights on oxygen to get used to the bulky facemasks and to learn how the blinker-type oxygen flow indicators worked. The oxygen masks and the extreme cold made it very difficult to move around and talk clearly. Fighting in all that equipment was going to be tough.

In the hours between missions we had some time to get to know the veterans from the 19th Bomb Group. Many of them were decorated, and a lot of them had been wounded. I noticed several long pinkish-red scars on them in the barracks showers. These men had flown the first bombing missions against Japanese bases around Rabaul, New Guinea, and they had suffered terrible losses. I began to see, for the first time, what fighting and killing does to men. They were very subdued, quiet almost to the point of rudeness. They had a hard glint in their eyes, and they smoked a lot. I noticed they never seemed to make an effort to get to know any of the men they were training.

They worked hard at showing the gunners how the Japanese fighters had flown at them. They patiently explained angles of attack and countertactics. They had lots of hard-won advice for us and cautioned us over and over to have everything ready, all the guns and ammo belts, because when it started, there wasn't time to fix anything or find extra belts.

"They're just there. They appear out of nowhere, zip past you so fast you get sick, then they're gone and your airplane is on fire." Their combat descriptions were short but plenty vivid.

They told us the fighters came in twisting and turning and usually attacked in groups of three and four, often working on one plane at a time. They had a lot of experience with wounded men aboard and showed us ways to keep them alive in the cold. We had to stop heavy bleeding at all costs and do everything possible to keep the wounded man warm. They also showed us what equipment to jettison if the plane was losing altitude, and they showed us several tricks for unbolting the guns and ammo boxes.

They told us how most of the missions were long, nerve-wracking experiences. I began to get an idea of the intensity of war. These men had a certain weariness about them. Sometimes they seemed to lose their focus for a moment, and their conversation would just trail off in midsentence. Then they would walk away.

We were assigned to Dalhart, Texas, for our final phase of training in July 1943. We spent four months in the suffocating heat, training constantly. We flew day and night practice bombing missions. The training was very intense, as they were trying to hurry us through it as fast as possible. They were losing a lot of planes in Europe, and they needed us badly.

Night missions were an important part of our training, and it was very difficult for many of the crews. The science of navigating at night and flying in tight formations was primitive, and the tension level was much higher. We all listened carefully to the navigator reading off landmarks and our position, and the gunners kept a lookout for planes flying too close to us. The possibility of a midair collision at night was on everyone's minds.

On one night mission, we were following the lead bombardier, who was trying to locate a lighted target, which he finally did. We lined up and carefully dropped our practice bombs and returned to the base. Practice bombs had flash powder and a white powder in them to mark the impact spot.

The CO's jeep pulled up to our plane before we had stopped moving. "All crew members in the briefing hut on the double!" the duty officer shouted at us.

The entire base was crowded in or around the briefing hut as we filed in. The brass not so casually informed us that we had just succeeded in bombing the town of Boise City, Oklahoma. Fortunately no one was hurt or killed, but there was plenty of hell raised by the base commanders. We all felt a little embarrassed. None of us were sure we could turn back the fascist tide, but we all knew we could knock the hell out of Boise City, Oklahoma. We were thankful that it happened in the last week of our training.

WE FINISHED up in mid-October and took a troop train to Kearney, Nebraska, in a blinding blizzard to pick up a new B-17. We arrived at the base just before dark. We were supposed to go out the next morning to look over the plane, but none of us could wait. We "found" a jeep and drove out to our assigned plane. We inspected our plane with flashlights like kids with a new bike. We looked at the improvements and changes. Our plane was a new G model with a chin turret. This gave the plane much better firepower to fend off head-on attacks, which was the favored killing method of the Luftwaffe.

We found some writing inside the fuselage from the workers who had built our plane. I found a message from a woman named Mary, which said, "To the men who fly this plane I send my best wishes and may God bless you and protect you." Seeing these little notes made us feel important, and we realized that these people had taken a lot of extra care to make this plane safe for us. After that, every time we got a new plane, we would scramble around looking for these messages.

We spent that evening just hanging around the plane and appreciating what a great machine it was. I felt like I was going to war the way I wanted to, as an American airman in the best plane ever built. The B-17 was just that kind of a plane. We wanted to call her "The Pistol Packin' Mama," but we didn't have the time or paint to get the nose art done.

We flew the new plane to Wilmington, Delaware, nonstop—a very long trip. Wilmington was the headquarters of the Ferry Command. There we got some idea of the scale of the European air war. There were just planes everywhere, as far as you could see, almost all new, all headed for England. Six of our crew left from Wilmington for England by ship, which was a big disappointment to them. "I didn't join no damned Air Corps to wallow around on no damn ship in no damn ocean," Robert said. "Hell, that water out there is over my little pumpkin head, and I can't even swim." All the men were shaking their heads and running a little complaint contest as they got into the trucks to go to the ships.

The Air Force used civilian ferry pilots to get the planes to England, and the gunners were not needed on the flight over. I flew the trip because they wanted an observer in the rear of the plane.

We flew next to Presque Isle, Maine, then over the St. Lawrence River on our way to Goose Bay, Labrador. Goose Bay was the coldest, most desolate place I had ever seen. There were just miles and miles of snowfields, with no trees, nothing. The cold was terrible. It was so cold your skull ached, even indoors. They issued us heated engine covers for the plane, and we waited for orders to fly on to England. I wanted to get over to a nearby Indian village to see how the local people lived, but we had no way to get there.

We had five long, cold, boring days at Goose Bay, probably the only place in the world where sleeping is considered a sport.

On the fifth night it was bitter cold, and we were all in the base theater watching a movie about ten-thirty when they came in and stopped the film and told us to report to briefing immediately. As we walked to the briefing hut, the cold closed around us and then stabbed right through us. It felt like the air was made of some hard glass that had been frozen for centuries. They told us our takeoff time was midnight. A ripple of fear passed through us. *Midnight?* We all wondered, *Why at night?* We quickly learned that U-boats were patrolling the waters between Labrador and Greenland. During daytime the U-boats were surfacing, shooting at the unarmed B-17s, and collecting information on plane movements.

We piled into jeeps and drove out to the plane in a daze and checked everything. Johnny Yergo checked his radio set over and over. The anxiety was terrible. We were all churning inside. It was 20° below, pitch black, with a harsh, steady wind. All we could see were the small lights on the field. We wondered, *Will these engines run right in this vicious cold? Will they get the plane in the air?*

We started down the runway, and my ears were tuned to every little sound from those engines. One missed beat and I knew we were in trouble. We were loaded to the maximum with fuel, and we used every inch of that rough runway to get in the air. We finally lifted off and got the landing gear up.

I was just beginning to relax a little, looking back at the runway, when I saw a huge, dazzling explosion. The flash was like a giant Fourth of July rocket. The whole sky was lit up. A plane taking off behind us had crashed and exploded.

"Large explosion on the runway behind us," I sputtered into the intercom.

"Roger, we can see it from the cockpit," Bowen replied slowly.

The explosion just kept going and going, with waves of dark orange flames and purple clouds. I stared for a long time, but there is a point when you don't see what you are looking at anymore, because you are thinking about what you are seeing. When I realized that the men on that plane had just been killed, I suddenly felt empty and bewildered. All those men. Gone forever. Men we had just been in the theater with. The feelings kind of roll up in a ball in your stomach, and then expand in your chest until it is hard to breathe. You start to think about what death must be like, then you stop yourself.

I spent some of that long, black night up in the radio room with Johnny. It was warmer, and I was glad for the company. We both started to say something at the same time, but I don't think either of us finished a sentence. We wanted to talk, but we didn't want to say anything. Most of all we didn't want to be alone.

A lot of planes were going off course that night and calling on the radio for help in getting a fix. The calls slowly became more frantic. Lieutenant Bowen called to Jim Pilger every fifteen minutes for a fix and a heading check. His reassuring voice helped us all. "Hold course one one zero. One one zero." Jim was quietly confident in his navigation. He worked and reworked our position all night without stopping. That night went on until it seemed like the world would be black and cold forever.

WHEN DAYLIGHT finally arrived in grudging shades of dark gray, we were over the coast of Ireland. The land looked different somehow. The greens looked greener, and the rock formations looked older than they do at home. We landed at Valley Wales, England, after bouncing around in big, sticky clouds for two hours. As we taxied in, we all thought the same thing: *Here we are. Finally. Hope everything works out for us.*

There were planes everywhere. Planes coming in, planes taking off. Jeeps. Air crews. Shouting, confusion, and bicycles. The ground crews all had black bicycles. They were leaning against every building and jeep around.

We finally found our parking spot and got the B-17 shut down. We tried to walk off some of the stiffness, but there were trucks and jeeps and bicycles zooming around everywhere. We felt like little kids in Grand Central Station.

We were loaded on a couple of smoking British army trucks and taken to a train bound for Stoke-on-Trent, near Staffordshire. The small town had been famous for many years as a pottery center, which was news to all of us. The famous Staffordshire ceramics works had been turned into a large munitions factory staffed by hardworking British artisans, who just happened to be women. Pretty, friendly, lonely Englishwomen. Only six thousand or so. It sounded like a job for the Eighth Air Force to us.

"Come on in for a spot of tea, Yank!" We heard this everywhere. The English went out of their way to welcome us and let us know how much we were appreciated. England is a beautiful country with lovely trees and warm, friendly people. I felt like the country was a big, comfortable house, where the lawn was always mowed and there was plenty of time for the little pleasantries.

The war had been very traumatic for the Brits, and they greatly appreciated what we were doing. They had come damn close to experiencing what the French and most of Europe were living with: occupation by a tyrannical German people, high on master-race ideology, mean as hell, and armed to the teeth. Every time the Germans were discussed, there was a real appreciation of their capacity for evil. The "Huns," as the Brits called them, were the real thing.

The pubs were warm and friendly places, too, much homier than our bars. They served restaurant-type food right in the pub, and it was very good. Whenever we went into a pub, one of the local guys would challenge us to a game of darts. This was their game, and they always wanted to play for a pint of bitter beer. Since we considered ourselves professionals at punching holes in things, we accepted the darts challenge and usually ended up buying the locals a lot of beer.

The Chinese fire drill chaos that we knew stateside was just as bad in England. Our orders were changed every hour for about two weeks until we were finally put on a train to Bovingdon, about twenty-five miles north of London. We picked up a different B-17 and took it to Ridgewell, a very small town about fifty miles northeast of London.

The weather was terrible. English fog is colder and English rain is wetter than American fog and rain. The wet gets into your clothes and boots and glasses until you can't seem to find anything dry no matter what you do.

We heard that there had been very serious losses on American daylight missions, and our mission planners were scrambling to find a way to cut down on losses. They were beginning to learn what the veterans of the Pacific war had learned: If a bomber's gunners were quick and accurate, they could do a lot toward bringing a plane home.

A huge new gunnery range had just been set up on the east coast of England, and they wanted all the crews cycled through this course, right away as always.

The Wash was a big bay on England's east coast. It was desolate, windy, cold, and gray. The British had gun turrets and
mounts set up in actual sections of the bombers, and we fired live
ammunition at silhouettes about four hundred yards across the
range which were motorized and moved very rapidly. They wanted results.

"Can't believe they would junk a B-17 just for training," the
gunner next to me said one morning as we prepared for drills.

"Don't think they junked this one, mate. I think the Jerries
might have helped a bit," said a short, red-haired British gunner,
leaning over and putting his finger through a jagged hole in the
bottom of the fuselage. We called the Germans Krauts, but the
British always called them "Jerries," and in a somewhat polite
way as well.

We fired lots of ammunition. Then we'd tear our guns down
and reassemble them, over and over. They brought in every kind
of emergency situation that could happen to us in the air. They
staged gun jams, broken belts, frozen mounts, power outages to
the turrets, and more. That was great for me, because I was able to
show them a few shortcuts and tricks. A month's armament
course was compressed into four or five days. It was valuable
training and gave us the kind of extended live fire training we
needed. They wanted us to fire plenty of ammunition, and we
did. I saw dump trucks full of .50 shell casings leaving The Wash.

Just as we were finishing up at The Wash, a crippled British
Lancaster four-engine bomber passed overhead, trailing black
smoke. A large piece of the belly had been shot off and was flapping violently against the fuselage. The pilot tried to line it up
with the beach, but he lost too much altitude in the turn and
crash-landed, half in the water and half on the beach. We raced
out there in a jeep, but the crew were all killed in the crash. We
did what we could, but the men didn't stand a chance.

That was my first experience with what could happen, and what was happening, in the war. I felt helpless again, like I had after the tornado in Clyde. I wanted so much for these men to live and to be all right, and when I saw their faces, it tore a piece right out of me. They'd been just like us. Young and invincible, but they were dead. Forever.

RIDGEWELL WAS a very busy base. Most of the bomb groups there had just arrived, and most of the planes were the new G model B-17s. There were B-17s landing on the runway all day, from dawn until late at night. Muddy jeeps full of flight crews whined around the tarmac constantly. Fuel trucks, bomb wagons, fire trucks, and ambulances drowned out most conversations.

We heard a lot about the losses on recent missions, and there was a feeling of real urgency, that maybe the outcome of the air war was seriously in doubt. The scuttlebutt was that the Nazis had moved a lot of fighter units from the Russian front to France to shoot us down. There was some big talk about "getting Krauts" and all, but I kept thinking about the men who had trained us in Texas. When they used the word Jap, or Jap fighters, they said it quietly.

The anxiety and anticipation began to build. We flew training missions for about three weeks. We sat in on briefings when the other crews went on missions, and we all gathered at the field when the planes came back.

I saw many planes shooting off red flares in the landing pattern, which meant they had wounded aboard. They were ordered not to report this on the radio, because the Germans were listening, and casualty figures would be helpful to them. There were more of these red flares than I expected, about one in every four or five planes. Everyone was silently pulling for the wounded men on the planes. We all knew how tough it was to keep a wounded man alive in the cold and how long those hours of flying could be for a man in pain.

When the planes started to return, everyone on the base quietly appeared at the control tower. The mechanics and bomb loaders and truck drivers rode up on black bicycles. Jeeps rolled quietly up and parked, and men in green overalls started to fill the duckboard walkways. Some of the guys had binoculars and called out the ships' names. There wasn't much talking, and later, after my combat missions, I realized that we were all there to pray for the men in the planes.

The crippled planes had priority and came in first. Sometimes the crews would bail out over the base if they couldn't land. Often these planes would have landing gear shot away or armed bombs hung up in the bomb bay. The men drifted down on the wet grass and tried to roll with the fall, but a lot of them injured their legs. Usually the pilot and copilot stayed in the plane and headed it out over the Channel and bailed out there.

Everyone tried to wish the planes down safely, especially when a ship came in with its wheels up. This was the best way to get a badly shot-up plane down. They had tried wheels-down landings and seen many bad crashes. Sometimes the landing gear would collapse or not lock properly, or the pilot would get a little sideways coming in, bounce, and flip the plane. A wheels-up landing slowed the plane faster and prevented a lot of deaths.

Sometimes it would look like everything was going fine, the plane skidding down the runway, then the plane would just blow up in a huge ball of angry orange flames. The firefighters were fearless and dove right into the flaming wrecks, fire hoses blasting water, trying against the odds to save the burning men inside. Those of us watching would often start walking, walking anywhere, in short steps. We coughed softly to ease the clenching in our chests and looked up at the clouds.

I spent a lot of time in the war room looking at photos of past missions. There were amazingly detailed pictures of targets, pictures of the small black clouds from antiaircraft guns they called flak, and lots of pictures of German fighters attacking the formations. I tried to learn all I could. I was beginning to see how the fighters would twist as they flew through the formations to give the gunners a narrow target profile.

I started looking for activities to soak up the time as the apprehension built. All we thought about was our first mission. *What would it really be like? What would happen to us?*

THREE

MISSIONS

"GET UP, LaMore. You're gonna fly today, you're gonna go see Hitler. Let's go."

The voice was right in my ear, and I could tell the duty officer was trying not to wake up anyone else. He told me I was going to fly as a replacement, in an experienced crew.

I walked through the bitter cold to the chow hut, where they served coffee and real eggs for the flight crews. I had both. That was my first mistake.

I tried to fit in with my crew and not say much. They were a good bunch of guys and had flown a lot of missions together. They were good-humored, but there was a limit to the joking around. I could hear a strain of nervousness in their voices.

The briefing room seemed different this time. I was going on this mission. This target was my target. This information was for me. All eyes tried to stare through the black curtain that covered the mission map. "Probably France. U-boat pens again," someone said. "I heard the U-boats have been sinking a lot of ships, they want them hit hard. They won't send us out of fighter range again. Last week was bad." Little snippets of wishful thinking rose above the nervous chatter.

When the operations officer pulled back the curtain and we first saw how long that red line was, there was a low groan in the room. Brunswick, Germany. A munitions plant and an aircraft parts plant. Right smack dab in the middle of Germany. I looked around at the faces of the experienced crews and saw real trepidation. The men kept their eyes open for a long time, then looked down at their feet.

The operations officer detailed how the flying formations would be assigned. They called them "upper box" and "lower box." The names of the planes' commanders and positions in the box formations were called off quickly. The pace increased as his pointer got closer to the end of the formation. The men shot glances at each other. There was a lot of sweating about who was going to be "tail end Charlie"—the last outside position in the box formation. When he called that pilot's name off, a tiny ripple of terror and compassion passed through the room. The odds of a plane returning after flying that position in a raid like this were nil closing on zero.

"You can expect to encounter heavy fighter opposition from about this point on your mission," the briefing officer said loudly and clearly. The point he tapped on the big map looked like it was a long way from the target. "All gunners make certain your position is supplied with the maximum number of ammo belts." He talked about where we would encounter flak, then covered the egress route and fighter escort rendezvous point very carefully. I kept hearing the words "maximum number of ammo belts" over and over.

The briefing officer told us they had several reports of "ghost ships" shadowing the formations on the last two missions. These were B-17s and B-24s that had been forced down and captured by the Germans. They would slowly join up with our formations right up to the flak belts. They stayed out about a half-mile from the formation, just out of the range of our .50s. They gave the German ground controllers accurate information on the formation's speed, heading, and altitude.

"We want detailed information on the types and markings of these planes, where you see them and where they leave your formation," he said, walking to the side of the room. That was as scary as anything we'd heard, and there was talk about the possibility of one of them appearing in the formation with the proper markings and opening up on our planes. A B-17's guns could shoot up four or five planes before anyone caught on. I talked to one of the men who had seen one, and he said it sure made the crews feel funny, knowing the Krauts were flying a Fort. "We arced a few rounds in their direction, just to say hello," he said.

We left the briefing room quietly. We boarded the trucks and rattled out to the flight line as the darkness was giving way to a weak gray light. The blue oil smoke from the trucks hung in the cold air and made me slightly nauseous. There were big clear areas in the clouds and for some reason the tarmac was dry. So was my throat.

I checked all the guns on the plane with the crew. I noticed that the guns showed a lot of wear, but they were set up right and they weren't overlubricated. My little tool for setting the headspace was a big hit with the gunners, and I promised to make several for them.

I looked at the bombs for a few minutes. Then I tried not to look at them. For a brief moment I tried to imagine just how big a blast five hundred pounds of TNT would make. The biggest thing we'd detonated in armament school was about twenty-five pounds, and that blast had seemed like the end of the world to me. Someone in Germany was going to hear a very, very loud noise that day. Six of them.

When the pilots, bombardier, and navigator showed up and pulled the hatches closed, I realized just what I had gotten into. We went through a final check and inspection before takeoff. Our pilot was Captain Withers. The plane was named "This Is It!" I guess they picked that name because when we would walk out to the flight line on the morning of a mission, the guys would usually say, "This is it!"

I prayed a little and asked God to be with me that day. I thought about the old expression "nothing sharpens the mind like a hanging." Going down a runway with a load of gasoline, high explosives, and ammunition to fly into enemy territory at 35,000 feet in broad daylight against the toughest, most experienced fighter pilots in the world and through the kill zones of several thousand 88-mm cannon, does roughly the same thing. My mind was very, very sharp.

When it was our turn to take off, I had to fight the memory of the plane that had exploded behind us in Goose Bay. This was the first time I had taken off with a full load of bombs and fuel. I was praying this old gal would get us into the air. We roared down that runway for what seemed like hours. My mind was pulling back on an imaginary stick the whole way. We bounced a few times, then, finally, we were up. It seemed like we were flying way too slowly, but we started to climb. The engines roared and roared under the heavy strain, and I just prayed that the people who had designed and built these planes and their engines did their jobs well.

The rendezvous operations took quite a while, but we finally formed up and headed east. It was bright and clear. The sun felt warm on my face. I said a quiet farewell to the White Cliffs of Dover below. It was the first time I had seen them. They were very striking and beautiful.

We slowly flew over the dark gray-green English Channel. Then, suddenly, there it was. Enemy territory. It didn't really look any different, it just seemed like it looked different. When you looked at the country from the air, with the endless green and brown fields and black lines of roads stretching to the horizon, it seemed impossible that it was a vast prison, ruled by evil people. I caught myself thinking, *What is life like for those people? What are the Nazis like up close?* Then I figured I would probably never see one face-to-face anyway.

The pilot ordered us to test our guns, to make sure they were loaded and firing properly. The noise and vibration woke us up a little, and it felt good to say, "Tail guns good" into the intercom. We flew on, still climbing, with our P-47 fighter escorts above and below us. We saw some small dark bursts of flak from the German 88s, but they were exploding way below us and scattered. Flak scared me and made me angry in a way, because we couldn't fight back against it. I put my flak jacket under my seat, as I just wanted a little more protection in that area.

Somewhere over Holland, I realized that I had ignored important advice from my fellow crewmembers. They had all told me not to drink the coffee, but I had anyway, and now I had some very serious human engineering problems to solve. Everyone had his own approach to this problem, and later I cut up some rubber tubing and covered the rim of some flare cans, but on my first mission I had to improvise, as I was sure the rising tide of coffee was going to affect my vision.

I heard a little chatter on the intercom and realized our escorting fighters were turning back. "Man, why can't they get a bigger gas tank in them beauties," our copilot said. The big, plug-ugly P-47s made a long lazy turn and wagged their wings. I hadn't expected this to affect me, but it did. It was like losing your whole family. Then the full realization hit me. This Flying Fortress idea was for real. We were going to literally fight our way into Hitler's Germany—alone. I could feel my own doubts rising. *Was it possible? Could we do it?*

It was very cold. I tried to stay warm and to stay sharp by rehearsing with my guns. I swung and tilted them over and over, trying to find the right positions to brace myself and getting my reaction times down as fast as possible. The cold penetrated my body like invisible X-rays until I could feel my skull, and my ears burned. The knuckles in my hands felt brittle, and it seemed like there was a high-intensity vibration deep in my body.

Then the navigator called out so loud his voice was distorted on the intercom. "Fighters! Fighters at twelve o'clock high!" There they were. Two black specks streaking away from us at unbelievable speed. They moved as fast across the sky as you could wave your arm. They were rolling and making tight, twisting turns in order to present the smallest outline to the gunners in the B-17s. It looked like a kid's hand, playing in the wind out a car window. *How can we ever hit anything going that fast?* I thought.

The first fighters approaching our plane were two twin-engine Me-110s, coming up fast from six o'clock low. "Fighters at six o'clock low!" I hollered into my intercom, my voice cracking. The plane next to us started firing, but I felt they were out of range. Two more Me-110s joined them, and they made their firing pass in a rippling, roller-coaster line. They closed on us in a heartbeat. Bright yellow and red flashes lit up their wings. I opened up, and so did the upper turret and the lower ball turret. The noise and vibration were overwhelming, as if your head were inside a jack-hammer. I thought the plane was going to shake apart.

I fired short bursts and tried to reacquire them as fast as I could, but they flashed past us, half-rolled, and dove off to my right.

In a strange way I felt better. All the anxiety of wondering what it was like slipped away. It was many times faster than I could have possibly imagined. But I was okay. I was doing okay. *Slap. Slap. Slap.* My oxygen breathing bag was running wild by itself! No, it was me. I was breathing as hard as I could, hyperventilating. My skin got very clammy and cold. The sweat started running down my back. The intercom went quiet for a minute.

Then I caught something out of the corner of my left eye, something black. I leaned forward and twisted around to look up over the engines. Flak. Not just scattered bursts here and there, but hundreds and hundreds of tight little black clouds neatly outlining our course. The burst altitude was exactly where we were flying. *Whump. Whump.* We were in it. The black oily clouds zipped past the plane and showed our speed through the air, which disoriented me for a second.

I couldn't let myself start thinking about it, but my mind got ahead of me a little as I imagined the deafening crash, the hole in the plane, the shrapnel tearing my life away, and the shrieking wind. I snatched control back and just prayed and hoped. I realized that my life was out of my hands. I talked to God again, softly.

We flew on for what seemed like a week through the flak. Then I saw the bomb bay doors open on the plane next to us, then felt our doors open. This was it. We were lining up on the bomb run. Those minutes from the time the doors opened until the bombs dropped seemed like hours. The flak got thicker and thicker. The German fighters peeled off when the flak got thick. They didn't like it either.

At first I thought something was wrong. The plane lurched violently up in the air, and my heart almost popped out of my mouth. I had to quickly brace myself to keep from banging my head. The bombs were away. We could go home.

We had done it. We had done what the plane was built to do and what we were trained to do. Pick up the war and deliver it right to the enemy's kitchen table. We winged over hard and set course for the nearest rendezvous point with our P-47 escorts. Below, I could just see the bright yellow flashes and black billowing clouds of the bombs through the clouds. Somehow, it didn't seem very important. It was old business.

The flak bursts came faster and tighter together now. For the first time chunks of shrapnel hit the plane forward with a sharp metallic crack. "Fighters! Fighters! Three o'clock high! Fighters! Twelve o'clock! Fighters six o'clock low, two of them. Nail 'em, nail 'em!" The intercom was one long excited shout. The sky was suddenly full of German fighters screaming through our formation, twisting, firing, rolling over, and looping around. They had tightened up their passes, and they were flying faster and closer to us than before.

"Fighters six o'clock low!"

"Where?" I yelled, banging my head as I tried to look down out of the tiny window. *Where? There! Me-109. Fast.* I jerked the guns down with every bit of speed and strength I had and fired. *I can't see! Where is he? Let up! Too long. Too long a burst! Too much ammo. Where did he go? Fighters five o'clock low! There! Wait, wait— hold. Hold. Now!*

After all of my practice, I was still too slow. My brace points inside the fuselage cut into my shoulders. I slipped on the seat and on the kneeboards. My kneecaps were on fire. I tried to look the bursts right into the fighters, but the tracers slipped all around them as they bored in, firing and twisting and closing. Bright red tracers and white trails of smoke blazed past my window. *They're gonna kill me. They're shooting right at me!* Was I talking out loud or to myself? "You will not kill me, you sons of bitches!" I yelled. The guns became part of my eyesight and my muscles and body didn't exist apart from the guns. I reached that point of absolute alertness that can only exist during battle. The exact second an attack broke off I started looking for the next one. *Where? Where now? Come on. Come on!*

"Six o'clock low!" I yelled into the intercom. Two Me-109s close together, just starting their firing pass. *Hold the guns steady. Come up on them, more lead, more lead, there!* It felt like I had pulled the triggers out of the guns. The front plane suddenly broke off, and something flew off the plane. The second one didn't break. *Fire. Fire. Fire! Is he gone? Too long. Too long a burst. How much ammo belt is left? Where are they?* Finally I heard the intercom again. "Fighters twelve o'clock high!" *Fighters everywhere. How many could there be?*

I could hear the lower ball turret spinning and firing. *Where were they?* I smacked my face against the small window trying to get a closer look. All the planes to our left were firing. I jerked my eyes down to the six o'clock low position. Nothing. *Where? Where are they?*

Then the slapping of my breathing bag slowed. The cold sweat between my shoulder blades made me shudder. The intercom was quiet. A dark black cloud erupted to my left as a B-17 from the 91st Squadron suddenly pulled back from the formation, rapidly slowing down, and burning a fierce yellow-orange from both starboard engines. The number three engine broke away in an explosion of debris and flame. The air drag from the mangled nacelle pulled the plane into a vicious clockwise spin. "Get outta that plane, you guys. Come on. Get out! Two. Two chutes. Come on you guys!" The voices on the intercom had the same tense pleading tone. The B-17 broke out of its spin and headed straight down, leaving a black, twisting cloud behind it that hung in the air for a long time.

"LaMore. Did you see whose plane that was?" Hearing my name jolted me back.

"No, sir. I didn't," I replied, breathing heavily.

"Any more chutes, more than two?" The pilot asked.

"I just saw the two." I watched the smoke rise from the impact point. Somewhere in all that cold, noise, and vibration there was a quiet moment in all of us. I was just able to catch my mind this time, before it got ahead of me. I tried not to think about what it was like for those men.

The Germans hit the formation again in a swarm. It looked like the entire Luftwaffe was in the air. They were flying everything, FW-190s, Me-109s, Me-110s, and they were pushing their attacks relentlessly. I watched one FW-190 dive through the formation next to us and roll off underneath me. I could see the pilot's face, he was so close. I got two short bursts in, but he was gone. They were diving at over 400 MPH, and away from our direction, which added another 170 MPH. This was so fast it was almost impossible for us to lock on them.

Then it stopped. The intercom was quiet again. They were gone. A few minutes later the big, beautiful P-47s and the sleek new P-51s appeared, and we could see the Channel ahead. We couldn't relax yet, but the worst was definitely over. As we crossed the English Channel, another ship ran out of fuel and crash-landed in the water. We learned later that the pilot,

Lieutenant Carl Baer of the 535th Squadron, was killed and the crew captured.

Now I knew what the guys meant when they said there was nothing better than seeing the White Cliffs of Dover. I've never seen anything prettier in my life. It was like they were welcoming us back home. It was hard to believe everything had happened in just one day. My sense of time was completely gone. It seemed like we had been flying for days.

When we landed, the Red Cross women had tables set up for us, with donuts and hot coffee. They knew not to ask questions about the mission, but their warm smiles sure made us feel better.

"When did you first see fighters? How many were there? Did you see the bombs hit the target? Did you see any ships go down? Where did they go down? How many men got out?" The voice of the intelligence officer was steady and even. They knew exactly what to ask us. They offered us some brandy after the mission. That helped a little. Some of the men had a hard time settling down enough to answer the questions. Several hours of flying— extreme cold, bone-jarring vibration, intense gunfire, and the constant fear that every second might be your last—can key you up a bit.

A PUB called The Fox was really home for me. It was right behind my hut, so I could always make it home to bed. The proprietor, Mr. Kemp, was a big, ruddy-faced German who had lived in England his entire life. He sort of adopted me. "Tommy! Mr. Tommy LaMore! Did you ruin Herr Hitler's day today?" He always said that. He had a bottle of my favorite brandy stashed behind the bar. That day the brandy got to the bar before I did. "Here's to your first mission!" Mr. Kemp boomed out to everyone in the pub. The guys who hadn't flown yet came right over.

"How was it? Did you shoot down any Krauts?" I tried to

answer their real question—"What is it really like?"—but I began to realize there was no way. Just no way.

I was jumpy and tired, and it surprised me to see the glass shaking a little in my hand. I tried to be nonchalant about the mission, but there was a hell of a mess going on in my mind. It was as if I had two minds. One was replaying the extraordinary terror I had just experienced, and one was trying to operate my body and relate to the people around me. I found myself slipping back and forth between these two minds. I kept thinking about the planes that had gone down and what had happened to those men. For a brief minute I thought, *Man, how am I going to survive twenty-four more of these missions?*

The brass must have known how severe the stress was going to be for the crews when they introduced the concept of limiting an airman's combat to twenty-five missions. This policy gave us a goal, something for our minds to work with. We got on a treadmill after the first mission. There was a lot of strange, superstitious behavior and religious thoughts, too. Some of the guys had rabbit's feet, lucky neck chains, pictures, you name it.

I finally made it back to my original crew the following month. It was like coming home. Our crew tended to skip the superstitious stuff, although we would pray together just before the mission. We were led by the soft low voice of Lieutenant Armour Bowen. We wanted to be in touch with our God.

THE BIG moment was always when the briefing officer drew back the curtain covering the mission map. He always did this with a flourish. When the red line was short, the tension level in the room dropped right away. We would have fighter escorts on these missions and the Luftwaffe didn't like to deal with American fighters on top of the gunners in the bombers.

My next two missions were runs over St. Avord and Nancy,

both in France. We flew in to bomb Luftwaffe airfields, to stir up Goering's Abbeville boys. Abbeville is a small town about thirty-five miles east of Dieppe, which was famous in World War I as the great hinge point of the Allied armies. Now it was the home base of Goering's pet Luftwaffe fighter group.

The flak wasn't nearly as bad on the St. Avord mission, and the German fighters didn't have much of a chance to get to us, because we had fighter escorts the whole way, and they were getting to be very good. We had several fighter aces by this time, especially Colonels Zimke and Spicer. These guys were racking up kills in double digits, which did a lot to lift our spirits.

On the Nancy mission the P-51s did a great job of eating up Goering's boys. Those Luftwaffe pilots were the toughest, most aggressive pilots we encountered. They were the most experienced outfit in the Luftwaffe, and they were good. They attacked straight through the formation, half-rolling and firing all the way. Many times they would fly straight at us until a collision was almost unavoidable, then pull the plane up into a steep climb that would expose their underbellies. They would "flood the zone" by coming in from the same position at different levels, which meant that the gunners could engage only one of them. They held their firing buttons down to the last second, and they were very accurate with their fire. They didn't waste a round. We had a lot of respect for this outfit.

I saw the wildest dogfights of any of my missions on February 6, 1944, over France. The P-51s flew straight into the Luftwaffe fighters, head-on, full throttle. Goering's boys hesitated, then peeled off and engaged in several individual dogfights. It was an incredible sight. There were about fifty German fighters and an equal number of P-51s. The sky was full of twisting, wheeling fighters, spraying tracers everywhere. I counted eleven German fighters knocked down in the first few minutes, and only one smoking P-51 headed for home. I saw two Me-109s collide and explode in a huge black-orange fireball.

I got to the intercom first. "Whew! I bet that smarted! Scratch two 109s."

Buzzy checked in. "Hope that fighter tactic catches on with the Luftwaffe!"

"These Krauts have to be wondering, just what is a Mustang anyway? Eat 'em up, baby! Eat 'em right up!"

The intercom was a joy to listen to that day.

There were very few chutes coming out of the burning German fighters. When the six .50s of the Mustangs hit a Luftwaffe fighter, they just disintegrated, with pieces flying everywhere. White smoke followed, then a big ball of fire.

You could tell those guys were going at each other for all the marbles. The fight lasted about thirty minutes, and there wasn't a time when any of the German fighters could get free to make a firing pass at the formation. We began to notice that the P-51 had turning and speed advantages over the Me-109s. Our guys had just reached the point where they could fly those Mustangs to their absolute limit and then some. The German planes seemed a little stiffer, a little slower coming out of turns—except the FW-190s, which were smaller and seemed to be much more agile. We noticed that the Germans matched the FW-190s with the P-51s, and the Me-109s with the P-47s.

With our strong fighter escorts, it was beginning to seem like we might actually make this whole thing work. I began to think maybe I might survive twenty-five missions.

The days and missions went by in a long blur. On February 11, we hit Ludwigshaven, on the Rhine, and on February 20, Leipzig, which was just ninety miles south of Berlin. Those were long missions with relentless fighter attacks and nightmarish flak. We all wondered why they didn't keep us on shorter missions until the P-51s were ready to escort us all the way into Germany.

We encountered something new on these missions that bothered me a great deal. Air-to-air rockets. Pairs of Junkers 88s would hang out on the sides of the formation, out of gun range, and lob in these large rockets with long whitish streams that came through the formations in the blink of an eye. They weren't guided, but they were lethal. When I saw them, I called them out on the intercom, but there wasn't much we could do. We couldn't shoot at them, because they were moving so fast. All we could do was watch. I saw one hit a B-17 behind us. It blew the wing off with a big explosion, which threw the plane into a violent spin. There were no chutes.

WE CAME through those missions okay, and I had the short walk to The Fox pub virtually memorized. There was a long plank over a muddy ditch that was slippery and twisted. For some reason, it was more difficult to maintain course and altitude coming back to the hut.

Mr. Kemp would always have my brandy waiting for me, and we would clink our glasses and toast to the success of the mission. He knew not to ask too much about the mission. He knew it was an effort to keep up the illusion that not much was really wrong.

All of us airmen were slowly changing. Slowly becoming more serious, less carefree. There was a certain look that developed in the men who were flying combat missions. It was a hard look. Our mannerisms were changing, too. We were edgy, prone to sudden outbursts and long periods of quiet, even in a crowded pub. The war was like a corrosive liquid that seeped into us, and hardened us, and made us shrink away from the world, then rush back into it, talking much too loud.

Sometimes there was a mission where everything seemed awkward and wrong, right from the start. The February 22, 1944, mission to Oscherslabon, Germany was one. It was my seventh mission, and I thought it would be a lucky one.

When the curtain was pulled back, the red line looked like it stretched all the way to Poland. Oschersleben, Germany, was about 100 miles west of Berlin. The target was a BMW engine plant, which elicited a long groan in the briefing room. These engines powered the FW-190 fighters, and this would be a high-priority target to protect. They told us to expect heavy fighter opposition and to take maximum ammo. The target was at the extreme end of our range, and there was a lot of muffled discussion among the pilots about the length of the mission. Everyone in the room stared at the navigators. All I heard was "maximum fuel . . . maximum load . . . maximum range . . ." Maximum.

The weather was terrible. The cloud cover was right on the deck and dark with rain, which forced our escorts back early. The taxi and takeoff operations were all snarled up, and several planes didn't make the rendezvous point. Everyone was grouchy as hell. Nothing seemed to be going right.

Our takeoff was somehow longer and more nerve-wracking than usual. We lifted off about three feet before the end of that runway. Everyone in our plane was so tense our voices sounded different. Higher pitched, fearful. I felt like I was made out of steel cables. I just couldn't loosen up. I was trying to limber up a little when I thought I felt the plane slow down slightly. "Boost dropping on number two. Boost down to seven pounds. Boost zero. Oil temperature rising fast on number two, Lieutenant," copilot O'Neal's voice was steady but tense. "Sir, we have to shut down number two." The words stayed on the intercom for a long time. We were just passing over the French coast, bouncing around in big, sticky clouds.

"Feather number two." We all waited for Lieutenant Bowen to finish the sentence with, "Men, we are forced to return to base with a dead engine." Nothing. We droned on, with a steady beating vibration from the feathered prop. We were going on. No one said anything, but we all were thinking the same thing. Lunchtime for the Luftwaffe. But Lieutenant Bowen was a "get the job done" kind of guy who didn't like starting things twice. That's just how he was, and he was our leader.

There had been talk that the Luftwaffe was moving even more fighter squadrons back to Germany from Russia, and today that was an easy rumor to believe. The fighters were everywhere. For the first time I saw waves of six and seven fighters. They streaked through the formations from every imaginable angle, and they never let up. I was sweating heavily and breathing hard from the extended work of flinging the guns around for so long. With ammo belts, the twin fifties weighed over 130 pounds each, which was more than I weighed.

"Fighters! Fighters!" The intercom never stopped. Fighters everywhere. Every gun on every ship was firing. "I don't know which way to go with these bastards. Tommy! Six! Six o'clock!" Buzzy screamed.

"I got you, Buzzy. Terry! Fighters at nine low. Nine low!" I tried to get the words out between bursts. The Me-109 was boring straight in at me from six o'clock low. I lined him up in the ring sight and waited until I knew he was in range, then started firing short bursts. The yellow and red blinking on his wings began just as my red tracers arced out to him, tearing pieces of black metal off the plane. He broke off, pulled up, and exploded.

"Fighters at one o'clock!" Jim Pilger yelled in the mike. We had every gun firing on that plane, and I felt like I was a small rock in a large can. The fighters came at us and came at us and came at us. I saw a Fortress behind us and to my left attacked by a stream of fighters. A big ball of fire suddenly erupted from its number-one engine, and a black stream of smoke started coming out of number two. The pilot slowly winged the plane out of the formation, and chutes started popping out. I counted seven.

"You got seven chutes back there, Tommy?" Julian said.

"Yeah, seven." Seven was good. Real good. Usually there were only two or three, and they would come out before the plane headed into the inevitable steep, sickening spiral that made it almost impossible for the crew to get out. We all wondered what it was like, being pinned inside the plane, thrown around and slammed into the fuselage, knowing that death was a few long minutes away. Our minds stopped this thinking up there, on the mission, but later, in odd moments and in crystal clear night-mares, we finished the process. The plane suddenly snapped into a tight spin and headed straight down, streaming black smoke and flames.

The flak was an almost solid dark cloud over the target. It was hard to imagine that anything could fly through it. I had arranged two flak vests under me, and that gave me some comfort. Suddenly there was a loud sound like someone hitting a giant fry-ing pan with a huge spoon, and the ship shuddered slightly.

The explosion slammed my head into the fuselage. An icy blast of air hit me from behind and whipped me around like a doll. The cold air was like an invisible fire hose, tearing my face apart, rip-ping at my ears, and slamming me into the fuselage. There was a large hole in my left window. I couldn't hear the intercom. I tried to get my helmet to cover my face, but it wouldn't reach. Then I felt nothing, and I couldn't hear the noise anymore.

They were still coming, still attacking from six o'clock low. I grabbed the guns and held on and fired. Just as one Me-109 screamed past, another one took its place. They must have seen our dead engine and my shot-up position. They were working us over good. I fired short bursts, then even shorter bursts, one eye on the ammo belts. The familiar *chang chang chang* of my guns changed for the first time. They slowed down. I pulled the triggers and held them down, but the guns just fired a few lazy rounds. Then a few more. Then they stopped. *Would they notice? Would the German pilots see I wasn't firing?* I wondered. I frantically yanked the charging levers on the guns, but they were frozen. White smoke poured from the receiver slots.

Then we were over the target. The plane jumped up as we dropped our bombs. It seemed like we had flown halfway around the world to get to the IP, the initial point of release. We wheeled around and headed home, and there was a little break in the fighter attacks. Then I felt a tremendous shudder in the plane. It felt like a boat that had run aground at full speed. I was thrown backwards to the floor of the plane.

"We've lost number-four engine to flak," Lieutenant Bowen called out. I could barely hear him with my right ear. I twisted around to look through the hole in my enclosure. We'd lost it, all right—number-four engine was gone. Wires and tubing from the jagged nacelle were violently whipping the wing in the black smoke.

"Crew, prepare to bail out!" Bowen's usually soft voice was high-pitched. We dropped out of formation trailing heavy black smoke.

Parachute. Harness. I tried to think clearly in the noise and blowing debris. I tried to find the triangle of the ripcord, tried to remember the bailout procedure. As I looked back, I saw the formation heading off with swarms of German fighters tearing at them. I had never thought about leaving the protection of the formation. It was like being in a life raft and watching a ship sail away.

Lieutenant Bowen eased the plane down in a controlled spiral and lowered the landing gear to slow our descent. Every time we came out of the clouds, the fighters were there. I felt something hit the plane hard from above and heard a new commotion on the intercom. There was a lot of yelling and garbled talk. "Stuart hit! Top ball out, top ball out!" Oliver Stuart, our top ball turret gunner, had been hit and was down on the floor of the plane between the pilot and copilot.

The fighters kept coming. My guns still wouldn't put out more than three rounds before they stopped. An FW-190 must have figured it out and flew by so close I could have touched his wingtip.

"Lower ball out of ammo!" I heard Buzzy call out. Both turrets out. We were finished now. I did all I could to keep firing and spread the short bursts around. We were in and out of the clouds, hoping to get away, hoping the fighters would turn back to the formation. A lone Me-109 dove on my position out of a cloud bank and started firing. The two or three tracers from my guns arced over his canopy, and he was gone.

At ten thousand feet copilot O'Neal tried to restart number-two engine. We could run the engine now, because we didn't need the turbocharger at this lower altitude. It finally caught. We hopped from cloud to cloud, flying level now, with three engines. Every time we came out of the clouds, the fighters jumped us. They couldn't leave a cripple alone. I fired, then fired some more. My guns slowed down, stuttered, and stopped. I tried to clear both guns, but they were locked up solid and pouring white smoke. I pulled the two short ammo belts off the guns and scrambled up to the waist gunners' position.

A trip I had made a hundred times was now like swimming through water. The air stream from the blown-out top turret was roaring through the fuselage. Pieces of wire, insulation, and dirt were blowing past me like they were shot out of a cannon. Both waist gunners were out of ammo and were attacking their mounts to jettison their guns. Any less weight in the plane would help us stay in the air. I helped Buzzy out of the lower turret by hand-cranking the turret.

"Man, am I glad to get the hell out of this turret! I'm out of ammo, and I don't have any power!" Buzzy yelled. He and the waist gunners started the tough job of unbolting the lower turret right away. We popped out of the clouds again, and it was clear. We all stuck our heads out of the waist gun ports. No fighters! They had lost us.

Once I got past the radio room and the bomb bay, I saw the blood. It was everywhere in the cockpit area. Thick, red, in big smears. Stuart was laying on his back facing me. His face was a bloody pulp, and he was breathing in shallow short breaths. I knew that controlling the bleeding was the key to keeping him alive. Matty, our bombardier, rolled a bandage and compress around his head as tight as he dared. Matty and Jim Pilger propped him up behind the pilot's seat and zipped up his B-10 jacket tight to keep him warm. I said a quick prayer for Stuart. It was up to God now.

"You got the RAF (Royal Air Force) yet, Johnny?" Lieutenant Bowen asked the radio operator.

"Roger, Lieutenant, they're trying to get something in the air for us. I'll know in five minutes."

They were trying to set up a rendezvous with British fighters. We were in a very bad spot. We couldn't bail out and leave our wounded crewman in the plane. Lieutenant Bowen and the navigator worked out the shortest course back.

"We think we can make it back. It's about fifty-fifty, men," Lieutenant Bowen said almost nonchalantly. "Get everything out. Everything."

Unbolting the lower turret was a tough job, and one of the bolts was seized. They finally got it, and Buzzy pulled the safety pin. The plane lurched up slightly, and Buzzy almost slipped out the hole. I grabbed his arms, but his head hit the fuselage with a loud whack.

"Thank you, Tommy. I almost joined the 101st Airborne on that caper!" he said, still dazed.

"Come to two four seven, two four seven, hold two four seven. Hold two four seven." Jim Pilger called compass headings to Bowen, who was trying to hold the weaving, vibrating plane on course.

Johnny was working feverishly, first contacting the rescue groups and trying to work out a rendezvous point for fighter escorts. This was very tricky. The Germans had radios, too, and they had fighter strips all over that area. He had to use several different codes. There was nothing for the gunners to do. We were not only out of ammo, we were out of guns. All we could do was sweat it out. No one said a word.

The plane wasn't really flying, it was just tearing a big hole in the sky. The vibration and sound from the ripped-out engine and shot-out turret were together a shrieking, chattering roar.

"We are forty miles east of RAF intercept," Johnny said. We poked our heads out just as the RAF came over the horizon at full speed. Spitfires! They flew around us and closed up. One of the pilots took a good look at us and shook his head. *Don't you Americans ever give up?* he seemed to say. We could have kissed those guys. I noticed for a second how beat-up the Spitfires were. At least now we wouldn't be captured, and it looked like we were going to make it to the Channel.

We all cheered out loud when we crossed over the French coast. They said you could wish a B-17 home, and that's what we did. Fortunately for us, the Eighth Air Force had just opened a new fighter strip on the south coast of England, and Jim had us right on top it.

We circled the field once, dropped red flares, and lined up on the runway. All eight of us hunched up in the radio compartment and braced ourselves for the wheels-up landing. We squeezed Stuart in between us. He was like a rag doll, quietly coughing blood.

Bowen set the plane down in the mud next to the runway with just a couple of loud whacks as the props hit the ground. Big chunks of mud and grass flew past the window as the plane slid along.

Suddenly it was quiet. We struggled up and made for the waist gunner's doors as white, oily smoke began to fill the plane. We quickly carried Stuart out and moved off about fifty yards from the plane. An ambulance lurched to a halt alongside, and we carefully loaded Stuart in. He was white as a sheet and shivering terribly. Stuart would live, but he would never fly again.

We took off our flight jackets and started looking at the smoking ship. The number-four engine mount was a black, twisted hole with wires and lines and mangled tubing hanging out. There were over two hundred holes in the plane. She never flew again.

"Tommy boy, your little home away from home got chewed up some," Buzzy said, as we looked at the bowling-ball-size hole in the left window of my position. I had almost forgotten. I suddenly tried to touch my face to see if I was wounded, but it wasn't there. It didn't feel like it was there at all. I finally got a look at my face in a truck mirror and saw the whole left side of my face was pure white and was just beginning to blister. My face had been frozen solid.

■ ■ ■

THE 381ST Squadron sent a plane down that afternoon to bring us back to Ridgewell. My face began to throb, then pound, then settled into a deep, searing ache. They took me straight to the base hospital, where the last word I heard was morphine.

The next day they treated the frostbite blister with a salve to take the tension off my face. They tried several packs and treatments in the next six days, but I really didn't care. That was it for me. I never wanted to fly again. I wanted to give it up. How the hell could we possibly live through twenty-five of these missions? I had flown seven missions in three weeks, five of them deep missions into central and east Germany. I was really shook up, exhausted, and depressed. The weariness in me made me feel like I weighed a thousand pounds, and every thought was just a long headache. As far as I was concerned, Tommy LaMore was finished.

Our navigator, Jim Pilger, came up to see me on a rainy, dark Tuesday. Jim was a wonderful fellow, a man I admired and respected.

"I never want to fly again," I told him. "I never want to go up again. That's it for me, Jim. I just don't think I can do her."

Jim listened and didn't say much. I rambled on for a while, blurting out similar statements one after another. It felt good to say what you were thinking. My mind was going a hundred miles an hour, and the pain had worn me out. Hearing myself speak helped organize the confusion in my mind.

Jim listened for a long time. When I finally finished, he said, "We need you, Tommy. You've got too much to offer the crew just to go and give up on it." He was a soft-spoken man who didn't say much. Then he shook his head. "You're just not a quitter, Tommy. Some men are, but you're not."

I realized some of the things I had been saying didn't sound like me. I decided the only way I could do it was to get away from the hospital and get right back in the air. I walked straight up to HQ and told them I had been released and I wanted to go on the next mission. That kind of request was a little out of place in those days.

Two days later, on March 2, 1944, I flew a mission to Frankfurt with Lieutenant Milton Fastrup's crew. I couldn't get back with my old crew for scheduling reasons. Once I got back in the plane, I felt like I belonged there. I took a lot of deep breaths, and I talked to my God. The mission seemed like it lasted for a week, but we weren't hit, and I saw a beautiful rainbow in the clouds just before we landed. It seemed like it was just for me.

WE BEGAN to hear about a mission to Berlin. Everyone wondered when we were going to hit the German capital. The Nazis were at the height of their power, and hitting Berlin in broad daylight would be a huge psychological victory for the Allies. The British had hit Berlin a few times at night, but they were very small raids. We all wanted to ruin Hilter's day, big time.

On the morning of March 6, there was a buzz of excitement running around the base. The briefing officer pulled back the curtain with an extra flourish, almost like a bullfighter with a cape, and there it was. BERLIN. For all the anticipation and desire to hit Berlin, when it was really up there the men suddenly became very quiet. The big one. The really big one. They told us it would be like the Fourth of July.

They said that we could expect the heaviest fighter opposition and the heaviest flak of the war over the target. They told us to take max ammo belts, and we would be flying with max bomb loads and max fuel. They had planned a circuitous route that might help throw the Germans off a little, but it would add a lot of

flying time to the mission. We left the briefing with mixed feelings. We wanted to take the war to Berlin, but the realization of
the coming punishment left everyone somber.

I was flying with Lieutenant Robert W. Mayburn's crew. We
took off just before dawn and used every foot of the runway to get
off the ground. Man, we were going to do it. A big daylight raid on
Berlin, right in front of the eyeballs of the entire German nation.
We felt like we were writing history. Our escorts joined up with
us as we left the Channel. I noticed something different on this
mission, after we had formed up and turned east. It took me a
long time to realize that I couldn't see to the end of the formation!
The contrails went all the way to the horizon. We all wondered
how many ships were on this mission, and the guesses went from
150 to 500 ships. Whatever the number was, it filled the entire
sky with B-17s. Years later, I learned that there were about 670
B-17s on this mission, with 69 lost. This was a very loud and clear
message to the Nazis. This seemingly endless stream of bombers
made the Luftwaffe pilots realize that they were being overwhelmed by sheer numbers of aircraft.

Our escorts had belly tanks, but they finally had to turn back
about an hour into the mission.

About thirty seconds after our escorts left us, the Luftwaffe
came at us from everywhere. Hundreds and hundreds of fighters.
I saw one plane take a hit on its number-one and number-two
engines. Huge balls of fire came off the wing. Then the wing came
off, and the plane immediately snapped into a twisting, sickening
dive. I yelled, "Get out, get out of that plane, you bastards!" Not a
single chute came out. Everything welled up in me. I began to cry.
I was mad. I wanted to kill some German pilots. I wanted to kill a
lot of German pilots that day.

Once we turned for Berlin and it became obvious what the target was, the fighters multiplied to the point where they were almost running into each other. There was no favored firing pass now. They came from everywhere, singly, in twos, threes, and fours. And something new. They came at us in swarms, like bees. They seemed to pick out a plane and attack it from several directions simultaneously. Once they started on a ship, it went down. That was it. They dove through us, weaving and turning, they climbed up through us, firing and twisting all the way. They made head-on firing passes, streaking away from us at over 600 MPH.

Just as we approached the IP, one of the planes behind us was hit in its number-four engine, which immediately erupted in a white-yellow ball of flame. Then number-three engine took a hit, and the whole right wing burst into a huge wall of flame. The pilot held it on course, desperately trying to correct the wigwag motion until the men bailed out. They jumped out right through the flames and held their ripcords until they were clear. "Two, no three, there's four. Five! Six. Come on! Come on, you guys!" The intercom became quiet when it nosed over and plunged down. The pilots did a hell of a job holding that plane steady while the crew got out. They didn't.

When we neared the target, there was a lot of chatter on the intercom. "We are on the IP. Flak. Very heavy. Flak . . . Hang on, men." The bombardier's voice was serious and tense. The sky was black with flak. It looked like nothing any of us had ever seen. *How many guns did the Germans have?* There must have been thousands of guns firing at us, and they were right on the altitude. Once we got into the flak, the German fighters broke off to refuel, which was a relief for the gunners. All we could do then was hope, pray, and sit on our flak jackets.

Berlin from the air was a huge, dark city. I couldn't make out any landmarks, but I did get a rush of excitement. This was

Hitler's town. The big bad boys lived in this neighborhood. For the first time, I felt a little cocky. Go ahead, send the Luftwaffe up, go ahead, shoot at us with everything you've got, but here we are, blowing up your houses in front of your master-race eyeballs. I cheered when the bombs left the racks. "Hold on to your sauerkraut, Adolf!" I yelled.

"Heil, Hitler, your mama!" Buzzy added.

"Explain this little problem, Goebbels!"

"Vat vas dat boom-boom-boom, Broomhilde? Is your sister here?" Everyone had worked out a special little comment.

As we winged over and pulled away, I saw hundreds of bright yellow flashes followed by thousands of tiny red explosions from the bomblets. I wondered briefly what it must be like for the people below. There wasn't much sympathy in me for them. They had started this damn war. These people had dished out plenty of this medicine for half the world and never once shown a trace of mercy. The hell with them.

Coming back was better than we thought it would be. We were running low on oxygen and had uneasy thoughts about what that might mean. The fighters had just begun hitting us again when we saw a big flight of shiny new P-51s. Those P-51 pilots tore after the Germans with every bit of speed they had. Full-throttle dives head-on, no breaking off, no pulling up. They were all over the sky. Some of the German fighters actually ran. We couldn't believe it. We felt like we were seeing a miracle. "Eat 'em up, baby! Eat 'em right up!" I didn't usually yell into the intercom, but I couldn't help myself. Seeing the guts and tenacity of our fighter pilots was like watching your football team win the homecoming game.

I thought the wings were going to rip off some of the P-51s when they dived on the Germans. Man, those pilots could fly those Mustangs. It looked like some invisible hand was flinging them around the sky. They dove right into the Germans, until it seemed like that big four-blade prop was going to chew the Me-109s apart. Then they would follow the Germans turn-for-turn in tight, violent diving S turns, firing in quick bursts. Every time a German fighter disintegrated into a ball of fire and black smoking debris, the guys would whoop and cheer. It was almost fun.

Once the P-51s met us, the flight back was easy. We tried to lay in a few long-range bursts at the German fighters as they twisted and wheeled around the sky, but mostly we just watched. This was an important milestone for us in the air war. We knew it was going to be easier for us from here on out.

WE SPENT eleven hours and fifty minutes in the air that day, and we were really beat up when we lined up on the runway. I just wanted to get down and hit The Fox pub.

Ridgewell never looked better when we flew over, so green and peaceful. But there was something going on. Something big. When we were rolling down the runway, I saw a huge crowd of people on the tarmac. There were people everywhere, civilians and women in dresses and Red Cross workers. There were reporters in trenchcoats with big cameras, and men on the tops of cars with movie cameras.

I kidded Buzzy. "Check your makeup, Buzzy. Looks like we're gonna be in the movies!" Bombing Berlin in daylight in 1944 was a real crowd pleaser.

As we taxied in, a big cheer went up. We could just hear it over the engines. We waved and almost burst out of our flight suits with pride. We taxied past the gray Rolls Royce of the royal family, and several big black cars from Churchill's office.

Our ground crew had set up banquet tables, and the Red Cross women were decked out in their best clothes. "Well done, airmen. Well done indeed!" they said with big smiles and warm spontaneous hugs. There was cold beer and toddies for everyone. I had two drinks, and I felt like I had been drinking all day. We had never seen anything like this.

Everyone knew this was an important turning point. There had been a lot of concern that the Germans might shoot down many of the Forts, but the losses had been lighter than expected. We had a few flak holes in the plane, but Lady Luck had been with us that day. I found myself watching the long line of B-17s coming in to land, and all at once I realized that there were very few red flares.

"Tommy! How did it go? Berlin today! Think of it. Berlin! Drinks for everyone tonight." Mr. Kemp bought a round for everyone in that smoky little pub that night. That was the second big shock of the day for me. Living through the mission was the first, and watching Mr. Kemp give away drinks was the second. Mr. Kemp was tighter than a tied ballgame.

I got pretty smashed that night, like everyone else. There was a tiny moment, one of those moments you have when you're really tanked, when you find yourself looking at the edge of the bar, not thinking, just waiting for the next thought. I had just reached the point where I had stopped thinking about the men who died in front of my eyes that day. I was thinking nothing. Then I heard some one say, "After the war, I'm going into my dad's tire business." Then someone else said, "After the war, I'm going out to California." *After the war, I'm.* There it was! Two magnificent new ideas. *After the war, I'm. This war might end! I'm! I might live. I might live to go home and enjoy life and be somebody. I might live! The war might end!* I stood straight up and smiled and laughed, and then I stood on the bar and starting laughing crazily. I looked around and saw other guys laughing crazily, too. It was really possible. It was really, really possible. We might just live.

WE EAGERLY waited the posting of the strike photos the next day. There was a big crowd around them. Berlin looked a lot better to us with big, nasty bomb craters where long, orderly buildings had been. The strike was a great success, and most of the bombs were on target. "Six months, it's over. Six, maybe five." The wishful thinking even got down to sixty days.

We hit Berlin again two days later, on March 8, and hit the city again the next day. The Luftwaffe had lost a lot of planes to the B-17 gunners and the P-51s, and the number of fighters was visibly diminished. The opposition was still fierce, and the flak was bad, but somehow the tide had turned. Everything seemed possible now.

I became fatalistic after a while. I gave up all the thinking and calculating, and even the fear seemed forgotten. I figured if I was going to make it, I was going to make it, and if I didn't, well . . . I didn't. At that time, some of the first men who had completed their twenty-five missions were heading home, and that lifted morale considerably. I actually began to think I might survive my twenty-five missions.

But the wear and tear on the crews was bad, and some of the men just couldn't take it. One of these men came up to me one day and asked if he could talk. I didn't quite realize it then, but I was considered a seasoned veteran—I'd flown about eighteen missions, and I tried to help out the green crewmembers when I could. He told me that he didn't think he could stand any more flying. The worrying and the fear made it hard for him to eat, and he looked very thin. He just said point-blank, "I'm so afraid of dying on these missions, it's all I think about, and I can hardly get through the day. What do you think I should do?" I felt a little uncomfortable. I told him that I had felt the same way after Oschersleben, and that Jim Pilger had helped me out a lot. I told him he was needed, and the job he was doing was important. Keeping busy helped me manage some of the anxiety, and I told him this. He didn't say much, but I think he felt a little better. He walked away slowly, clenching his hands under his armpits as he walked.

"OKAY, YOU heroes, get up. You're going to go see Hitler today. Let's go, angels!" The officer of the day seemed louder than normal, and it seemed like we should have a day off. It was about three weeks after the first Berlin raid. We had hit Ahlen, Germany, in the Ruhr Valley, the day before on a long, difficult mission, and Berlin the day before that. We were all tired, and I just didn't feel like flying.

Nothing seemed right that day. My clothes went on slow, I couldn't seem to wake up, and when we got outside, the weather was completely closed in. There was a lot of muttering about why were we flying in such lousy weather.

After we sat down in the briefing room, the curtain came back kind of slowly, almost sadly. The red line was a long one, and at the end was a name that we all knew and dreaded. Schweinfurt. Schweinfurt was a word that usually came at the end of a sentence that began, "As bad as. . . ." Schweinfurt was a bad target. The first Schweinfurt raid was referred to as Black Thursday, because sixty Forts had gone down. That meant six hundred crewmen lost.

Schweinfurt was a small town about seventy miles due east of Frankfurt am Main. The area was highly important to the Germans because their ball bearing manufacturing industry was there. The idea behind strategic bombing was to cripple the enemy's industrial base, and the target pickers loved the idea of stopping the factory production lines in Germany because of a shortage of ball bearings.

Everyone was on edge that day. We could almost reach up and touch the dark gray clouds. I got out to the plane and ran through the guns and checked the bomb rack. I kept looking out at the clouds. The weather was right on the deck, and the clouds had become fog. You could see all the men looking up, all thinking the same thing. We just shook our heads.

I was standing by the tail next to my hatch when I saw someone waving at me. It was the guy I had talked to who was so afraid of dying. I gave him the thumbs-up sign, and he smiled.

"We're cleared for takeoff, men. Here we go," Lieutenant Rickerson called out on the intercom a short time later. We thundered down the runway until it seemed like we couldn't possibly make it. We lifted off right at the end of that runway. We pulled up into the overcast, climbing very slowly. From my tail gunner position I watched the second plane behind us going down the runway. He lifted slowly, then veered drunkenly to the right, finally dragging the wingtip into the plowed field. The plane pinwheeled and exploded. The explosion was a long, rippling, bright orange explosion that engulfed the trees and the brush. Then a flash of white light obliterated the whole area, throwing trees hundreds of feet into the air as the bomb load exploded. Much later I learned that the young guy I had talked to about fear was on that plane.

The clouds just wouldn't quit. We climbed and climbed, but the clouds extended all the way up. They were huge, thick, billowy clouds. Our escort fighters picked us up over the Channel, but they were having trouble with the clouds as well. Everyone was shook up that day. We would fly into clouds and stay in them for several minutes. A few ships aborted, citing weather. We heard on the radio that there had been several near collisions.

The feeling of flying in clouds is like driving way too fast with no headlights. The anxiety builds to the point where you can't sit still. Every sound, every movement, tells you death is near.

We flew like that for hours. My back began to ache from the anxiety. We would break out of the clouds for a few seconds and start to adjust to the sunlight and visibility, hoping the clouds were behind us, then the engine noise would suddenly quiet down and the air suddenly became an ocean of white-gray nothingness. Somehow you felt if you kept quiet, it would go away.

When we got close to the IP, there weren't breaks anymore, just solid white clouds. "Abort. Abort! Why the hell don't they abort this mission?" I said to no one in particular. "How can we hit anything in this weather?"

As if in a dream, I saw a ship looming out of the clouds to my right. They were way too close, only two hundred feet away, but the pilot saw us and corrected. I waved to the tail gunner, who held both palms upward as if to say, *What the hell are we doing here?* The plane slipped off to my right and picked up a little altitude.

I was desperately trying to settle down, trying to find a way to deal with my fear. I remembered a saying from my childhood:

Come one, come all, this rock shall fly from its firm base, and so shall I.

I silently repeated it over and over. The seconds passed by a little easier. I don't know why.

I looked out the left window trying to see where our wingman was when a B-17 tail section loomed up right underneath me.

"Aircraft directly under—" I tried to call out to the pilot, but it was too late. There was a loud, scraping metallic noise and a grinding crunch. Our plane shuddered violently and pitched into a sharp dive, slamming me into the ceiling. Our number-three and number-four engines had hit the other plane from above, severing their cockpit. Their number-one prop had cut the nose of our plane completely off. We were locked together and falling rapidly.

My head was slammed into the left window as we collided. I hit so hard that all I saw was a bright blue flash that slowly gave way to black, then light blue, then white. I opened my eyes, blinking as hard as I could, but everything was a white blur with bright red streaks billowing violently around me. The plane was shaking so hard I couldn't tell if I was seeing or if I just thought I was seeing. Then panic shot through me like a jolt of electricity. *We're going down! Out, gotta get out!*

I desperately grabbed at the flapping white blur, suddenly realizing I didn't know what it was, but it was real! I could touch it. It was tearing at me, smothering me. *We're crashing! Down! Going down!* My breathing bag slapped loudly. One second I could move, the next I was pinned so hard to the ceiling I couldn't breathe. Finally, the plane dipped and dropped me on my gunner's seat. The white blur slapped me so hard now that it stung my face and woke me up a little. I grabbed at it, tearing it from my face. A chute! My chute had popped open and filled my enclosure. I couldn't get past it. It was slippery and covered with blood and the lines tangled around my feet. All I could think about was getting out, getting to the hatch. I tried to pull myself down to the hatch, but it was impossible. My muscles weren't working. Then I realized I couldn't bail out. My chute was gone.

We were falling fast, dipping and rolling left and right. I was slammed around the fuselage. There was a loud pop, and we lurched left and up. Then we stopped. It was as if the plane had rolled up and parked. We were gliding.

I could feel the pilot struggling to get control of the plane, and he finally leveled it out and brought the power up on engines one and two. I slammed into the floor and hit my shoulder on the gunner's seat. I wiped the blood off the window with my chute and looked out and saw the other plane in a sharp right bank, debris streaming out of the huge gash in the cockpit. I thought maybe they were okay until a bright white light and a monstrous red and black explosion took the place of the damaged plane.

I struggled past the tail wheel to the waist gunner area into so much wind I could hardly stand. The entire nose section was gone, and there were large chunks of debris blasting through the plane. There was blood running into my eyes, and I couldn't stand. *This is it,* I thought.

I must have looked like a ghost to the waist gunners. They helped me get the chute lines off my legs and handed me a compress for my head wound.

"Pilot says we're gonna try and make it back," the gunner nearest to me yelled over the screaming wind.

"We gotta dump everything if we're gonna make it," I yelled, turning around to look out at the engines on the right wing. Number three was on fire, and four was dead, with a mangled prop windmilling dangerously. We quickly cranked the ball turret around and got the gunner out.

"Are we going, are we bailing out?" he yelled.

"Not now," I told him.

He looked out at the right wing and shook his head. "You sure?"

Lieutenant Wilson, the copilot, finally got the fire on number three out, then told us we were going to try to get the plane back. I didn't see how.

"Salvo the bombs! Salvo the bombs!" Lieutenant Rickerson yelled over the intercom, and there was a loud tearing sound as the bombs crashed through the bomb bay doors. The plane lurched up and pitched to the left.

We were barely flying, pitching and rolling on engines one and two. We flew along for about an hour, frantically throwing guns and ammo out of the plane. We had lost a lot of altitude and were down to about 10,000 feet. We dumped everything, including the ball turret. We had a tool kit to unbolt the turret in an emergency, but it took forever. Now we were too low to bail out, but I couldn't bail out anyway because of my chute.

"We're not going to make it, everyone prepare to crash-land!" Lieutenant Wilson called out. Everyone got into the radio room and tried to find a spot to brace for the crash. "Get in, get braced, boys. Here it is. Hold on!" the pilot yelled.

I helped the guys around me get settled into a crash position, then tried to brace myself outside the radio room. There was a lurch and a bump, then the earth grabbed the plane all at once with a vengeance. I could feel the bones in my shoulder grind and crunch. The pain tore through my body. I closed my eyes so tight I could see the waves of pain pulsing in bright red sheets of light. The B-17 finally shuddered to a halt in a last grinding metallic crunch.

For a few moments it was quiet. Then, "Get out, everyone, get out quick!" We all yelled the same thing. We had been trained to burn the plane to destroy the bombsight if we crash-landed in enemy territory. This was my job, and I started fires with magnesium flares around the bombsight. Don Wilson stayed with me and helped me get out, because my right arm and left shoulder were injured.

I slid down the side of the plane and looked around. We were in a very large field somewhere in France. The front section of the plane was glowing a brilliant white from the magnesium flares.

"We gotta get the hell outta here, Tommy, everyone has already scattered," Don said.

"Go ahead, I'm gonna be movin' slow, and it's better that they catch one of us instead of two," I croaked.

"You sure you can make her on your own?" Don replied.

"Yeah, go on and take off, that's what they told us to do in briefing, scatter and run like hell," I reminded him.

I staggered away as fast as I could, but the pain in my shoulder was so bad I couldn't stand up. I sat down in the plowed field for a minute and watched the men run off in different directions. The plane was making loud snaps and cracks now, like a motorcycle engine cooling off. Big red flames were curling out of the cockpit. "At least they won't get the bombsight," I said woozily.

The smell of newly plowed earth helped me pull myself together. I needed a minute where nothing was moving, not my body, or my surroundings. I touched the earth and held it tightly with my hands. The spinning and the ringing in my ears slowly stopped. I held my left arm up a little, and that eased some of the pain. I pulled myself up. There were hardly any trees to be seen, but there were a few houses in one direction and a church steeple in the other.

There was some kind of a hedge about a quarter of a mile away. Then it struck me. I realized that I was about to be captured. A new fear. The Nazi enemy, up close. Prison camp. Beatings. Torture. Deprivation. Death. The pain receded, my heart began to pound, and I began to run.

FOUR

THE FREEDOM FIGHTERS

I HALF WALKED, half dragged myself toward the hedge. The pain started up again. The soil had just been plowed and was like soft sand. Each step seemed to take forever. I finally reached the dark, twisted hedge and collapsed in a heaving lump. It was quiet. I saw a small gravel road about a quarter of a mile off and slowly made my way down to it. I felt like a rabbit in a big, empty field. I could feel eyes on me, lots of them.

I started up the small road and met two Frenchmen on bicycles. They must have come from a coal mine, as their faces were covered in black soot. I didn't know what to do. "American airman," I said. They walked their bikes around me, looking back at me and talking. Finally they stopped and motioned for me to go to the left, rapidly. I staggered down that road as far as I could until I started to get light-headed. I figured I was going to pass out, so I crawled into a hedgerow and tried to cover myself up. I lay there and just listened to my heartbeat for about fifteen minutes.

When I could sit up, I noticed there was a farmer plowing a small field about half a mile away. He was headed in my direction.

I'll wait here for him to come by, I thought—and passed out cold.

When I came to, I noticed the farmer was much closer. I was suddenly terribly thirsty and very dizzy. When he got close, I whistled softly. When he saw me, he almost jumped out of his shoes. He was a big, broad-chested man with a red face and short, straight hair. He quickly looked in every direction and motioned for me to stay down.

"American . . . airman," I croaked.

"Marmuse, Monsieur Marmuse," he said in a very soft, kind voice.

"Water?" I croaked. My thirst was consuming me. He quickly pulled a battered aluminum canteen out of a box on the tractor and gave it to me. With broad gestures he indicated that he was leaving, but that he would be back. I crawled as far into the hedge as I could and drifted off with a loud buzz in my ears. A wall of silent blackness dropped around me.

A FAMILIAR sound awoke me. A faraway dim roar with a crunching sound at the edges. The buzzing in my ears and the throbbing in my head lifted slowly as I struggled to place the sound. *Texas. I'm in Texas. Good. A car. A car in Texas on a gravel road. I'm home.* I pulled myself up and looked down the road. About half a mile away there was a dark military car that looked like a jeep with a big black cross on it. It was moving fast. I wormed farther into the hedge. It had felt so good, the brief moment I thought I was in Texas. Now I felt so far away and so lost I got dizzy again.

In the field, the big white ox plodded along, pulling a small cart piled high with hay. I tried to keep my eyes open to watch, but the pain washed over me in waves, taking a layer of my strength with every surge. The cart seemed like a dream. It moved and moved and never went anywhere.

Finally, I looked up into the ruddy face and kind brown eyes of Marmuse. He helped me get on the cart, then pulled a tarp over me and pushed the hay over that. The movement made me feel better somehow. I was going somewhere, maybe a place where there was water and no pain.

"Halta! Halta!" A harsh German voice ordered Marmuse to stop while a motorcycle engine idled. He yelled at Marmuse and shot vicious questions at him, one after the other. I heard a few French words in a resigned, innocent voice. I almost stopped breathing. I was sure the soldier had a bayonet and would stab the hay pile. But the cart was very small, and I was rolled up in a ball. I hoped maybe, just maybe, the guard figured there wasn't room for a man under the hay. The German seemed convinced by Marmuse and roared off on his motorcycle. The cold malice in the voice of the first live Nazi I heard went right through me. It said, "Fear me, fear me, fear me."

WE TRAVELED about three kilometers. Marmuse rolled the cart into a large barn and helped me off the cart. My left arm was the worst. Every little movement was grinding, crunching pain. I almost passed out just standing there. Marmuse brought me some water, which I drank as fast as I could. He brought some blankets and made a place for me to lie down in the hay. The faint smell of a home clung to the warm blankets. I thought of Texas as I fell asleep.

When I woke up, my mind frantically tried to find my place in the world, but there was nothing. I just blinked and stared. There was a short man with a white mustache standing with Marmuse. He was holding a lantern and talking softly. He had a medical satchel in one hand and a bottle of wine in the other.

"Monsieur, we must set your broken shoulder," he said in good English. He wrapped a splint around my upper right arm and tried to reset my dislocated left shoulder, but nothing seemed to work. He put a small bag of sand under my arm and pulled carefully. I thought I knew what pain was until that moment. Just as I thought my arm was going to tear off, I heard a loud pop, and he let go. The relief was immediate. He removed a small piece of metal from my right eye and cleaned and bandaged the puncture wound in my forehead.

I looked up at his kind face as he handed me a small wine bottle and two pills and asked me if I could take these pills. I got them in my mouth and washed them around with the wine. I was feebly trying to thank him and shake his hand when the lights faded out again.

THE NEXT time I awoke, there was a short moment of terror. I couldn't seem to put together the pieces. I started to sit bolt upright, but the pain in my shoulder seized my upper body. I panicked for a minute, fearing everything at once.

Marmuse ran into the barn wearing a dark raincoat. "Must go now. Nazis coming here. Must to go," he said. The fear was all over his face. The Germans were searching everywhere for the crew of the downed B-17, and they were on their way to the farm.

He helped me into the haycart again, then quickly moved me to the basement of a winery a few hundred yards away. The fear had changed his face, and he moved in quick, jerky steps. I spent a day there, then they moved me to a large barn on his farm nearby.

I slept for what seemed like a week. My shoulder was much better, and I ate all the food he gave me. I could feel the food giving me strength. The gravy and potatoes and meat were warm and tasted wonderful.

On the third day, about three in the afternoon, I was standing by the hayloft window thinking about how I might get back to England. I heard the clattering engine of a truck barreling down the long driveway at full speed. The driver slammed on the brakes, showering gravel, mud, and geese everywhere. The soldiers jumped out of the truck and fanned out, quickly surrounding the barn. I was trapped.

One of the Germans began banging on the barn door with his fist and yelling something in German. I took a long look around the hayloft and realized that it was the only logical place to hide in the barn. So the Germans would probe there first. They were noisily working the slide bolt that held the doors shut as Marmuse hurried over.

I jumped down to the dirt floor and looked around. There was no place to go. Wait—there was a large pool of water for the cows in the corner of the barn. About ten white and black cows were standing around it. I wasn't sure how deep it was, but I hurried over to the water and looked around for some kind of breathing tube. The door started to open. I slipped into the water, took a deep breath, and submerged.

The pool was about four feet deep and built so that half of it was outside the barn. I could see the daylight easily. I ducked under the barn wall and quietly surfaced on the outside just as two German soldiers ran past the cows standing two feet from me at the pool's edge. I listened while the Germans tore the haystack apart with bayonets and pitchforks. I could hear Marmuse pleading in French, but they kept attacking the haystack. Suddenly I heard the squishing of boots coming down the side of the barn toward me. I took a deep breath and pulled myself under the water and back into the barn. I held myself down as long as I could, then quietly surfaced.

I tried to smother my gasp for air. The big doors banged shut just as I opened my eyes. I could hear the soldiers outside the barn talking. They seemed to be in a hurry and talked rapidly as they clambered into the truck and departed.

The water was so cold it brought the pain in my shoulder back in throbbing waves. My bones felt as if they had been broken with lead pipes. I dragged myself out of the pool and lay there gasping.

Marmuse walked in and grinned when he saw me. He said something like, "Not bad, Monsieur Flyer, not bad." He quickly brought me some dry clothes. I changed into them and crawled back under the warm hay as a steady rain began.

THE NEXT few days I was alone the entire time. Marmuse came in once a day with food, late at night in case he was being watched. We talked a little about the Germans. I asked him what would have happened if they found me. He made a little noose with hay-wire and put it around his finger, jerking it violently.

"Many of us, already," he said. "*Boche,* terrible. Terrible people. All, all *Boche*. Terrible. Like Frankenstein monsters," he said over and over. I saw a steely hardness and hatred in this kind man's eyes.

A few days later, a tiny, battered van pulled into the barnyard late at night. It was clear and almost warm, with just a sliver of a moon. The little van was so small it looked like a child's ride at a county fair in Texas. There were signs on the side, something to do with electricity service, and it smoked badly. A tall, middle-aged man got out and talked quietly with Marmuse. He had a very stern and sincere bearing and impressed me right away as a man to be reckoned with. He was introduced to me as Jules Carpentier. Marmuse seemed to have great respect for this man.

Carpentier asked me a few questions and told me in good English that they were going to move me to the nearby town of

Carvin, which was about twelve miles south of Lille. I vaguely remembered seeing Lille on the silk maps of France they gave us, but I couldn't quite remember where it was, so I asked Carpentier. "Lille is in the lion's mouth, again." He growled. "Lille is about 130 kilometers east of Calais, on the English Channel. It is there the *Boche* believe the allied invasion will come, so poor Lille, the birthplace of Charles DeGaulle, is in the lion's mouth, as it was in the Great War." I started to ask what happened there in World War I, but decided not to. The beef between the French and the Germans goes way, way back.

"The *Boche* searched everywhere for your crew, but they have tapered off now," he said.

I thanked Marmuse for helping me as Jules arranged a place for me in the back of the van, which was filled with spools of wire and ladders. Jules handed me a small Walther automatic pistol. He assumed I knew how to shoot and quickly showed me it was chambered and would fire after it was cocked. He covered me with a heavy blanket and pulled some large loops of wire over me.

We rattled along in the van for about half an hour. It was very dark, and the only traffic seemed to be an occasional truck. I had just dozed off when I heard the van slow down and a loud voice shout *"Halten! Halten!"*

The harsh voice shouted in German, but I could pick out a few of the words. "Why are you out at this time? What are you doing?" The questions came loudly. My heart stopped, and I broke out in a cold sweat. Jules calmly replied in French, which the German had trouble understanding. He banged on the top of the van with something hard and started to walk to the rear. He couldn't possibly miss me. This was it.

I pulled the blanket off and cocked the pistol. The German sentry pulled open the door and flashed his light right in my eyes. I couldn't see to fire, so I kept the pistol under my right leg. He stuck the rifle barrel under my chin and reached over to pull me out of the van. As he leaned over, I stuck the gun up to his chest and pulled the trigger. His mouth jerked open and a gush of bright red blood spurted out, covering me. Jules had stabbed him in the side just as I shot him. I was ready to shoot again, when Jules yelled at me, "Get out! Let's pull him off the road and hide him." Jules bent down and knifed him again several times. "The shot might have been heard. Hurry. We have to get out of here!" We quickly pulled him off the road, took his rifle and pistol, and rolled him down the embankment. I barely got the rear door closed before Jules screeched off.

The smell of the blood on my face was beginning to make me sick as we pulled into the rear driveway of a large building, jumped out, and ran into an entrance. Jules introduced me to M. Henri Perlot, who showed me to a sink to clean up. M. Perlot was a short, very trim man with a clipped white mustache and white hair. He must have been about seventy-five, and his wife was very elderly and in a wheelchair. He was distinguished looking, like a movie star or a famous doctor.

M. Perlot was as gentlemanly as he appeared, and he immediately offered me a warm meal. They already had clothes for me, laid out in a small room in the attic on the third floor. I quickly ate the big plate of meat loaf and potatoes and slept almost normally that night, in a real bed that felt like heaven. The face of the German patrolman we had killed woke me up once, but I was able to keep from shouting. It was hard to forget the smell of his blood.

M. Perlot called me softly from below just after dawn. I woke up slowly and ate the excellent breakfast he brought up. I couldn't leave the attic room—one of the Germans' favorite tactics was to burst into a house at any time of the day or night hoping to catch people using radios or sheltering fliers.

On the second day, a kind-looking older Frenchman was brought up and introduced to me as Dr. Baker. He came from the Carvin hospital nearby and tended to my shoulder, arm, and back. He put drops in my eye and left medication for me. He spoke a little English and asked me where I was from. When I said Texas, he laughed.

"Texas, you are then a cowboy?" he asked.

"I feel like a cowboy who was thrown by a horse, a big horse," I said.

He laughed quietly. "A very big horse," he said.

I HAD a small window in my room which looked out on the street of Rue de la Lille, the main road to Lille. I would just sit there hour after hour, watching the daily life in this small French town. It felt so good to be able to rest. Just watching people walk down the street in the sunlight was a pleasure. Life is more precious, more enjoyable when you have survived a few bad scrapes.

The weather was warming after a long, wet winter, and the birds sang all day. I worked on my French with three little prewar phrase books M. Perlot gave me. I learned fast. There wasn't much else for me to do, and every word I understood helped. Dr. Baker came back several times to treat me and to ask me about cowboys, rattlesnakes, banditos, six-shooters, and the Alamo. I asked him to speak slowly, which he did.

I asked him about the Resistance movement, the *Marti* as they called it. He told me how the Nazis had mounted a political operation in France before the war, which was highly successful. They had succeeded in dividing the French people and establishing a fascist political movement in the late thirties. This became the Vichy government after 1940. The hardest part for Dr. Baker was the issue of Marshal Petain, the great hero of World War I, who had become the leader of the Vichy government. He was a hero to the whole country in 1918, and he wasn't much older than Dr. Baker. He said the name "Petain" with a barely controlled disgust that made him shake a little. He finally told me to be very careful. "We are not one people, now," he said sadly.

I began to develop a deep respect for these brave people. They never hesitated to fight the Germans, even though many of their friends had been tortured and shot. The Germans were cruel, arrogant people in those years. You really had to admire anyone who stood up to their terrifying brand of harshness and cruelty.

M. Perlot had hired a lovely young girl, Leone, to help care for his invalid wife. She prepared and delivered my meals as well. "This is a brave girl. She can be trusted," is all M. Perlot said. She was eighteen, with lovely brown hair and soft brown eyes. We talked a little, and she brought me a French–English dictionary, which helped a great deal.

"Is it possible that girls are also with the cows in Texas?" she asked one day.

I laboriously tried to formulate an answer in French, but it didn't work. "Cowgirls, yes, they call them cowgirls," I said finally.

She laughed. "This I would like!"

I WAS watching the street a few days later when I heard one of the heavy German trucks coming through the village. People started to point and gesture at the truck as it came down the street. When it passed below, I could see a section of a B-17 on the trailer. It took me a minute to realize that this was my plane, all sliced up. I almost yelled out, *Hey, that's my plane!*—but caught myself. Then a wave of depression washed over me, as I thought about Ridgewell, the war, missions, and flying again.

When I felt my strength coming back, I began to wonder what I should do next. I asked both Jules and M. Perlot what they were going to do with me. They said it seemed like the best thing to do would be to wait for the Allies to liberate the country.

About a week later M. Perlot and Jules talked to me about going south, over the Pyrenees and out to the Spanish coast. They brought me some heavy sweaters and a leather coat, but a few days later they told me several flyers had been captured on that route, so they decided to wait.

I began talking to M. Perlot, Jules Carpentier, and several of the Freedom Fighters with my barnyard French. One of them was named Roussell, and another was Joe Martin. They were highly decorated French veterans of WWI, tough, smart men who had survived almost five years of underground fighting in this war. I marveled at how smooth and quiet they were, how confident, how resourceful. I realized that they were the best. The smartest. The Germans had shot the rest a long time ago.

I wanted to help these brave people all I could, and I told them that I had received some explosives training. This raised their eyebrows, and without saying much they indicated they could use help in that area.

They told me bluntly that they couldn't tell me very much, because I might be captured at any time. They were very concerned about their friends who had been picked up, and there was a lot of discussion about what, and who, these people knew. The Gestapo had just intensified their campaign against the Resistance because of the anticipated Allied invasion, and many, many people had been picked up.

A week or so later, they began letting me join them in the evenings in the basement of the house, where a shortwave radio was hidden behind a rock wall. The radio antenna ran from the basement up through the house to the roof; it was completely undetectable.

The BBC in London was our only contact with the outside world. Listening to the BBC was the highlight of the day. That took place about nine o'clock at night. We hung on every word. It was like a ray of truth and sunshine in a dark, cold world.

These basement sessions helped me with my French, and also provided some much needed comic relief for the Freedom Fighters. I would trot out a sentence, and they would look at each other, say the words, then start laughing. I was like the carpenter who was only a few inches away from perfect.

I was allowed to listen in while they planned missions, which surprised me. I took this as a real gesture of trust, and I repeatedly asked if there was anything I could do to help. One evening they asked me if I wanted to go with them to observe a new weapon the Germans were testing. They were guessing it was a new robot airplane and wanted to know if I knew anything about this weapon, which was pilotless and was fired from a ramp. I had no idea what it was, which seemed to surprise them.

One of the men who came to the house had a farm near the testing area, and he offered to take us to a place where we could observe the Germans. A mission was planned for three days later. I thought very seriously about the mission, as I knew that spies were shot if captured, but I wanted to do anything I could to help these brave people. The Germans had already tried to shoot me anyway. Lots of times.

Jules Carpentier picked me up a few days later just after ten o'clock at night. We drove several kilometers to a small farm surrounded by poplar trees. The night was windy and moonless. We gathered in a small stone building that was very damp despite the hot iron cookstove in the corner. There were two men I hadn't seen before sitting on a wooden bench, listening as the farmer described where the test site was. It was about three miles away, so we would need to leave by about two A.M.

Jules opened a small briefcase and handed me my new French ID card, picture and all. My name was Maurice Dupiere, and the pass indicated I was a deaf-mute. This meant I could move around and travel. I had seen French police and Gestapo agents check these cards on the streets of Carvin from my window. They checked everyone, constantly, and you could go nowhere without a card. "Now you are one of us," M. Perlot said, somewhat ominously.

We started walking in the pitch-black darkness, through large fields and black hedgerows. We stumbled several times but made very little noise. We finally came to a large hedgerow where a man was waiting. How these men found this place in the dark was beyond me. We hid there and waited for dawn.

In the gray light of early dawn, we could see where the Germans had set up three long wooden ramps in the fields below us, about three hundred feet away. They showed up right at dawn in two big green Wehrmacht trucks and three battered cars. They seemed to be mostly civilians, with a few soldiers and several thin laborers in blue overalls. They began unloading large black cylinders amid constant shouting and clanging. When the cigarette smoke from the Germans reached us, the Frenchmen rolled their eyes and sighed. We couldn't smoke in our hideout, and it drove them crazy.

The Germans were obviously in a hurry or behind schedule. They pulled a tarp off a strange-looking little plane with stubby wings and installed one of the cylinders on top of it.

We watched them launch one rocket, which took off with a big *whoooooosh*. They had started work on one of the other rockets when something went wrong. A technician in a white coat was standing behind the rocket when it ignited. The rocket took off and left him in a ball of white and red flame. He began screaming and flapping his arms, and finally he collapsed. They tried to put out the flames, but it was too late. I was looking through the binoculars when I heard muffled applause. The French farmer who had brought us here was clapping and laughing quietly. Jules was smiling from ear to ear. They all said variations of the same thing: "That's one less *Boche* we'll have to kill."

I didn't know what these rockets were, but we carefully noted their size and basic configuration and slipped away. When we got back to M. Perlot's home, we all agreed that we had to notify the British. I figured it was some kind of new rocket that was being readied to oppose the invasion. We wrote up the exact location and described the rockets and how they were launched. We would radio this out that night with the radio set in the basement. Jules said, "Tell them they burn German technicians very nicely."

When we were finished with the mission, I felt a lot better. It was good to get out, and I felt trusted and included by the French. I found that Jules and M. Perlot were including me in more and more of their discussions, and I worked harder than ever on my French.

M. PERLOT took me into town one day to see the cathedral. It was a beautiful, quiet place. We climbed into the bell tower, and I carved my name into a beam. M. Perlot seemed older that afternoon, and we spent quite a bit of time sitting up there.

M. Perlot told me how to stay alive and survive the war. He said, "Your best protection is to keep your mouth shut and talk to no one outside of our small group. Just go along with what I tell you. We have people that we can't trust. Don't feel like you have to confide in anyone. Put your trust in me and no one else. If we go on a mission, I want you to be with someone from our group at all times, and do not allow yourself to talk to any of the other men."

I told him I was just glad to be able to help. "We have lost a lot of good men, Tommy, and your help is needed here. Just be careful and listen to me." He looked right at me and seemed to know something I didn't.

A few days later, Jules began talking about an operation against a potato distilling plant that was nearby. The Germans were short of fuel, and they had been distilling the French potato crop into alcohol. They were using it for jeeps, half-tracks, and trucks.

This would be a big operation, and several men came through the house in the next few weeks for briefing and training by Jules. I was asked to help build the charges for the operation, and they brought out everything they had saved. We didn't need very big charges, because the alcohol itself would go up if we could get it started.

They had twelve sticks of dynamite that scared me because they looked like they had been stored for a long time and they might have gotten wet. They must have been buried in the ground. I could see where some small animal had been chewing at the heavy red paper in the wrapping.

I tried to remember everything I could about handling dynamite, which I had never liked. Dynamite can easily become unstable if it is contaminated. This batch looked as if it had been run over by a half-track.

Little pieces of fuse, blasting caps, and detonator wire appeared every time someone came through the house. I thought they would have a lot more ordnance, but Jules told me the Germans had intercepted nearly all the British airdrops for the last six months.

"It's all we have, this and a few German grenades. Will it do?" he asked.

I looked down at the mismatched array of explosives in front of me. "It will do," I said.

We planned the operation with the help of some people who had worked in the plant. They diagrammed the plant for us, their calloused hands shaking with fear. They showed us how to open the alcohol vats, so they would drain out into the plant. There was a long discussion of where the best place would be to set our charges. They asked me for my advice. I picked out the valve banks. I figured that a charge here would open all the vats and the transfer tanks at the same time. They agreed.

The tension became noticeably worse. Many members of the Resistance had recently been turned in by traitors, and everyone knew the Germans were paying big money for information that would prevent a major attack. Every day a black Mercedes would speed through town surrounded by motorcycles. The Gestapo wanted everyone to know they were on the job. They were picking up anyone and everyone.

After a few days of preparation, Jules told me we were going in that night. I was nervous. Watching a rocket launching was one thing, blowing up a heavily guarded synthetic fuel plant was another.

We left the house at dark in pairs and walked silently to another house near the alcohol plant. We waited in the basement until midnight. I stretched out and tried to sleep, but it was impossible. Then Jules tapped me on the shoulder. "It is time," he said. We left for the plant, two of us every three minutes. I went with Jules. My stomach was in knots, and my heart was pounding.

The plant was off the main road, set back about a quarter of a

mile. There was a large concrete main building and several out-
buildings surrounded by big silver pipes. A canal about fifty feet
across ran parallel to the plant. We waited next to a footbridge
while the first two men slipped in to take out the guards. They cut
a hole in the fence at a corner where it was dark. I just caught a
glimpse of them moving through the shadows.

The men had only been in there about three minutes when
one of them came back and signaled that the guards were down. I
was surprised how quickly they handled two Germans with
machine guns. Jules noticed my surprise. "They are the best," he
said. "They are fast."

We ran into the plant under the blazing lights, wondering if
some hidden machine gunner was going to open up on us.

The Resistance fighters had rounded up about twenty French
workers and were not too gently marching them past us as fast as
they could. The workers were scared to death. No matter what
happened, they would be in trouble with the Germans. They were
thin and dressed in ragged denim work clothes, with pathetically
thin sandals. They didn't want to look at us. Their sandals shuffled
and scratched along the ground as they hurried off.

The building was a lot bigger than I'd thought it was. The ceiling was very high, and there were six huge wooden vats, each
about twenty feet high. We found the release levers for the vats
and started turning them. The alcohol gushed out of the vats and
ran over the floor and into a concrete gutter that ran to the canal.
We watched it run while we wired the charges on each valve
block. The timers were set with a six-minute delay. I had never
seen timers like the ones they had. They made a loud ticking
sound when they were set, and they were cheap and crude. I finished placing the charges as the alcohol vapors began to make me
feel light-headed. We set six charges and ran like hell.

Tommy LaMore with new stripes in a pre-war photo.

Tommy with AT-6 on Matagordo Island, with parachute and life vest that would soon save his life.

Tommy's original aircrew, with Lt. Armour Bowen of Memphis, Tennessee. Tommy is third from the right on the bottom row.

Tommy being decorated in 1946. His wanness and distant expression reveal the detachment and confusion that was common in returning combat veterans.

This shot was taken after Tommy received his fifth medal. War is the most corrosive of all experiences.

Tommy and Gilbert Marmuse holding a photo of Tommy's B-17. The local farmer told Tommy they still find pieces of it every spring.

Tommy with Marmuse in 1995, toasting their success in eluding the German patrols.

Tommy with CAF honchos in 1996. Tommy was an honorary lifetime member. He experienced a terrifying flashback after one B-17 flight.

Tommy always wanted to meet John Browning and tell him just how good his guns were.

Leone Thierry in a wartime photo. Tommy saw clearly how the war had robbed her of her vivaciousness and youth.

Church tower in Carvin where Tommy was hidden. His initials are still there, carved in the bell supports. The WWI damage to this church bothered Tommy.

Tommy with Jules and Madame Carpentier looking at Tommy's fake ID photo, which Madame Carpentier saved after his departure—a dangerous notion.

The house in Carvin where Tommy was hidden.

The Ford Tri-Motor Tommy flew in as a child. He memorized the serial numbers of planes he flew in.

We made it to the other side of the canal and into the brush when the charges went off. There was a bright flash and a muffled *whummp*. Everybody jumped. Jules grabbed my shoulder, and I looked at him. He looked like a kid on Christmas morning. The flames jumped higher and higher, blue, white, and red at the edges. The flames raced out of the building and into the canal—it lit up the whole countryside.

There was a huge rumbling explosion as one of the vats blew up, then another blew out the front wall of the building and another launched sheets of tin off the roof that fluttered everywhere in the dazzling blue and orange light.

We walked away rapidly, cross-country in different directions, stealing looks at the burning plant whenever we could. There were huge red and purple sparks shooting out of the burning building like a Roman candle. Jules was giggling like a little kid, much louder than I thought was safe.

We took a winding route past several houses and farms, dodging in and out of the shadows. The farmers had been told to bring their dogs in until we had passed, and then let them out again. This would let us know where the Germans were, and if they were getting close.

The roads quickly filled with German patrols, driving fast. They sent everything they had to the plant, but it was already a burned-out mess. *We stuck it to the Germans tonight,* I thought. The French weren't too excited, though. They had conducted many of these operations and were just glad they had lived through another one. But for my money it was a big, splashy operation, and I was duly impressed, as were the Germans. Jules was impressed, too. He was finally quieting down, but his eyes twinkled for days.

We had a little celebration in the basement of Jules's house the next night, and everyone congratulated me on going on the mission. "*Viva* America! *Viva* Texas! *Viva* Tommy LaMore!" Jules said, as we raised our glasses. It was a special time, and for a moment the dark gravity of war lifted a little. I wondered briefly what peace was like. What was it like when people celebrated harmless little events and slept through the night?

THE NEXT morning Jules told me that they had to move me. The Germans were going door to door, searching every house. We drove about ten kilometers away to a house in the countryside. It was a plain little house on a small farm with a stock barn and a few fruit trees. Jules told me it was the home of Joe Martin. "He is a special man," he said in a very low voice.

As we got out of the car, a middle-aged man came out of the house and walked over to us. I was pulling my satchel out of the van when I looked at him. His eyes were so piercing and intense I froze when he was about fifteen feet away. I didn't feel fear, exactly, it was more like extreme caution, with a touch of reverence. This Joe Martin was a powerful man, with special abilities and a burning ferocity that pulsed just behind his eyes. To be this man's enemy was not something I ever wanted to experience. I wondered if he was unpredictable.

I stayed there for about five days, in the back of his barn. I slept close to a pile of hay. Under the hay was a small door down to a root cellar. I had to stay close to this day and night. The Germans were tearing the area to shreds looking for the Resistance. The patrols sped past the farm several times a day, raising dust and running the few cars on the road into the ditch. The heat was on.

Joe and I talked a little, but he was a distant, cautious man. I sat in the barn most of the day and worked on my French. The weather was good, and the sun and fresh air slowly renewed my spirits. My body had completely recovered, and that helped, too.

Jules drove in early one afternoon and told me to jump in the back of his truck. He looked very worried. He took me to a church in Carvin, driving very carefully and pulling over clumsily to let the German trucks pass. He played the part of a tottering old man perfectly, holding up the trucks until they honked their horns, acting confused, braking suddenly.

I stayed five days in the bell tower of the St. Martin Cathedral in Carvin. The Germans were pulling out all the stops, and this was the only safe place left. It was quiet and restful in the bell tower. The wind was warm and gentle, bringing the first barely perceptible smells of spring.

I had just fallen asleep reading a French textbook one afternoon when I heard a faint throbbing hum far away. *I know that sound, I know that sound . . .* The air raid alarm startled me wide-awake. So this is what it was like on the other end. I jumped up and finally located them. Neat little groups of black specks heading in from Holland. As they came closer I could make out the big heavy shapes of the B-17 wings. *Down.* I cursed myself. I was standing up in daylight!

I quickly crouched down and watched the B-17s. They crawled across the sky like an army of locusts. Several smaller specks of German fighters zipped in and out of the neat boxes, leaving little puffs of white smoke from their guns. They were headed toward Lille, and it looked like there were about a hundred bombers.

Everything came back to me at once. The B-17, the missions, the fighters, the intercom. I belonged up there. I wanted to pull myself up and jump into one of those planes. As they droned away, I felt truly homesick for the first time in my life. It was a desperate urge to be home, home with my friends and in my airplane.

As I sat there watching the B-17s drone out of sight, I noticed that there were bullet holes in the beams of the bell tower from WWI. I wondered, *How much longer can this old world take war? When will we find a better way?*

Jules came for me a few days later. *"Le Boche* have calmed down, finally. Several Nazi officers were called to Berlin because of the alcohol plant. None of them returned," he said as he winked at me. He drove me back to M. Perlot's.

I WAS invited down to the basement on a regular basis again after the attack on the fuel plant. I listened as the Frenchmen talked about the war. My French was much better now, and I could pick out most of the words. The Freedom Fighters felt like they had been betrayed by their own people and their government in this war. They hated the Germans with a visceral loathing that came out of them like an invisible sweat. They felt that the worst thing the Germans had done was to turn their own people against them.

They talked a lot about what would happen after the war, how those collaborators would be tried and hanged. One favorite diversion was a heated discussion on whether to use the guillotine instead of hanging. "It's much faster for large numbers," went one argument. "No, hanging is more painful for them, because we won't let them drop more than a meter. We could also use barbed wire, like the Gestapo. That would be good," others said, slowly peeling apples with their wood-handled Opinel knives.

As the pace of Rommel's buildup on the French coast continued, the British asked the Resistance if they could destroy some of the many small bridges that crossed rivers and canals in our area. Jules came to me in my room late one night and told me they needed help in making special charges to destroy some bridges. He brought some steel casings and assorted artillery shell powder and explosives to the basement the next day.

"Can you do it, Tommy? Will this be enough to bring down a small bridge?" he asked, looking much older. He was clearly worried about these operations.

"I think it will just be enough to blow two small wooden bridges," I said to Jules, who seemed relieved.

"We haven't had any proper explosives from the British in several months. *Le Boche* seem to know when and where the air drops are attempted," he said, looking directly at me. "They always seem to know." Jules warned me every time he could about traitors.

I spent several days in the basement making the best charges I could. I packed the pea-sized pellets of artillery powder into the ten-inch steel pipes around a half stick of dynamite and screwed the caps on with a little grease. I dripped candle wax around the holes in the end caps where the detonator wires exited to keep any water out. The powder looked like it may have gotten wet, but I did my best to dry it on metal cookie sheets in the basement.

There were two major bridges northeast of Carvin that were important. The Resistance decided to take both of them out at the same time, so they wouldn't have to revisit the area.

The French were very thorough in their intelligence gathering and mission planning. I listened in the basement as a very small man in greasy overalls briefed us on the guards. He said there were two guards on each bridge with a telephone on each end. The guards would call in to a duty officer at exact intervals of thirty minutes, all night. They would walk from the center of the bridge to the end, call in, and walk back to the center.

The plan called for Resistance fighters to attack the guards shortly after they called in. This would give the men about thirty minutes to set and detonate the charges before there was any alarm. They decided to blow the second bridge about thirty minutes after they blew the first one.

The plan was simple but inspired. They decided to blow one bridge first. The blast would hopefully draw the Germans to that area so they could blow the second bridge. There was a lot of back and forth about blowing them at the same time, but any slipup in timing could easily jeopardize the other operation.

On a rainy Thursday evening, Jules came up to my room and said simply, "Tonight we go." We left about ten o'clock, driving slowly through the downpour. A big thunderstorm had blown in from the west and soaked everything in a steady, driving rain.

We parked the van at the end of a dirt road and carried the charges cross-country for about two miles, slipping and sliding along a muddy path. We stopped just before the crest of a small hill and slowly looked over. The bridge was below us. The guards were hanging around the guard shacks at the ends of the bridges, trying to stay dry.

I saw two dark shapes move up behind the guard shack and heard a loud whack. I guess it was the helmet of one of the guards hitting the shack when he went down.

Our signal to set the charges was two quick flashes from a flashlight. But something had gone wrong. There was a scuffle at the other end of the bridge and suddenly a loud scream. Next to me Jules cursed in French. I looked up and saw a flashlight blink twice. We were on.

We scurried down the hill and under the bridge and wired the big charge where the supporting beams came together. We waited for the signal from the other end. Three flashes from a flashlight. We set the timer at four minutes, flashed a signal to the other end of the bridge, and took off.

When we reached the top of the small hill, we heard a motorcycle. Jules motioned for us to keep going and trotted back. I heard a German voice yelling questions, then a sharp pistol crack.

I was wondering if four minutes was enough delay when the charges went off just as Jules caught up with us. You could have heard them all the way to Texas. Chunks of wood rained down through the trees behind us as we ran along the muddy path.

Just as we got to the van, I heard another explosion in the distance. Right on time. I waited for Jules in the van, the rain hammering the roof. He finally appeared carrying a Schmeisser submachine gun and an ammunition belt. The whole operation was over in forty-five minutes. We wound through dirt roads and got back to the house about midnight.

"It's a good thing you sealed the charges with candle wax," Jules said to me outside the house. "Say nothing of this mission to anyone. We have been biting the *Boche* lately and they can bite back. Play your role as a French deaf-mute."

Upstairs I pulled off my wet clothes and tried to sleep. I was pleased and impressed with the results of my charges. I didn't know how much of that two-lane bridge was left, but it wasn't much. So far, so good.

I AWOKE to the rumbling of trucks in the street below. A convoy was going through the small town. The big German trucks were filled with soldiers, and they pulled trailers with tanks, guns, and what looked like fortification materials. Everyone knew the invasion was coming—and soon.

The flights of American and British bombers flying over seemed to increase also. Every time the air raid sirens howled, a cheer went up in my heart. *Eat 'em up baby, eat 'em up*, I would say to myself.

M. Perlot came up to my little room one day and handed me a small manila envelope. "A souvenir for you, Mr. Tommy," he said. I opened the envelope and found a black-and-white picture of my plane sitting in the field. I tucked it into my small Bible. My first souvenir.

"Merci beaucoup," I said without thinking. *"Merci beaucoup."*

The French asked me endlessly what the American people thought of the French. They were terrified that Americans thought they were with Hitler in this war. The Vichy government and Marshal Petain were an unspeakable disgrace to them, and they wondered if the Americans would identify them with the Nazis.

"You're sure they don't think we are fascists? Petain is a Frenchman in name only!" they would say, spitting the name Petain.

"No, we know the French were subjugated and overrun by the Nazis," I tried to reassure them.

"We will quickly kill all the traitors right after the war, and this Hitler business will finally be over. We are not fascists. We are just the proud French," they would say, looking closely for my reaction.

THE DAYS dragged by. There were more German soldiers patrolling the village now, and they walked right under my window several times a day. They had police dogs, and they seemed very wound up. They shouted up and down the street. They were looking. I had to stay on the third floor most of the time, and I found myself wondering when a German patrol would come crashing up the steps.

There had been several strange men stopping by the house lately, picking up my charges and dropping off small satchels of bomb-making supplies. The risk of informers in the midst of these men seemed very high. Jules told me to play the deaf-mute role with these men. "They don't know you are an American. Don't tell them," he said.

I had learned to read French pretty well, and they gave me issues of *The Voice of the North,* an underground newspaper which covered the Resistance movement and featured stories on Allied bombing targets. There were many stories on traitors they had captured and what these people had done. The French word for "liquidated" was often the last word in these stories. Leone helped me read these tattered papers. When I asked her about the collaborators, she became so angry she trembled. "It is not possible to talk of these things," she said.

I continued to listen to the BBC news broadcasts at night. Jules would operate the radio, and someone else would take notes. Another radio operator would stop by from time to time. The room would be as quiet as a church. We all listened intently when they discussed troop buildups in England. We even heard some sports news once in a while. When I heard the scores from the American baseball leagues, I tried hard to remember what that world was like. I tried to imagine what it was like to watch a baseball game and eat a hot dog. I tried to imagine what it was like not to live in fear. I tried, but I couldn't.

The war news droned on, and after several weeks I began to hear a pattern. *Calais.* The word would be dropped from time to time in reports of bombing raids and other matters. *Calais.* Everything seemed to point to Calais as the likely place for the big invasion.

We posted lookouts when the radio was transmitting, because the Germans used radio signal homing equipment in little black vans to find Resistance radios. It only took them about five minutes to get a fix, so outgoing messages were kept very short. I never knew what they were sending, and they didn't want me to know. They got the set ready, signaled to the lookouts, sent the message out as fast as they could, put the radio set away, and disappeared.

Henri and I were chatting with Jules at the table in the basement one balmy evening. They had been talking about messages that had been received from the BBC shortwave broadcasts. The British announcers would use code phrases that gave the Marti crucial information on airdrops and when to start planned operations. I asked Jules how we would know when the Allied invasion was going to start.

Jules looked at Henri for a long moment, then turned to me and said, "I will give you the code phrase for the invasion. This you must keep and protect with your life." They struggled a little with the translation. Henri went and got a book and showed me a picture of a peach. We finally got the exact wording. *The peaches are green.* This phrase would be heard on the BBC shortwave at the time of the invasion. It would signal all the Freedom Fighters to start a series of sabotage operations that had been planned earlier with British agents.

I was surprised. The answer to my casual question was probably one of the most important pieces of information in the world. I felt proud that they trusted me enough to share it. For a few minutes, I wasn't sure I really wanted this information. I don't know why they told me. I never asked, and they never offered a reason. My only guess was that they thought the Gestapo was closing in on them. If they were captured and shot and I escaped, I would know the code word and could help other units. Perhaps I was the only other member of the group they trusted with this information.

Leone continued to help me with my French. She asked me about New Orleans and the French Quarter there. "This was once France, you know," she said, looking for a response.

"Until we bought it," I said, finally getting a little smile from her.

"You Americans, you are always buying things. Even whole places!"

Leone was a sad reminder of how war withers even the brightest and youngest flower. She had become serious and withdrawn at the age of eighteen when she should have been enjoying the best years of her life. You could tell that she had been a bubbly teenager just a few years before.

M. Perlot again told me to be careful whom I talked to. It was a strange feeling, wanting to help these people liberate their country but not knowing who you could really trust.

The biggest concern for the Marti was when someone was picked up by the Gestapo. They never knew who would break under torture. There was constant talk about who had been picked up and what that person knew.

Many times these people wouldn't return. The Germans would simply kill them and let their families and the Marti wonder what happened to them. Several men had been picked up in the last week. Some of them had been to the house. All we could do was keep any explosives well hidden and wait.

Late Friday night after the BBC broadcast, a thin man in a suit came to the house. I was sent upstairs when he arrived. Later that night, they asked me to come down to the basement. The thin man had left. They told me he was from the north, near Ascq, a small village close to Lille. He had brought important news. The British had sent word that a Nazi train was in the rail yard near Ascq. The train was loaded with several large siege guns, which had been pulled out of Russia and were being sent to the French coast. The Germans moved these trains at night and camouflaged them carefully during the day. The RAF had missed the train several times already and aerial photos indicated the concrete emplacements for the guns were nearly complete.

The Resistance in that area had been asked to destroy this train. They had very few explosives, and their ranks had been decimated by recent arrests, so they had asked Jules for help.

This was going to be a big operation, involving several different cells of the Marti. Jules didn't like the idea of cooperating with Resistance units outside his own. The risk of betrayal was high, but this target was deemed to be very important. The British were pleading, promising to airdrop explosives and weapons.

All eyes in the room were on me. "What do you think, Mr. Tommy?" Jules asked.

I chose my words carefully. "Well, the British and the Americans know what these guns could mean in the invasion fighting. They could cover a lot of beach and maybe stop the invasion altogether. I think we need to help out, but we need good explosives to take out train tracks and rail bridges. We don't have much here after the bridges at Carvin."

Jules nodded. "Let's see what the British can deliver."

About five days later a flurry of late-night activity woke me up. I heard hushed voices and several people coming and going. The next morning Jules took me down to the basement.

"This is all we could get," he said, pulling a blanket off the table.

There were three small sacks of artillery powder, a box of about twenty sticks of dynamite, and something new: square gray blocks of plastic explosive and a small wooden box of detonators.

He smiled. "We finally got to a drop before the *Boche*."

I worked all that day and the next building charges from the artillery powder and dividing the blocks of TNT. I guessed about a softball-size chunk of TNT would blow the train tracks.

The next day Jules and I drove through Lille and on to the small town of Leers. We turned off and tore down a maze of country roads to a small, wooded clearing. I don't know how Jules knew this was the spot. I couldn't see any kind of sign anywhere.

"Quickly, under the tree," he said, his eyes darting around.

We took the charges and a small box of pistols out of the back and left them under a tree. Jules beat me back to the car.

"Hurry! Let's go!" he said.

We roared off and drove through another maze of dirt roads for more than an hour. I was surprised we didn't meet the local Resistance people and transfer the explosives to them.

"It is much better this way. No face-to-face moments. On this I insist," Jules said, curtly.

I wondered many times what forces had so divided the French, setting them against their own people. The Germans had found ways. I think they exploited old rivalries, gave the traitors land and farms, and used money, hostages, and blackmail. Whatever they did worked.

Three days later, a young girl on a bicycle stopped at the house for a few moments, before breakfast. Jules called me down after she left. I couldn't read his face. It was a strange mixture of excitement and sadness.

"Baguettes," Jules said.

"Bread?" I asked.

"Baguettes, Mr. Tommy. They say the guns looked like baguettes."

"The charges worked okay, then?"

"Yes, they split the rails on a downhill grade and dropped the entire train into a gorge. About three hundred Germans troops went with them."

I couldn't figure out why he didn't give me his little wink. He just walked off.

The next day I heard the full story. The SS had marched to the little village of Ascq that night and shot one in every ten of the boys and men in the village as a reprisal for bombing the train. They shot them in the street. In the middle of the night. In front of their families. One after another.

The deaths in Ascq affected everyone. There was no celebration this time, even though the operation had been a big success.

Gestapo activity reached a feverish level. The black cars roared through town several times a day now, with two or three people crammed into the back seat. They picked up hundreds of people and shot many of them. It was a good time for the Resistance to lie low and bide their time.

"Stay away from the window," was all Jules said to me.

THE NEXT few weeks dragged by. Very few people came to the house, and food became harder to get. Leone came only one day a week and seemed more and more distant. We didn't use the radio for several days.

Wondering what was going on in the war started to occupy most of my time. When would the invasion start? What was taking our guys so long?

One day Jules said, "It's time for you to go to Lille, Mr. Tommy. The British are going to take you to England. You leave tonight."

I was ready to make a break. I said good-bye to everyone and thanked them for helping me. It was a very subdued time. The French had been exhausted by four years of fighting, and there wasn't much emotion left in them. The bone-deep weariness of war was visible in everyone.

That night we drove through the drizzle to Lille in M. Perlot's little van. The trip took hours because there were so many German trucks on the road. I noticed German messenger motorcycles roaring up and down the road in both directions, spewing blue smoke. The French never looked at the Germans sitting in the cars next to them in the stalled traffic. They lived in parallel worlds of mutual hatred.

Jules dropped me off at a small two-story house in Lille and quickly drove away. He didn't wave. The door opened, and a young women gestured me to step in. She was about twenty-five, with dark-brown hair tied up in a very neat ponytail. She closed the door and hurried me upstairs to a small room with a cot.

"You will stay here until your contacts arrive," she said in English, then she closed the door.

She left the house and didn't return until late at night. Another man was brought up to the room. He was a small, wiry man with bushy eyebrows and yellow teeth. He slept on the floor. I was still trying to follow Jules's advice and keep my mouth shut, and this man apparently had been given the same advice. We didn't even say hello.

I lay awake all night trying to remember what England and Ridgewell and flying would be like again. It all seemed so far away. I had just dozed off, wondering if the P-51s would make my remaining missions easier, when a big car tore down the street and slammed on the brakes. Moments later, two doors slammed, and the car screeched off. The bad guys were busy. They were always busy, and they were always noisy.

The next morning the young woman brought up a small breakfast for us. She returned in an hour and motioned for the man with the bushy eyebrows to come with her. They left silently. No one wanted to try small talk. I was slowly getting scared and beginning to wonder why I wasn't allowed to stay with Jules until the invasion.

The day dragged on. All I had to read was my small Bible. I

read Genesis and dozed off wondering what life was like in those times.

As the second day slowly turned to evening, I began to squirm. The room started to close in on me. I pretended I was blind for a while, concentrating on the noises from the street, but nothing helped. I finally decided I couldn't take another day in that room. About eleven o'clock that night, the woman suddenly ran up the stairs and opened the door. I was sweating bullets.

"It is time for you to meet the British agents who will take you out of the country," she said sharply.

I followed her downstairs. A few minutes later a small, fat Frenchman entered the house and talked quietly with the woman in the kitchen. I waited by the door. I didn't like him. His eyes flicked from side to side, and he chewed gum constantly. He was trying to appear relaxed, bored by the whole thing, but I could tell he was nervous. He never once looked me straight in the eye.

We trudged several blocks in the light rain to a large square with lovely young maple trees and walked up to a man sitting on a bench.

"This is the man who will take you to England," the Frenchman said, then hurried off, glancing back several times.

I expected the man to tell me what was going to happen, but he said nothing. He got up and motioned for me to follow him. We walked a block down the street to a long black Citroen that was idling by the curb.

There was a woman with bright red lipstick in the front seat. There was a tall man in an expensive suit and gray hat in the back seat. They both stared straight ahead and smoked quietly. My heart pounded, and something told me this was all wrong. The agent opened the door, half pushed me in, and jumped in beside me as the driver peeled away from the curb.

"Hello, Mr. LaMore, how did you get to us? Who have you been staying with? Where have you been?" Their British accent was so badly faked I almost laughed. The car fishtailed a few times, as we raced through the rainy streets. I looked over at the man next to me. He was clenching his teeth, looking out the window.

We rounded a corner and pulled up to a pair of towering black iron gates with bright lights on each side. Two SS guards swung open the gates, and we drove in.

In a cold voice the woman said, "For you, the war is over."

FIVE

INTO THE ARMS OF THE GESTAPO

"AS YOU can see, Mr. LaMore, this is no place to try anything. If you want to live, just cooperate," the man sitting next to me in the back seat said dryly. My stomach was a hard knot. The anger started to build when the door flew open and two big Germans in black uniforms pulled me out and dragged me up several flights of stone stairs. I glanced at them quickly. Their faces were pink with scrubbing, and they were very close-shaven. They were detached, hard looking. Their hands felt like steel hooks.

I was passed from person to person for a few minutes, then taken to a room where I was ordered to strip. They searched everything. I didn't have much, just the small pocket Bible, one dog tag, and my clothes. I stood there naked, watching them. Then they grabbed me and hustled me, still naked, down a long hall. For a terrifying moment I thought they were going to shoot me. We reached two doors that were about ten feet tall. They shoved them open and threw me in.

At a long table sat seven people in various uniforms. One of them was a woman, which surprised me. They stood me against a wall next to a guard with a dog on a big leather leash. Two large mounted lights stood on each side of the desk and were pointed at me. The big clear bulbs created a wall of light so bright and hard you could see the dust on the floor.

A deep voice boomed, "How was your jump, Mr. LaMore? Did you meet your contacts here in France right away, or was it difficult for you?"

Then the woman spoke. "We've found your parachute, and we have the people who helped you downstairs, Mr. LaMore. We are quite within our rights to shoot you tonight, but we are willing to treat you better than a spy. You could live if you so choose. . . ." Her voice was strained, as if she could hardly control herself.

"What was your target in this area, Mr. LaMore? A train, perhaps?"

"Where are the other men you jumped with?"

"Where is your equipment, your radio, and your bombs?"

The voices were shrill and demanding. They were more like orders than questions. They were clearly trying to establish me as a spy. "My name is Thomas L. LaMore, my serial number is 18026043, I am a member of the Eighth Air—"

"You are an American agent! You are here to kill and to destroy!" A voice cut me off. "You have brought explosives and radio equipment into this country. You are a spy!"

My heart was pounding like a jackhammer. "I am Thomas L. LaMore, my serial number is—"

"Members of the Eighth Air Force have uniforms and jackets, Mr. LaMore, and you have civilian clothing. What is your real mission in France?"

I continued to answer with my name, rank, and serial number.

They would shoot back a question. The room was cold, and when the dog snarled, the guard would snap the heavy leash much harder than necessary.

It was hard to see past the light, but I was able to see the woman. She was dressed in a black SS uniform with a white shirt and black tie. She had very short black hair, and she stared at me without blinking. She never moved in her chair. Her questioning was especially belligerent.

"How do you feel, standing here before us, lying to us, with no clothes on, claiming to be an American airman? You are a spy. You would be much better off if you cooperated with us and told us the truth." She always said something about my nakedness.

The questions hammered on until just before dawn, when the woman shot a diatribe at me that really got under my skin. She said, "You are an enemy of the Fatherland. You are fighting against the German people, who are striving to make this a better world. Look at you now! You are standing before us, looking ridiculous, like a monkey. Lying to us. The people who are going to make this a new world!"

"You're a whore!" I yelled.

"What was that you said, spy?" she hissed.

"In Texas, we would call you a whore," I said loudly.

She yelled something in German, and the guard hit me so fast I never saw it coming. He hit me with the butt of his pistol, which broke my front tooth and split the side of my mouth. I fell to my hands and knees, spitting blood and waiting for the next blow. Through the buzzing in my ears I could hear several of the officers berating the guard for hitting me. They were furious that he had hit me in the mouth, which prevented me from talking. The dog was barking right in my ear, his warm saliva spraying my face.

I don't get mad too often, but when I do, someone usually remembers it. I decided right then I would fight them every step of the way and be just as mean and ornery as I could. I figured they were going to kill me anyway. But when it became obvious I couldn't talk, they finally quit asking me questions and ordered the guard to take me down to a small cell. At the entrance, he gave me a hard shove that knocked me into the far wall. He slammed the steel door so hard the dust on the floor blew up into my face.

I figured that was it. They could easily execute me as a spy if they wanted to. They could make me disappear if they wanted to. My life was completely out of my own hands, and I was just about resigned to dying. Now I knew what it was we were fighting against. These people were just plain evil. They thought they were the chosen ones and everyone else was just there for them to exploit. I guess that's the thing that made me the maddest. Being treated like an animal. Stripped, insulted, threatened, pushed around, and beaten like a dog.

They sent a medic in about eleven o'clock in the morning to look at my mouth. The cut was bad, so they brought in another man who had a small medical kit. I watched him take out a curved needle and some suture.

He looked at me coldly and said in French, "Get ready for it." He roughly stitched up the cut right there, no anesthetic, nothing, then slammed the door hard on his way out. That's one thing I noticed about those people, they never seemed to just close a damned door.

I waited all day, my face throbbing with pain. Still naked, I shivered on the cell's single wooden shelf with half a smelly gray blanket. They brought me some stale bread and a whitish soup that tasted like the dust in Pyote. I heard the loud *clomp clomp clomp* of boots all day and all night. I was sure they were coming for me, coming to shoot me, every time.

Sometime early the next morning, the door opened slowly,

and the guard told me I was going to Brussels. The way he said Brussel*s* woke me up. I asked him what was in Brussels, and he muttered, "Gestapo Headquarters is in Brussels. That's where you are going, Brussels, yes, for you, Brussels." He threw me my pants and someone else's dirty shirt. "Hurry up, spy, the professionals are waiting in Brussels."

They threw me into the same black Citroen I'd been captured in, and we drove from Lille to Brussels, about eighty-five miles. I thought about escape, but I was helpless. There were German troops hurrying everywhere, tearing up the roads in mud-splattered trucks and gray half-tracks.

We drove up to a large, yellow castle-like building, with towers and small slits for windows. I felt like saying something to the Gestapo driver like, "You bastards really like melodrama, don't you?" But this place was ominous. Even my guards seemed to react to it. I didn't say a thing.

They took me down long flights of stone stairs and threw me into a cold, dark cell. The walls were made from huge wooden planks, and the floor was cobblestone. I asked them for water and food before they closed the door, because my mouth was hurting. They looked right at me and slammed the door.

There were large cracks in the walls where the planks had warped. I peeked through and saw a man in the cell next to me. He was a young man, very thin, with long brown hair. He was slowly rocking back and forth on his bunk, his knees to his chest.

I sat there for a couple of hours trying to gather some strength. Two big uniformed guards jerked open the door and grabbed me. They took me up several flights of stone stairs and into a large room. There was only one man in the room, but he was quite a figure. He was a tall red-haired SS major, with a round pasty face and deep-set, watery blue eyes. His uniform sent a shock of fear up my spine: black wool with silver piping and some kind of bright red ribbon. The SS emblems on the neck said something familiar: *Fear me.*

He started slowly, in English, after a long silence. "What do you want the most? What do you want out of life, Mr. LaMore?" He looked at me as if he actually expected an answer. "Here you are, picked up as a spy in France, an enemy of the Reich, what can you expect? What do you want?"

I looked at him and said, "I want a cigarette."

He said, "Okay, I'll cooperate with you, and you can cooperate with me. Here is a cigarette."

The German cigarette was harsh, but the smoke was a small luxury. He waited a few minutes, then started asking me questions.

"What was your assignment here in France? How many men were with you?" He repeated every question in a slightly different way. I didn't say anything. I wanted to finish the cigarette before he hit me. I stalled as long as I could, and finally he snapped.

"You are going to cooperate with me! I gave you what you wanted, now you give me nothing!" He hit me so hard it dislocated my jaw. He was a much more powerful man than he looked. He slammed me back into the chair and told the guard to take me into another room. My jaw was pounding. I sat on a bench, wiping the blood from my mouth with my shirt sleeve.

Then he stormed in and shouted at me. "I am going to give you a second chance. I want you to answer these questions or you will never live to leave this place! We are going to try you tomorrow. Do you want that? Do you want to be tried and shot as a spy? What group are you working with? What was your assignment?" He was really riled up now, and he stared right through me with those watery eyes. I got halfway through my serial number when he suddenly grabbed me and popped my head back against the wall. He held me for a minute, and I looked right at him. *I could kill this man in an equal fight,* I thought. I almost hit him, but something deep inside held me back. He stormed out of the room, and the guard took me back to my cell.

I'd been alone before, but that night the solitude bored into me and froze my insides. I was in some real trouble this time. It was raining again, and the water was pattering on something metal outside my cell. My jaw was pounding, aching, and I began to feel like it was over. I felt good about my missions and about blowing the fuel plant and bridges. *Well, I did my best,* I thought. I almost felt like telling them, just to see the look on their faces.

THE MYSTERY of who could have betrayed me went around and around in my mind. I did everything Jules told me to do, and still I had been betrayed. I wondered if the traitor was in Lille, someone in the house there. I couldn't imagine any of the French people I had met cooperating with these brutish, arrogant bastards, but many did. The Germans gave them money, and the land and houses of people they betrayed. *Enjoy it while you can,* I thought, knowing what would happen to them when they were discovered.

I tried to talk to the Frenchman in the cell next to me, but he wouldn't respond. He didn't trust me. I felt completely alone and lost.

I was so caught up in the pain in my jaw that I had forgotten what the SS major said about my being tried. It flooded back to me, and I began to realize that if they were going to go through the charade of a trial, they must be planning to shoot me.

Your mind does strange things when you're pretty sure you are going to die. You try not to think about what it will be like, what the bullets will feel like when they hit you, and what happens after that. Then you think about what life has been like, and you're really glad that you haven't done any terrible things. What these Gestapo bastards would feel like when it was their turn to die interested me in a strange way. Would they think about the people they beat up and shot? Would they have a moment of terror, wondering if there was a judgment in the hereafter? I hoped so. I wanted them to sweat big, cold bullets when their lights went out.

They came for the Frenchman very early, about six o'clock the next morning. He said nothing as they led him down the hallway.

I realized suddenly that I hadn't had a bath in several days. I hadn't shaved, my face and my hair were greasy, and my hands were dirty. I wanted to be clean when I was shot. I started to get mad as hell again. It's one thing to beat and kill a man, but for some reason the Germans seemed to specialize in humiliating and degrading people. I was a soldier, a military man, and I felt I had the right to be clean and dignified when I was executed.

My cell door opened with the usual finesse, and two guards ordered me out. They looked at me a little differently, as if they were enjoying the idea of my trial. They led me into a large, cold room with a long desk. There were four men and one woman seated at this table, all in uniform. I noticed for the first time how clean and well groomed they were. The guards pushed me down into a large wooden chair with no arms.

A tall man in civilian clothes stood to the side. He wore a baggy, gray suit jacket and trousers that were too short for him, and he wore a black fedora hat that was way too big for him. He was very tall, with a long, gaunt face. He looked like a scarecrow. I knew what he was. Gestapo.

The female officer in the middle began almost softly, in

English. "We're here to be fair with you, and show you legal consideration where you have shown our country none."

I caught that one. France was now their country. I hadn't thought of it before, but that's how they looked at it.

"We know you are a spy and a saboteur. We know you were parachuted into France. Ordinarily we do not go to these lengths with people like yourself. We shoot spies immediately on direct orders from Berlin. But we are taking mercy on you here. All you have to do is tell us who you are working with, and you will be spared. You will live." She looked at me while she said this, trying her best to appear human.

"I am Staff Sergeant Thomas L. LaMore, serial number 18026043," I said slowly, my jaw starting to lock up.

Her eyes began to glaze over. Everyone at the table looked to the Gestapo agent for cues. He crossed his arms. Then he slammed his hat on the table and wheeled around, pointing a long finger at me.

"This man is a spy. Are we going to let him get away with these crimes against the Reich? He was captured with photographs of enemy aircraft. Here, look!" he said, slamming down a small piece of paper. He was actually turning red. The tribunal seemed to be terrified of this man. They passed around the paper and looked intently at it. Finally the woman handed it to the guard to show to me. It was the little photo of my plane in the potato field. My shredded Bible was left on the table.

One of the officers began questioning me in a rapid-fire manner. "How did you get into this country? What plane dropped you here? What unit are you attached to? What was your assignment?" They waited about five seconds, then cut my reply off. Down the line they went, asking variations of the same questions. Finally the woman, after glancing at the Gestapo agent, jumped in. Her voice had changed from a soft pleading tone to a piercing screech.

"Tell us what you know about the murderous plans of your troops to land on the shores of France. The army of the Fatherland will slaughter them and wipe them from the face of the earth! How do you know the date and time of the landings that you are so foolishly hiding? What is the signal for the beginning of the landings? We already know much from your captured comrades. They have told us nearly all. If you value your life at this moment, tell us everything. Later will be too late. You will be shot! You tell me this now! Do you want to die? *Do you want to be shot? DO YOU WANT TO DIE TODAY?*"

I wondered how bad the torture would be. I had to protect the code words with my life, and now I was beginning to realize what that might mean. I thought about the trust that Jules had placed in me and how brave those men were.

They didn't stop, varying the questions and the threats, telling me they knew I was a spy. After a while all I heard was spy, spy, spy. They spit this word out with special bile. I briefly thought about the Ascq operation and inwardly chuckled a little. We must have really knotted their underwear with that mission. I was glad for every charge I packed and every fuse I wired.

The harangue dragged on and on. My jaw was throbbing and locking up, which made it hard to swallow. My body ached from lying on the bare wooden shelf in the cell. I thought about spitting on them, just to speed things up.

The scarecrow leaped up and slammed his hat on the floor. "You are not doing your jobs here! You are not getting what we need from this spy. The Fatherland deserves better than what you are doing here. Our soldiers are being killed by men like this. Killed!" This time he actually took his long coat off and flung that onto the ground. He turned to the tribunal and pointed at me and screamed, "Shoot him! He's a spy! Shoot him! Shoot him!"

The tribunal huddled for a few moments, then quickly reached a consensus. They ordered me to stand. The woman looked straight at me. This was the first time I was really able to look at her. She wore an SS uniform. She was in her early thirties and very short, but she stood up straight. Her face was so translucent you could almost see through her skin to the bone beneath her face. There was a hard glitter in her eyes.

She tried to boom out the sentence, but her voice cracked. "We have found you guilty of espionage against the Reich and the German people, and we hereby sentence you to be shot, at a date to be designated."

The scarecrow leaped up. "He will be shot tomorrow! Tomorrow! There will be no designated date. He will be shot tomorrow morning. That is it!" He stormed out of the room and slammed the door. They motioned for the guards to take me back to my cell.

The guards held me for a minute in the doorway of the cell and then whipsawed me into the stone wall so hard it knocked the wind out of me. They laughed loudly and slammed the door. Those boys were just short on manners.

SOMEHOW, THE pain didn't help me focus on the minute-by-minute reality anymore. I began to slip into an emotional swamp of fear, a childlike feeling of being lost and abandoned. I held my breath while the worst waves of fear washed over me. I knew something else was coming, and I waited for it. I felt that sudden hot flash of anger I had felt in combat. I leaped up and pounded the door. "Come on, you bastards. Come on! Let's go! You want to shoot? Let's shoot. You want to kill? Let's kill. We'll bomb every house in Germany into matchsticks! We'll kill every one of you Hun bastards! You'll be sleeping in the rain for five hundred years!" I yelled out that keyhole for what seemed like hours until my jaw locked up.

"*Viva!* Good cursing! Good job of telling the *Boche* off. Did you blow up some German houses?" To my astonishment the Frenchman was back in the cell next to me. He was still alive, and he began talking, in good English. He told me he had been sentenced to be shot as a spy by the same Gestapo tribunal. Then he asked about me. He seemed a little surprised when I told him I, too, had been sentenced to be shot. We compared our experiences with the tribunal. We even managed a little laugh at the antics of the scarecrow.

Later that night, I asked him if he liked peaches. He came back with the rest of the code phrase: "Only if they are green." With that we were friends. We shook hands with our eyes through the small crack in the wall. I told him my name, and he told me his name was Lauren. We talked quietly all night.

We talked about our families. He described his wife, and her wonderful little mannerisms. We talked about our people, the French and the Americans, and we decided we had a lot in common. We cherished many of the same things and believed in the same God. He felt like his country had been betrayed and until this was righted, he had nothing to offer his wife or his child. No future to build for them. I felt the same way.

"The *Boche,* they have only hate. They give only hate to all the other people in the world," Lauren whispered. "Why, why are they this way? We've asked ourselves for generations. My father fought them, and his father fought them, too. They took our country over in 1870, and we worked like dogs for years to pay their tribute. How can they be so advanced a people in science and knowledge and then follow a stupid man of hate like Hitler? All we can do is kill them now. We don't want to kill anyone. It is such sad business, killing," he said, his voice trailing off to a whisper.

I said, "Do you know who Jesse Owens is?"

"Jesse Owens? Yes! He was a sensation, no? We all clapped when he beat the German runners. They say Hitler blew a fuse. Ha! Good for him. Four gold medals, it was unbelievable," he replied and started laughing quietly. "I would like to make Hitler blow a fuse." His laughing slowly stopped.

I was surprised that he knew all about Jesse Owens. It never occurred to me that he was a hero in France as well. We talked about American music for a long time.

"You Americans don't know what you have in the jazz music. It is pure art and very sophisticated," he said. "There is so much life in that music. So much life. To hear the playing of Errol Garner, it is heaven." His voice became even softer. "It is heaven."

We talked on. The darkness in our cell started to go away, the blackness becoming shades of gray. Tiny noises started, then stopped. Then there were more that didn't stop. It was morning. Something had moved through us. We prayed together, asking our God to help us to be brave in the face of our cruel enemy. We prayed for our families and prayed that God would take our souls after we were shot.

THE BOOTS came down the steps in a flourish. These were boots in a hurry, with a purpose. We sat silently wondering who would go first.

Come one, come all. This rock shall fly from its firm base, and so shall I, I said silently, over and over.

They pulled open Lauren's door as if they were trying to pull the hinges off. I jumped, and my ears hurt from the noise.

Through the wall I could just see the big red-haired major standing there in his long black leather coat. He half-ceremoniously read out a proclamation to the Frenchman. He droned on, then almost shouted the last words: "And we will forthwith carry out the sentence of execution!"

Lauren jumped up, stood at attention, faced my cell, and shouted, "*Viva* France! *Viva* America, and *Viva* Tommy LaMore!"

They grabbed him in a rush, and he shouted, "God bless you, Tommy!"

I shouted back, "God bless you, Lauren!"

They dragged him down the hall and up the steps. I wondered if I would hear the execution. I hoped I wouldn't. It was quiet for a few minutes, then I heard a command shouted in German, then another, then another. The rifle blasts sounded as one and echoed off the walls and the surrounding buildings. They were so loud they reverberated in my cell. A part of me died then.

My hatred for the Germans reached a level I couldn't have imagined. Somehow I had wanted to believe that these Germans must have some good in them, that they wouldn't really do these things. To shoot a man like a dog, to take him from his family forever, to stab the hearts of every person who ever knew this man for years to come, how could they do this? Then I heard those shots again. I realized that they had crossed that line so many times that it was easy for them. Then I hated them for that.

I waited. I prayed for strength. I was tired now, worn out. I kept wondering, *How will I go? Will I feel it? Will I beg for mercy when I hear the firing squad chamber their Mausers?*

Four hours later, they came. They opened the door, and the major held up a paper. He didn't read from it, he just said, "I have come to spare your life. We are not going to shoot you. We are going to send you into the Fatherland into a POW camp."

I told him, "You didn't save my life. I died a thousand times last night." He said nothing. I thought it was probably a trick, and by this time I was at the point where I didn't really give a damn what they did.

They took me out and let me bathe and gave me some clothes. They walked me out of the prison, through the courtyard, and past a thick wooden pole. There was a pool of dark blood on the ground, and the pole was riddled with bullet holes and badly splintered. They let me stop in front of it for a few seconds. I felt weak and small. For a strange second the feeling I had when I looked at the V-8 Ford that Bonnie and Clyde were killed in came back to me. My mind slipped a little. Then they pulled me away.

A big, heavyset German guard took me to the train station in Brussels. I was handcuffed, and all the passengers stared at me. *"Ja, Oberursel. Ja. POW Stalag Luft,"* the guard said. It took me a full day to find out that the camp was north of Frankfurt.

WE CLATTERED through Holland on a bright spring day. There were tulips right by the tracks, which cheered me up a little. There were windmills, too. They were much bigger than I thought they would be, and they stood out starkly against the featureless lowlands. They looked just like they did on Aunt Florence's plates, but they weren't blue. We followed the Rhine River, past many of the famed castles. They seemed like dark, brooding monstrosities to me. I had the feeling that this world-conquest idea wasn't a new thing for the Germans.

We arrived in Frankfurt around noon the next day. There were about six British airmen there in a small holding area for prisoners.

Frankfurt had been badly bombed both by the Americans and the British. I thought about my mission to Frankfurt, wondering what the guard would say if I told him I had bombed this city.

Overhead, in the train station ceiling, there were thousands of panes of glass shattered by the bombing. A light rain falling through the roof made the platforms slippery. I thought about what I had yelled through the keyhole of my cell. *You'll be sleeping in the rain for five hundred years!* I was beginning to believe it.

We were waiting on a platform when suddenly a skinny old man with a black umbrella started screaming at me. *"Luftgangster! Luftgangster!"* Then he started swinging the umbrella. He began yelling something about how we had killed his family and ruined his house. The crowd gathered around him instead of leaving the area, which surprised me. They, too, began yelling and throwing small pieces of trash. People began to close in and started kicking and punching at me. Their faces were all twisted up in hatred, and some of the women had tears in their eyes. They were big women, with scuffed shoes and loud voices.

"Raus! Halten! Raus!" My guard started shouting at the crowd, but they were really going now, and most of them didn't hear him. They were trying to spit at us. Finally the crowd surged in, and my guard slipped his Schmeisser off his shoulder and chambered it loudly. He waved it at the crowd just as they began to tear at my clothes. The old man somehow whacked my shin with his umbrella and knocked me down. It took several threats from the guard to move them back. I covered my face from the spit and punches. The guard was shaken up. He wasn't too sure what to do. He was shocked when they didn't respond to his first commands, but they responded when he chambered his weapon.

We stood there for a while, hoping the train would arrive soon. A large group of Hitler Youth came through the station. They were wearing white shirts with swastika armbands. They must have heard that we were captured flyers, because they ran straight toward us and screamed in English and German, "You are

bombing our homes and killing women and children! You are
murderers! Nothing more than filthy murderers! *Luftgangsters!*
You are bombing homes and hospitals!"

Those kids would have torn our hearts out. To see viciousness
and naked hatred in faces so young terrified me. I noticed that
many of their faces were already deeply lined with pinched,
severe expressions.

Right in the middle of this melee, a British prisoner elbowed
me, looked up, and said, "Look at that, mate. There's still one
pane of glass unbroken up there. You bloody Americans are no
good at all with bombing, are you?"

I couldn't believe it. There we were surrounded by teenage
monster Nazis, desperately trying to kill us, and this Brit casually
makes a bad joke.

"We left that one for the British, just to give you something to
do," I said.

Then the guard slapped one of the Hitler Youths and ordered
them off the platform just as our train pulled in. They stayed back
a few feet, but close enough to scream insults. I was never so glad
to see a train in my life.

The small train pulled into Oberursel just before dark. The
town was surrounded by forests of tall pine trees. When we got
off the train, the smell of evergreen trees washed over us. It was
like washing your face after a long drive. We breathed in deeply
and felt better for it. There were about fifteen of us on the cold,
wet platform, about half British and half American. The rain
increased as a Wehrmacht truck pulled up to take us to Oberursel.
The guards wouldn't let us talk for some reason.

Oberursel was an interrogation and classification center for
captured Allied flyers. The building itself was an old castle of some
kind. We rolled in through the barbed wire gates and were

marched into a barrack with cots and good Wehrmacht wool blankets. We quickly found out who had been shot down the most recently and pumped him for war news.

"We've mostly been flying a lot of missions over France, near the coast," Bobby, a tall kid from Fresno, California, told us. His B-17 had been shot down by flak only two days before. "Hell, some guys are getting ten, fifteen of their missions in on these milk runs. The Mustangs have the Luftwaffe on the mat now. It's all over for the Germans." We all silently hoped he was right.

The questioning session began right after breakfast, which was hot porridge and toast. I noisily ate several bowls.

"Ain't they been feeding you, Tex?" the men asked me. I still found it hard to say much after my conditioning with the Resistance. I had learned to pause for a long while, carefully considering my response before saying anything, and usually the conversation would move on by the time I replied. But it was great to see Americans and hear English again after the months in France.

BUT SOON I was alone again, in a room with a single German. "Who is your commanding officer, Sergeant LaMore? What is your bomb group? It is not so bad for you now, is it, Sergeant LaMore? We in the Luftwaffe treat you as fellow flyers here. You can relax now. You know, I was just wondering, what is the difference between a B-17G and a B-17F?" The interrogation officer droned on, smoking and looking out the window. He went on and on, hoping to engage me in a little airplane talk. "We really have to hand it to you Americans. How do you get those guns to fire so reliably in the cold? We hear you are using a new bombsight, the Sperry. Is it much better?"

I found myself looking at his uniform. It must have been specially made. The wool cloth was beautiful, and the seams were perfect. "Come, Mr. LaMore. Help me a little here. We are giving you good food and a clean place to sleep. Help me a little." It didn't take them long to find out who would talk and who wouldn't.

It was a relief to be dealing with military people again. The Luftwaffe were professionals and never got into the threats and insults the Gestapo and the SS threw around. I never heard the word "spy" at Oberursel, but the face of the scarecrow Gestapo agent stayed in my mind for a very long time. I was able to rest up and put on some weight. After a few days, my jaw was much better and my lip had almost healed up.

They gave me some Wehrmacht pants and a British airman's wool shirt. I was beginning to realize that the less I said to the other men, the safer I felt. The suspicion and mistrust I had lived with in Carvin was hard to shake. I slept well for the first time in months, listening to the wind in the trees around the camp as I fell asleep.

I was in Oberursel about a week. I rested and ate everything I could. I listened in on the discussions around me, but I still found it hard to say much. I was wondering what the POW camp would be like. I never stopped thinking about the men I had talked to in the Philippines. They had been captured by the Japanese, and most of their comrades had died on the Bataan death march. I just hoped the Germans were a little more civilized.

EARLY ON a dark, overcast Saturday morning, they put me on a train with about fifty other prisoners going to a POW camp called Stalag Luft 4 near Stargard, close to the town of Stettin. We were all sure that the treatment there would be the same. The train chugged on through the rolling country of eastern Germany. My guard dozed off several times, even leaning against me and snoring. I could have reached the handcuff key and seized his weapon, but then what? Jump off the train, in the middle of Germany, surrounded by eighty million angry Germans? The scene at the train station came back to me vividly, and I just closed my eyes.

We were close to the town of Erfurt when I heard a distant humming sound. In a flash it was right on top of us. Planes! The train lurched to a halt, the iron wheels screeching and throwing sparks. The guards shouted at everyone to leave the train. I craned my neck out the window and saw a bright silver P-51 winging over, going around for another firing pass. My heart leaped into my throat. What a glorious sight. The supercharged Merlin V-12 engines made a loud *whoom*. "Eat 'em up, baby!" I shouted, suddenly realizing I was the last one on the train.

The Germans were scared to death of the planes, and they flew off that train. I was too excited to be scared—until I heard the .50s tearing up the cars at the back of the train. I looked back and saw wood splinters and glass flying everywhere as the cars disintegrated, like some giant invisible chainsaw was slashing through them. Then I realized the rounds were marching toward me. Fast.

I leaped off the train and ran for a ditch about fifty yards from the tracks. I dove head first into the ditch as the P-51s came around again. The noise was incredible. The *blam-blam-blam-blam* of the .50s was so loud my ears began to ring. There was a brief lull, and my guard ran back to the train for some reason.

The last of the P-51s looped back and hit the train again just as he was jumping off the car. The devastating firepower of the six .50s tore that car to shreds in a flurry of wood splinters and dirt. The chunks of wood and pieces of metal had just stopped falling when I heard the P-51s returning from behind me. They were lining up for a pass diagonal to the tracks to hit the engine. They came in at full throttle. The first rounds hit the dirt right in front

of me with a loud *thack-thack-thack*. Then they hit the engine with
a *whang-whang-whang* that was so loud it was like being in a
church bell. Bright sparks hissed past my head, but I couldn't take
my eyes off the spectacle. The boiler blew up in a booming
whooosshhh that forced me to hug the ground. Suddenly the
Mustangs were gone, and a strange light rain began to fall from
the steam cloud above us. No one moved for a long time.

"Where is our Luftwaffe? Where is our Luftwaffe?" the
German civilians on the train asked each other in whispers, while
they tried to find their luggage in the shattered cars. They couldn't
believe that American fighter planes could fly with impunity that
deep into Germany. I very much wanted to tell them where their
Luftwaffe was, but I still wanted to live.

My guard had been killed outright. He lay in the dirt face up
with his chest blown out. Pieces of vertebrae littered the steps to
the car.

The rail workers finally arrived at dusk with a towing rig for
the locomotive. It was a hell of a mess. You could see where the
.50 rounds had gone all the way through the boiler, through two
half-inch pieces of steel plate and hundreds of heavy-gauge pipes.
The hitting power of John Browning's pride and joy had to be
seen to be believed. No wonder the Luftwaffe fighter pilots
worked so hard to avoid our B-17 gunners.

The guards kept us away from the German civilians, who
glowered at us as they waited in one of the few undamaged cars.
It took two days to get up to Stettin, where they put us on a small
train that took us directly to Stargard.

STARGARD WAS a marshaling point for Allied flyers—and the
end of any semblance of civilization for us. There were about 150
POWs there. Our guards were men who had been wounded on
the eastern front, and they were mean, hardened men who

shouted and pushed us constantly. Many of them had pink and white scars on their faces and hands. They herded all of us into filthy boxcars with no windows or water and bolted the doors. We didn't know how far we were going, and the claustrophobia began to affect several men. They started sweating and crying and had to be held down. The idea of what the P-51s could do to one of these cattle cars flashed into my mind.

We were terribly cramped in those stinking cars. We didn't even have a bucket to relieve ourselves in. We had to back up to a crack in the side, and the stench was unbearable. Our clothes were covered in filth, and many men were vomiting. There was no way to keep from spewing on the other men. The acrid vomit ran all over the floor, which made it hard to stand up in the sway-ing, screeching car. The stench was unbearable, and the heat in the car quickly increased to the point where we were all sweating profusely.

I began to wonder if they were planning to kill us all. This was the first time we had been treated badly by the Luftwaffe, and the tension was terrible. We called out to the guards, asking them for water, asking them if we could get out, anything. I thought about Bataan and wondered if the worst was yet to come.

Many of the men shouted insults at the guards, and there was a collective search for fitting insults in German. We called them *hundogs,* a slang insult, like calling someone a pig. They hollered back at us. *"Luftgangsters,* murderers of women and children!" they shouted, over and over. We finally arrived at Kiefheide, a small station near Gross Tychow.

We exploded out of the cars when the doors opened. "Start marching!" the guards yelled as they moved down the line. These guards were older men, part of the Home Guard. Several of them were meaner than hell and couldn't wait to beat a prisoner.

We weren't allowed to relieve ourselves at the station, and

everyone was in real pain. Many of our men were in very bad shape. We had to stop and help the men who were too sick to keep up. For some reason, the guards would rush over and start slapping and hitting the men helping the others.

We marched about three miles through a heavily wooded area until we reached a clearing of around twenty acres. The camp had just been completed. The crude, unpainted wooden buildings were surrounded with barbed wire fences on concrete poles, with guard towers at each corner. We could see the machine guns in the guard towers from where we stood. The areas around the buildings were plain dirt, which was blowing around in little clouds. It looked like what it was: a hellhole.

We were finally allowed to relieve ourselves at a big log pile while they readied the camp for our arrival. I headed up there. To our surprise, there was a bunch of German or Polish women working in a field next to the log pile. They pointed at us as we bent over the logs relieving ourselves. They laughed and giggled. I had never felt so humiliated.

SIX

STALAG LUFT 4

STALAG LUFT 4 was a camp for enlisted airmen located in western Poland near the town of Belgard. The Germans let us know right away this camp was meant to punish us.

"Stand at attention! Straighten up these lines. We will stand here until these lines are straight!" the German officer shouted in English. The guards would run up and down the ragged lines, letting the dogs nip the behinds of prisoners who were out of line. Many of the men were weak and sick from the cattle car nightmare and could barely stand. When the dogs bit them, they responded with a choked, weak cry that revealed the depth of their exhaustion. We were told we would be assigned to barracks and that there would be about sixty men to a barrack.

"This low wire you see here before the outer wire is the warning wire. Cross this wire and you will be shot immediately. Leave your barracks after lights out and you will be shot!" Commandant Pickhardt was a tall, thin man with a scrubbed, pink face, and he wore a full dress uniform with a big red diagonal ribbon with lots of medals. He tried to boom out his words, but his voice was very high-pitched and thin. He would rise up on his feet to hurl the words at us as his voice rose. He looked like some nut in a cheap Halloween costume, but one message came across loud and clear: This was a dangerous, disturbed, and angry man. He held his P-38 pistol at his side and would suddenly point it at us and then wave it around. He waved in the direction of the tower, and they opened up with a ten-round burst that kicked the dust up right behind the wire and sent ricochets buzzing off across the field. The muzzle blasts startled us awake and put tight little knots of fear right where he wanted it, deep in our guts.

Pickhardt watched the color drain from our faces and smiled to himself. He looked over at us and moved his head slowly as the machine gun silently swept from left to right. He was far beyond trying to mask his warped mind. He wanted to advertise it.

We were all pretty shaken up when we got to the barracks. The wood was so rough sawn that little splinters would poke through our shirts if we leaned against a wall or doorway. The bunks were just large wooden shelves. There were no lights, no wash basins, no soap, nothing. Each barrack had a latrine behind it with a long board with six holes in it. We couldn't believe these were going to be our living conditions. "Is this it? Is this how we're gonna live? Hell, our cows back home live better than this." The muttered comments hung in the air as the crude conditions, and what they meant, set in. Two questions hit all of us then: *How long would the war would last, and how long would we last?*

The degradation of imprisonment is very hard on men who have never been on the wrong side of the law. We all had a terrible time accepting the constant humiliation of being counted, ordered around, shouted at, stripped, searched, and locked up. I saw many men struggling to control themselves, trying not to attack a guard. The guards couldn't wait for that. They tried to find big, tough men who couldn't take humiliation. They would kick these men and follow them closely, shouting in their ears, hoping they would attack. The men clenched their fists and rolled back their shoulders, but for the time being they took it.

We began to notice that the Germans flipped the safeties off on their Mausers when they started in on a man. We passed this information around, and it helped the men get through it. No one wanted to give the Germans what they wanted. We all had a lot to learn at Stalag Luft 4, and there was a test every day.

We soon learned that there was one guard that even the other guards stayed away from. We called him Big Stoop. He was a huge, heavily built man with rounded shoulders that pointed inward, almost comically. He walked with a shuffling lumber and kept turning his head from side to side. He had small, bulging eyes that blinked constantly. His helmet barely fit over his head, and he had huge hands. His favorite trick was to cuff a prisoner on the sides of his head with both hands to rupture an eardrum.

The Germans used "goons" to patrol inside the camp. These were men who were borderline retarded or otherwise not fit for military service. They roamed around the camp and tried to find activity to inform the guards about. They were a source of amusement for us, at least in the beginning.

The days at Stalag Luft 4 were long and monotonous. Each day began with a general muster and head count that dragged on for hours. They would count us, and count us, and count us again. If there was the slightest error, they would start the whole thing over. We would sometimes stand in muster for two hours while they ran around and added counts and ran around some more.

Hunger was the one thing that kept everyone occupied. We were hungry all the time. We ate what we called "slop" twice a day. Slop was a heavy, whitish soup made primarily from a *kalarabi*, a local term for an overgrown turnip. Every once in a while they would kill a cow somewhere, and we would get a few bones in the soup and little shreds of purple meat. We had ersatz bread made from sawdust, a little flour, and what tasted like dirt. The slices would crumble before we could get them to our mouths, they were so dry. The calorie level was just enough to keep us on our feet. The subject of food, the whereabouts of food, the ways to get food, and the ways to make food occupied everyone's thoughts all day and all night.

Nighttime was the worst. There were no lights in the barracks. We were locked in just before dark each night. Later, there were a few candles, but mostly it was just dark, cold, and smelly. The bunks were hard as concrete, and we were only allowed one blanket and one thin pad.

Our thoughts turned to home, and we wondered what our families were doing and how comfortable a real bed was. I turned and turned in my bunk, trying to get the blanket to cover both feet at once. I half listened to some of the conversations around me, but I'd heard it all before.

"They gotta be hitting France with the big invasion soon."

"When the Krauts see the size of Eisenhower's Army they'll throw in the towel. They ain't that dumb."

"We'll be the first to be released. They won't want to piss off the Americans when they're trying to cut a deal to save their asses from the Russians. I heard the SS killed millions of Russians. Millions. Man, what they're gonna do to the Krauts if they get to Berlin ain't gonna be pretty."

The nights were the longest I ever lived through. Every night seemed like a week. I thought about the locked door, and I wanted to go outside, to feel the wind on my face. I wondered over and over, *How long will I be here? When, oh when, will this damned war end?* There were occasional muffled sobs. After all, we were only boys, fresh from high school and college, fighting a man's war in a faraway country full of strange, dangerous people. We just wanted to go home.

THE DAYS blurred together. After morning count and "breakfast" the long day began. The men drifted into small groups and pursued little diversions. Marbles, mumblety-peg, cards. Anything. Many men worked on detailed diaries with careful drawings. The discussions on when the war would end started when we woke up and ended when we fell asleep.

"Berlin must be a smoking rockpile by now. We hit it twice before I was shot down. They gotta look at that and guess the rest."

"There can't be much left of the Wehrmacht. The Russians have chewed up 150 divisions. At twenty thousand men a division that makes for a lot of job openings in the Wehrmacht."

The only real highlight was radio news. Some of the radiomen had cobbled a receiver together with a truck battery and some parts from Wehrmacht field radios. They paid a lot of cigarettes to the goons for these parts, but when they got the BBC on a dull, overcast day in May, it was big. The notes from the broadcast were written on scraps of paper with pencil so they could be erased for the next day. Runners were organized right away. They would get the news from one of the operators and take it to the shacks. It looked like a football huddle when they came in, with one guy at the door of the shack watching for goons. The news came out in quick excited bursts.

"The Russians have captured Sevastopol!"

"Where's that? Is it around here?"

"The Russians are headed into Czechoslovakia next."

"Monte Cassino has fallen! We captured the whole damn German Airborne. Mark Clark's boys are hauling ass for Rome."

"Esther Williams has a new movie, *Bathing Beauty*."

"When do we get it?"

"Shut up, ya mug."

"The Eighth hit Brunswick again."

"Attaboy!"

"Hitler arrested some general, a guy named Jaenecke, and locked him up for asking permission to surrender at Sevastopol. Bet the Krauts don't know that one."

Real news kept us all going, because it was all good. The Germans were reeling on the eastern front and the stalled invasion of Italy was picking up speed after the breakout at Anzio. The news we all waited for was the invasion. An entire industry sprang up in the form of pools to guess the date.

The radio was moved every day, and despite the "best" efforts of the commandant and his boys, they never found it. I think they faked their efforts to find the radio. The Nazi radio news was badly distorted, and news of Nazi defeats and the surrender of German forces was rarely reported. The Germans seemed very uneasy about how the war was going, especially in the east, and they needed information. None of us quite knew how the deal worked, but somehow the radio operators passed news to the Germans for little favors. The Germans knew who all their generals were, and the story of Hitler firing General Jaenecke at Sevastopol would be worth something.

ONE MORNING soon after I arrived, they called for anyone with medical training. Several of the men knew I'd had some, and they loudly volunteered me. After a short discussion with one of

Pickhardt's flunkies, I was led to a small building by the well that had been locked up.

"Infirmary," the sergeant said, and he walked off. I pushed open the door and looked in, expecting to see beds and a few bed stands. It was empty. There was nothing, not even a chair. There were 1,500 men in the camp with more coming, and a lot of them were wounded. As I stood there looking at the empty room, the helpless feeling from the Clyde tornado gripped me again. I could see the vacant, pleading eyes of the injured, looking at me. I felt the surge of guilt and bewilderment well up in my stomach. I walked out to the well and closed my eyes.

"*Ja, ja, ja.*" I looked up to see an old German doctor. He must have been at least eighty years old. He had given up on the lower three buttons of his faded Wehrmacht uniform. His face was so red and puffy from years of schnapps, he looked like Santa Claus. We had to help him up the steps of the infirmary shack. Whatever you said to him or asked him, he would just say, "*Ja, ja, ja.*" It was all the same to him. I had the feeling he had been saying that all his life.

The sick and wounded began coming into the infirmary, expecting some kind of treatment. I felt terrible. I didn't even have an old medical chart to point to.

One man had landed on a high-tension wire after bailing out of a B-24, and his entire hip was a deep, badly infected third-degree burn. I begged the old doctor for medicine, for sulfa drugs, for dressings, for burn ointment. It was always the same thing: "*Ja, ja, ja.*" I picked the infected flesh out of the wound and cleaned it with towels and boiled water. The hipbone was just beginning to show through the angry red flesh. I finally got the old doctor to look at the wound. "*Ja, ja, ja,*" he mumbled and wandered off.

I tried everything. I cajoled him, I begged him, I pleaded, I humored. Finally there was nothing left, and I tore into him full bore. "I have nothing! Nothing to treat these men! They are sick and wounded. You tell the commandant I am angry! You ask him if he would treat his own soldiers this way. You tell him this immediately!" I screamed this in his face, backing him up against the wall. I knew he spoke some English and understood me perfectly. Business as usual was over.

He replied in perfect English. "I could never speak to the commandant on these matters. We are very short of medicine for our own soldiers."

"Well, you tell him I'm angry. Tell him this right away!" I yelled this in his good ear. He got one *"Ja"* out before I drilled him to the wall with an intense stare. He still had a look of surprise on his face when he left.

Big Stoop couldn't just walk into a room. He barged in and began bellowing in broken English. "I want to know about your complaining. What are you complaining? We owe you nothing. You are enemies of the Fatherland. You are lucky you are alive at all. And now you complain?" It was only a matter of how bad it would be. I tried a stall.

"We have men here who are suffering. Some are dying without any medical attention at all." I tried to show him the ward in a sweeping gesture, trying to get some distance from him.

"Good for them, good for them if they are dying. Good for them!" he shouted. If this man had any skill at all, it was picking the perfect moment to blindside a man. I don't know how he did it, but I never saw it coming. It felt like a wall falling on me. I sat on the floor for a long time until I realized there was no hearing in my left ear.

The hell I raised about the lack of medicine got around the

camp quickly. Then I heard that the radio operators had cut off the Germans from the news. The people who run prisons like to think it's a one-way street, but it never is.

A few days later I walked into the infirmary and saw two goons carrying a large cardboard box. They both had white powder sticking to the stubble around their mouths. They set the box down and told me loudly, in German, "We have not opened this box." I turned the box around. In crude letters the word MEDI-CIN was written with black paint. I opened it as fast as I could, hoping to find sulfa drugs, pain medication, and antiseptics. The boxes were the size of soap boxes, and there were two familiar words on them: Bayer and aspirin.

"Herr Doctor, there is only aspirin in this box. Are there other boxes?" I shouted as loud as I could to the old doctor, who dutifully shuffled over and looked in the box.

"*Ja, ja, ja.* Aspirin," he mumbled.

"I must have sulfa drugs, antiseptics, pain medications!" I shouted right in his ear.

"*Ja, ja, ja.* Sulfa, sulfa! I am sure it is coming soon. *Ja, ja, ja.*"

I used the aspirin for everything. I mashed it up and mixed it with warm water to make a paste and used it on burns and open wounds. It actually worked. The men I treated got better, and more started coming into the infirmary. I had about twenty patients and spent all my time in the small shack.

"MacArthur has landed on some island in New Guinea, Biak or something. The Japs are on the run. The Eighth hit Lyon, Nice, and Marseille. Must be a warm-up for the invasion." The news was good.

ABOUT THE last week of May we had a warm spell and several patients came in with high fevers and severe sore throats. I mixed the aspirin in warm water and had them gargle it. Two of these men had fevers so high that they were delirious. I looked down their throats, but I didn't see any swollen tonsils. The next day several more men came in with severe sore throats, and the first bunch came back choking and coughing up whitish mucus by the cupful. Several of the men were on the verge of choking to death. I thought we had an epidemic on our hands. I called for the old doctor.

"Herr Doctor! These men are dying. What is this illness? We must test these men and find out what they have." I tried to instill some real urgency in him.

"*Ja, ja, ja.*" He could somehow say this without moving his mouth.

I hammered at the old doctor every hour he was in the camp. I was terrified. These men had a serious disease, and I was sure they were going to die. They were choking for air, turning purple, and flailing around. The infirmary filled up, the little hall filled up. There was a line every day of more men in the early stages. These men were looking at me. Their lives were in my hands. They were pleading with their eyes. All I could do was keep cold water compresses on their burning foreheads.

The old doctor must have told the camp commandant we had a serious problem, because he came in the next day with a small glass jar of throat swabs. We carefully swabbed the men's throats and prepared samples to go to a laboratory. He had just started his muttering when I grabbed his arm and pushed him up against the wall. His bleary, half-closed eyes opened up for the first time.

I said, "We must help these men right away or they will all die, and I will not let them die!" I stared at him for a long time. I was ready. If they wanted to hand me the bodies of my countrymen, I could hand them the body of one of theirs.

He slowly raised his hands up. Then he said, "Okay." He

opened his bag and brought out a small black case with some surgical instruments in it. His hands began to shake more than usual when he handled them.

We took six of the worst cases and performed tracheotomies on them right away. They winced and writhed and tried to scream when he made the incision, but I told them that it would save their lives. We inserted a small piece of rubber tubing in the throat incisions so the men could breathe. The air rushed into their lungs in great heaves, and their color changed right away. We managed to stitch the tubes in place with cotton thread we had boiled. All we had was a small vial of alcohol and a few cotton balls to wipe off their throats, but it worked. It was a pitiful sight, but they were alive. The old doctor showed me how to perform this simple procedure, and I did several in the following days.

I figured we were looking at some kind of an exotic pneumonia-type disease, because the doctor didn't seem to know what it was. I asked him over and over what it was, but he just mumbled something about diphtheria. I wracked my brain to remember what I had learned at Baylor. All I could remember was that death from diphtheria was an agonizing combination of suffocation and drowning, and infection of the larynx results in a 90 percent death rate. The dread disease had been cured at the turn of the century with a simple, cheap drug. Diphtheria was now unknown in the U.S.

When word got out it was diphtheria, it had a devastating impact on the patients. No one really knew what diphtheria was, but everyone knew it was bad. The patients became despondent and worried for their lives. We worked night and day to save these men, and after a few weeks the epidemic seemed to slow down a little. I started stealing the little vial of alcohol from the doctor's bag every day to swab the tracheotomy incisions.

We had other pressing medical problems, including a man

whose hand had been badly mangled by a flak burst. His hand had swollen up into a purplish-black lump, and there were angry red streaks running up his arm. I convinced the doctor to operate on this man's hand the next morning. I begged him to bring some anesthetic for the operation as he tottered down the steps.

The next morning we got the patient ready by boiling towels and wrapping his hand. We waited and waited for the old doctor, but he didn't show up. The red streaks had reached about four inches past his elbow, and I knew that if the blood poisoning got much farther, this man would die.

I found the doctor's surgical kit and started to work. I cut in across the palm, and to my surprise there was very little blood. The tissue had died, and so had many of the nerves. The patient, Chuck, was from Louisiana, and he would drawl from time to time, "Damn, that hurts. Damn, that hurts, son."

I ended up cutting most of his hand away, except for the thumb. Without antiseptics the hand would surely get infected. I vaguely remembered that they used to cauterize wounds on the battlefield with hot irons to prevent infection and close blood vessels. I ran into the barracks and asked a couple of the guys if they could stoke up a fire and heat up an iron rod that I had found.

I decided it was best just to do it, instead of telling Chuck about it, so I walked in with this red hot rod and pressed it into as much of the wound as I could. To my surprise he yelped a little, but the nerves were so far gone in his hand that he didn't feel much of the burning. The smell made me sick. I washed his hand in a mixture of boiled water and aspirin, then bandaged it as best I could. The hand didn't get infected, and Chuck kept his arm, and his life.

"Someday, Tommy, we're gonna meet again, and I'm gonna buy ya a drink and a steak and tell you how much I appreciate what you've done for me," Chuck said, as he slipped a shirt on to leave the infirmary. It's a fine feeling, knowing you've helped someone survive.

AFTER A while the infirmary actually looked like an infirmary. We had cobbled together a few beds that had tilt-up sections to hold the patients in a half-sitting posture, and we had collected towels and a few small white bowls.

I noticed the men whose spirits were highest did the best. Anything helped their spirits. Any joke, any song, any little two-step. There had been so little in the way of bright moments for so long that even a little smile seemed wildly out of place. Chasing the gloom became almost as big a job as chasing the Grim Reaper.

"We welcome you all tonight! We are coming to you live, from Earl Carroll's restaurant, in Columbia Square, in Hollywood, California! And through these portals pass the most beautiful ladies in the world! Tonight we welcome you all, while you sip your fine wine at your table and enjoy your food—*wonderful food*, right? If your food is not perfect, just send it back to the chef!" That line would always get them. "Now we're going to introduce our musical host, from coast to coast, Mr. Tommy LaMore, with music galore!"

I set up a small stage in the ward, with a big curtain across the front. I would pull back the curtain and leap out on the stage. "Hi, folks! I'm Tommy LaMore, with music galore. Let's hear it! How about a little music? I'll bet everyone is thinking about their sweetheart right about now, and I'll bet they're thinking, *Is she thinking of me?* Well, I've got a little song to sing with the band, it goes something like this:

> *Is my baby blue tonight, is my baby thinking of me tonight?*
> *Now you know and I know we're not being smart,*

You might fool your friends, but you can't fool your heart . . ."

My voice wasn't the best in the world, but to see the looks on these men's faces, you would have thought I was Frankie Sinatra himself.

The radio operators would write down the lyrics from American songs on the BBC, and I would listen to the melody. We called it the "Stalag Luft 4 Hit Parade." I found some other men who could act, and they worked up a little comedy routine. Two guys had Abbott and Costello down pat, and they got the whole ward laughing loudly.

It was corny, really corny, but it was a big success. Laughter can give a sick, depressed, starved man just enough reason to sit up a little higher, smile a little, and start to live again. I did the show a couple of times a day, and I found that it made me feel better too.

THE INTERNATIONAL Red Cross made sustained efforts to help the POWs. They packaged parcels for us and diligently shipped these to as many camps as they could throughout the war. The parcels became a full-time occupation for us. The guards and the goons stripped the small cardboard boxes of cigarettes, chocolate, and soap, and we would get what was left.

Cigarettes became the common currency in the camp. They were hoarded, traded for food, and carefully, carefully smoked. They had another important function. The cigarettes could buy power. The goons were the weak link in the prison system. At first they were seen as drooling snitches, wandering around spying and listening to the prisoners. Later, they were seen as an opportunity, because of their weakness for American cigarettes.

The parcels came into the camp on large green wagons and

were stored right behind the infirmary. The guards and goons would always loot the parcels between the train and the camp.

One morning I was up early and saw a load of unopened parcels being loaded into the storage shed. Talk about good luck. I could just dodge into this shed on my way to the water well without being seen. Billy, one of my helpers, and I frantically stashed the cigarettes and chocolate and tins of Spam in every conceivable corner of the infirmary. We had lots and lots of cigarettes. The goons loved American cigarettes. We could own the goons with enough American cigarettes.

"American cigaretten?" we asked.

"Ja, okay! *American cigaretten."* We gave it a few days. They came by several times during the day, trying to look menacing, then we would offer them a nice, fresh Lucky Strike or Camel.

We quickly learned the fine art of manipulation. We owned the goons now. They had broken camp rules by taking bribes from us. We could threaten them by telling the commandant. One word and they were off to the Russian front. The sacks of dandelions we bought from the goons with cigarettes helped a lot. We made soup and tea from them, and the men responded immediately. Dandelions are very nutritious, and they gave the men the vitamins they needed to recover. Later we got mushrooms, wild onions, and even some potatoes.

ABOUT NINE o'clock on a cloudy, overcast Tuesday, I noticed the messengers from the radio operation were running instead of walking. Everyone they passed started smiling and jumping up and down.

"Ike's landed at Normandy on the French coast! The invasion was a success. They're on their way, men! Hitler's ass is between a rock and a hard place now, soldier!" The news electrified the camp and made several prisoners rich in cigarettes from the invasion date pools.

The Germans responded by making us stand in muster for four hours the next day. Commandant Pickhardt ranted for two hours and actually fired his pistol several times. We were beginning to wonder just how far the Germans would go when the other shoe dropped.

Bernie, one of the radio operators, showed me the piece of paper with Eisenhower's words:

This landing is but the opening phase of the campaign in Western Europe. Great battles lie ahead. I call upon all who love freedom to stand with us.

MY TEARS came so fast a few drops hit the smudged brown paper before I could move it.

My thoughts turned to the Resistance, to Jules and Henri. I hoped they would live. I hoped with everything in my heart that they would survive. I thought about them every night. I wondered what operations they had been conducting, and I prayed for their safety. They deserved to live.

The nagging preoccupation with food was overshadowed by an intense craving for news. Every news story was instantly circulated in the camp and analyzed in minute detail by the 1,500 military experts in the camp. Rumors ran wild, and there were experts in every area: strategy, timetables, the German response, you name it.

"The Russians just launched an offensive on the Karelian isthmus."

"Where the hell is that?"

"Somewhere around Leningrad, about seven hundred miles east of here. The Germans are in full retreat, fifty, a hundred miles a day. Man, they could be here in a week, ten days easy!"

"They used the Eighth Air Force to pulverize the Germans holding up the invasion in St. Lo. Attaboy, mighty Eighth! These Krauts ain't gonna last long trying to fight with a thousand B-17s over their jarheads!"

About June 12 I saw a story that froze me:

The French Resistance has reported today that the SS has killed all of the residents of the French town of Oradour in reprisal for the execution of an SS officer. Over six hundred people, including all the women and children of the town, were killed. The women and children were burned alive in the town's church.

My mind raced. *Would the Germans actually kill the entire population as they retreated?* A wave of panic rippled through me. *Would they kill us, too? Would they kill everyone in Carvin?*

Bernie shook his head. "Man, these Krauts are out to set the world's record for bad asses. Imagine herding women and children into a church and setting it on fire. Where do they get these monsters?"

"They make them. The factory is right around here," I said, trying to shake off the revulsion. I began to feel a strange fatigue in my mind from the months of fear and hatred of the Germans and what they were doing. I was beginning to feel a weariness, a choking nausea, and an almost frantic anxiety to be far away from this darkness and danger. Forever.

Everyone in the camp began to wonder what the Germans would do with us when the Russians arrived. Would they move us, leave us, or kill us?

"Why would they move us? It's just more work and manpower for them. Hell, they'll just leave us for the Russians," went one argument.

"No, they'll move us west. They need us as bargaining chips when they cut a deal with Ike."

No one wanted to voice the other possibilities.

JUNE 1944 passed quickly. The news was good. The Russians took Viborg, on the Gulf of Finland, and Ike's troops took Cherbourg. The radio boys cut a hell of a deal with the Germans to tell them the name of the general who surrendered Cherbourg. Lieutenant General von Schlieben. Ten pounds of potatoes, please, and thank you very much.

Around the fifteenth I read a few lines of news that made me sit upright:

British authorities today reported that an unmanned flying bomb fell on London and exploded. The plane is a small, jet-powered plane with stubby wings and was launched from France.

So that was it. The robot plane we had seen was a flying bomb. I was surprised the Germans were using it against London instead of against the invasion, but then trying to figure out a madman is impossible.

"THERE WILL be a large group of prisoners coming to the camp tomorrow from Stalag Luft 6. Some of these men may be ill. You will escort them to the camp and treat those who are ill or injured." The commandant's orderly told me this quietly, so the other men in the infirmary wouldn't hear.

There was our answer. The Germans were going to start moving us around. Stalag Luft 6 was up on the Baltic coast, about sixty miles north of Kaliningrad, Lithuania, and was in the path of the advancing Russian army. The Germans were going to move them down to our camp, which meant they planned to keep us.

Nearly two hundred of these men arrived at the Kiefheide station on the hot, dry morning of July 21, about eight o'clock. When they pulled back the doors on the train, I knew things had changed. These men were nearly dead. They crawled and fell out of the doors in sickening slow motion, yelling and crying.

"Go ahead and kill us now, you Kraut shitbags!"

"Water, oh God, give us water! We're dying! We're dying!" The men were beyond reason, ready to charge the guards. I was sure I was going to see a massacre.

The men were emaciated and bleeding from scrapes and sores on their heads, elbows, and knees. They had been locked in the hold of a filthy ship for several days with no food or water, then beaten and packed into the cattle cars. Vomit and excrement covered them. Their eyes darted everywhere, and in a frantic daze they stayed close to the cars for cover, sure they were going to be shot.

Commandant Pickhardt was there in his full dress uniform, standing in a small green Wehrmacht car and waving his pistol. He seemed extremely agitated and right in the face of everyone he talked to. Pickhardt snapped as he talked, like a Doberman on a short leash. We called him the Madman. He seemed insanely angry all the time, talking in a high-pitched, screeching series of urgent commands.

Pickhardt screamed at the guards. "Assemble the men at once! Get them together. Use your weapons! Don't give these murderers any mercy at all!" The men were sure he was ordering their executions. He sounded like Hitler. Harsh, relentless, and red-faced, he waved his pistol around wildly. "We're going to move these murderers to the camp at double time. If any of them fall or make a move to escape, use your bayonets!"

The guards who arrived with the prisoners were young recruits from the German Navy. They were just one step up

from the Hitler Youth. Pickhardt whipped them up with the
Luftgangster/murderer message, but this time he told them to use
their weapons. This was the first time I had seen Pickhardt in this
kind of all-consuming rage, and these prisoners were right on the
verge of collapse. The Kriegsmarines were getting the message.
"Raus! Raus! Get up off the ground!" they screamed at the men as
they prodded them with their bayonets.

Once the men were assembled, they were handcuffed in pairs
and lined up. Pickhardt wanted the men marched at double time,
which I couldn't believe. Most of these guys could barely stand. I
told the guard I was with that they couldn't do this, and I was
going to the commandant to tell him this. He quickly put his hand
over his mouth and warned me to shut up. Pickhardt was in no
mood to be approached with anything. The guard took me to the
rear of the line and told me to follow the group. Pickhardt gave
the order to move the men out, and the men started a pathetic
double-time march that was more of a mass stumble.

"Raus! Raus! Move! Move!" the young guards screamed at the
poor bastards. They were using their rifle butts to hit the men in
their lower backs. They had dogs everywhere that snapped and
tore at the men if they even slowed down. This was different, and
it scared the hell out of me. The Germans wanted to kill some
people that day. Several of the prisoners collapsed right away.

I tried to help one man who collapsed. His shackled partner
was trying to drag him along and was pleading with him to get up
before the guards and the dogs tore into them. I had just gotten
him to sit up when I saw a group of camp guards coming. Big
Stoop was with them. I had just about pulled the man up to his
feet when I saw Big Stoop's face. I remember thinking, *How could
anyone have a head so big?* I looked away for a fraction of a second
to get my balance. Big Stoop hit me on the side of the face with
his cupped hand so fast I never saw it coming. I collapsed on my

stomach and started to roll over, then doubled up when one of the young Kriegsmarines ran his bayonet into my right leg. The bayonet plunged deep into my calf and hit my leg bone with a jolt that blinded me with a searing flash of pain.

Big Stoop bellowed at me to get up. "Get up, you *luftgangster* crap! Get this scum up with you. You think you can kill German women? You think you can blow up German cities and everything is fine? Not so fine now, eh *luftgangster?* Get up now, you complaining shits! Now! Now! *Raus! Raus!*" His voice roared in my eyes. I could feel him thinking that he could kill me now, if I stayed down one more second. I grasped this thought and somehow pulled myself up and looked at him. His face was a quivering mass of hate and malice, his bleary blue eyes glazed over with rage.

Somehow, I threw my right leg forward and tried to put some weight on it. It held for a second, then spun out from under me. I tried again, but the blood was running out of my leg and into my shoe, which squished and sloshed around and made it even harder to walk. *They are going to kill us all,* I kept thinking.

The three kilometers to the camp dragged by in a blur of flashing dogs and the shrill shouts of young men just learning to hate. To this day I don't know how we made it.

I was taken back to the infirmary, where the newly arrived Dr. Wilbur McKee closed my leg up with about thirty stitches. "What the hell is going on? What was Stalag Luft 6 like? Did they treat you this badly up there?" I asked.

"This all started about three weeks ago, when the Russians broke through up north," he said. "I think they're finally realizing that they are going to lose this war, and they're plenty riled up." He pulled the stitches tight. I was really shook up, but more than that I was angry. I'd been told to go out and help these pitiful men, then they did this to me. The hot anger I felt in Brussels came flooding back.

. . .

DR. WILBUR E. McKEE was from Louisville, Kentucky, and was the chief camp doctor at Stalag Luft 6. Dr. Henry J. Wysen, from Youngstown, Ohio, was with him, and they were a godsend to us. They arrived a few days ahead of the rest of the men from Stalag Luft 6. I showed him what we had done to control the diphtheria outbreak and our efforts to treat the burned flyer. They were amazed at the effect the powdered aspirin had on the men with severe problems. They were also aghast at the virtual lack of any medical equipment or supplies. I guess they were hoping for better than they'd had at Stalag Luft 6. "We're going to have a hell of a time taking care of the men here with this little box of aspirin," Dr. Wysen said. "We're going to need your resourcefulness in here, airman. You've done a hell of a job taking care of these men with next to nothing."

My leg became infected, and I ran a fever for three days. I was trying to rest in my bunk in the late afternoon when I first felt the animal stir in my chest.

It began as a dry, incessant tickling cough. Then it began to feel like pieces of my lungs were tearing off when I coughed. I coughed for hours. I don't remember sleeping, it seemed like I just quit paying attention and drifted away somewhere.

I woke up thinking I was going to die. My solar plexus strained so hard to pull air into my lungs that my eyes bugged out. When I moved, every bone hurt, every joint burned. Time and place began to blur, and sounds grew louder.

The coughing didn't let up. The mucus splattered out in big yellow-white slimy chunks. I looked at the mess in my hands and on the blanket. *How much is there before there is no more animal, no more of my life? What do I do when I can't cough it out anymore? Will I choke on it? Will I die here? Did I do all I could? What day is this? Where am I now?*

Choking down the warm dandelion soup was almost impossible, but I could feel every atom of the vitamins. I lay awake at night and felt the atoms fighting each other. Every sip of dandelion soup brought in more good atoms. Every second of rest between coughing bouts helped the good atoms. I talked with God and asked to be saved. When I did, the good atoms became stronger.

Getting that close to death again changed me. I realized I might die here. But I didn't want to. I hated that camp. I decided not to die in that stinking camp. The German fighter pilots did not kill me. The German flak gunners did not kill me. The SS did not kill me, and I would not die for them in that hellhole.

I remember reading somewhere that the solution to your agony always lies somewhere in that agony. When the paralysis started in my left leg, I remembered that they had transferred some of the men with post-diphtheria paralysis to a real medical facility somewhere in Frankfurt an der Oder. I tried to remember what symptoms were prevalent in the men who were shipped out, and how these were manifested.

The three weeks I'd fought with the animal within me were a fuzzy blur. I waited until I could just move around a little to try my plan.

"Herr Doctor, I have become paralyzed!"

The old doctor looked at me. "*Ja, ja, ja.* Paralysis." He tapped around my legs and repeated himself. "Post-diphtheria paralysis. *Ja, ja, ja.*"

The homemade crutches came in one at a time. When I had two, I dragged myself into the infirmary and complained to the old doctor, and then to Dr. McKee and Dr. Wysen. They knew what I knew. Untreated, post-diphtheria paralysis was often fatal. I timed my worst complaints for the two days before the expected arrival of the Red Cross inspection teams.

When the day for the Red Cross inspection came during the last week in August, nothing happened. The camp buzzed with scuttlebutt. *Were we too close to the eastern front? Would they come again?* The visit was the only source of pressure I had on the Germans, and now their visit was off. No one knew anything.

"The Krauts are tightening up. They're getting their asses kicked all over the place, and it's no more Mr. Nice Guy with the Red Cross," was the only thing on the grapevine.

"The Red Cross is not coming, but we are sending you to Frankfurt for repatriation examination. You leave on the train tomorrow," the old doctor said, as Dr. McKee looked on. I had to try hard to contain my excitement and maintain my act. The word "repatriation" seemed like it was written everywhere.

THE GERMAN civilians on the train to Frankfurt were reading newspapers and passing them around. The news was bad, and they were worried. I could pick out a few sentences here and there. "The Wehrmacht really has their hands full on the eastern front. . . ." "I wonder why the Luftwaffe can't stop these cowardly air attacks by the Americans and the British." I loved it. Worry on, you bastards.

The face of a beautiful girl can take you away from your fear and your pain. Her face was proud and unlined. She looked at me and didn't make me feel inferior. She looked intelligent, as if she might have a mind of her own. She was about twenty, with long, wispy blonde hair and big, bright blue eyes. She passed by my seat silently, and a small orange fell from her hand into my lap. An orange. A round, orange-colored fruit. It lay there for a long moment. The guard looked at it. I looked at it. I looked at him. He looked away. I covered the orange with my hand and held it and tried to remember what an orange tasted like.

It was nice to know there were kind and decent German people who had resisted Hitler's poison. I peeled and ate the orange one section at a time. I could feel the good atoms surging through my body.

Repatriation. The word raced through my mind a hundred times a minute. *Was it possible? Would the Germans actually repatriate me? What would it take? How should I act? What must I say? How must I appear?* I agonized over every conceivable detail on the train. I mentally rehearsed my walk and my lines.

When we arrived in Frankfurt an der Oder, the station was quiet. The Germans moved along as if they were in a dream. Most of them knew the war was lost now, and the first traces of fear were in their faces. I heard the word *Ost* in muted conversations many times. They all seemed to be worried about the events in the east.

They took me to the hospital in a Wehrmacht truck that was barely running. The hospital was a huge building with peeling yellow paint and a lot of military activity. The ward for American POWs was in an isolated section of the hospital. We walked for what seemed like miles through corridor after corridor. There were about four men in the locked ward, and we skipped through the information game very rapidly. I knew more than they did because of our radio at the camp. The news that the Russians were shelling Warsaw was a big and welcome surprise, but I was saving the best for last. "Paris has been captured, and a bunch of Hitler's boys tried to blow him up," I told them, adding quickly, "and the Krauts had to close Stalag Luft 6 and send them down to Stalag Luft 4."

"Paris liberated, already? Say, Ike's boys have been busy!" a lanky kid from Oklahoma said from his wheelchair.

"Can't be long now, it just can't be. With France and Italy out of the war, hell, the Germans are fighting half the world alone, and that ain't gonna last long," I said, believing it myself.

"They moved Stalag Luft 6 already? Jeez, the Russians must really be on the move," said Tim, a short guy from Florida. "The Krauts will wise up and cut a deal with Ike any day now." That seemed to be the consensus. The Germans couldn't be dumb enough to let the Russians fight their way into the German home-land—or could they?

"Sending me back to England day after tomorrow. Guess they traded some shot-up Luftwaffe pilots for me." Benny, a P-47 pilot who was paralyzed from the waist down, said this quietly. Another man who was being repatriated was completely covered in bandages. He had severe head injuries and could barely talk, but he wanted to know the news.

"Paris! Warsaw! Man, these Kraut bastards must be sweating," he whispered, gritting his teeth against the pain. "I almost hate to miss the big party here when they give up. Maybe I'll refuse to be repatriated," he croaked. No one laughed.

Repatriation. The magic word. These men were actually going to be released. I looked at each one as if he were the kid who got the new bike for Christmas. I was envious down to my toes. *If these men were going back, why couldn't a paralyzed, dying airman go back?* It was possible. It could work.

"This doctor will assist in your examination," the nurse said in almost perfect English, which surprised me. The doctor, a sharp-eyed, elderly man with a tiny, white mustache, missed nothing. My stomach did a full turn when he looked at me. He tested my reflexes over and over and over. He tapped, I resisted. I did have a weakness in my left side which made it easier, but his eyes never left the rubber mallet when he tapped my knee.

"We will determine tomorrow what we recommend for you,"

the nurse said sweetly. Something about the way she said it alarmed me.

THE CAFETERIA for Allied POWs was surprisingly big. The tables were long, and there were several places on the walls where pictures had been removed. The linoleum was clean and highly polished. It took me a minute to realize how long it had been since I'd been in a clean, well-lighted room.

I took one of the few open seats and started to eat. One of the men spoke up in good English. "Welcome, welcome! You're an American? We're Polish here. We were fighting with the British and captured in North Africa, by Rommel's boys. There were four hundred of us at first, and there are now forty still alive." He said this almost gleefully, and it took me a minute to realize that he was impressed that forty of his men were still alive. They had been in some very bad camps for almost four years, in North Africa, Italy, and Germany. They were now in camps in Poland.

His name was Manuel, and he was the obvious leader of these men. A bright, happy-go-lucky man, Manuel had been a veterinarian in the Polish cavalry. I guessed he was about forty by his premature gray hair. He had some kind of serious sickness that the Germans had not been able to diagnose. They were sending him to one of the worst camps in the entire POW system. It was a camp that was filled mostly with Russian POWs, somewhere near Küstrin. I liked Manuel. He was a spark plug, and he kept all the men around him going with his wit. He made quite an impression on me. He looked just like James Cagney.

When I got back to the American ward, the men crowded around and asked, "Are you going to be repatriated?" I told them I didn't have any idea, but I sure as hell hoped so.

The next day they called me in for my report. The nurse

opened my chart with a quick flick of her wrist and began read-ing. "Airman Thomas L. LaMore. Diagnosis: Post-diphtheria paralysis. The medical staff have determined that your illness is in regression and that your life is not in any further danger. Therefore, you will be assigned to a POW camp immediately." She closed the file and walked out.

I tried to look on the bright side. The war was almost over any-way. I had tried. At least I had tried. I almost wanted to ask them what part of my act didn't work, but I had learned long ago that humor was not a big part of the Nazi mindset.

BARTH, GERMANY. They finally told me on the train where we were going. We went to Stargard, then to Stettin, then on to Barth. A truck met us at the station and took us to Stalag Luft 1. The camp looked almost identical to Stalag Luft 4. Stark, un-painted wooden buildings. Towers, guns, dogs, lice, dust, despair. When they told me it was a camp for officers, I didn't really care. It was a camp.

Colonel Spicer was a tall Air Force officer with graying hair and high cheekbones. He was of German descent and spoke the language fluently. I liked him right away. He had crash-landed a P-47 on a mission over Germany, and he welcomed me to the camp in an affable manner. He told me there was another famous ace at the camp, Colonel Zimke, who was also of German descent. Everyone knew about Zimke. He had been a leading ace when I crashed. They had all kinds of aces in that camp.

Spicer and I chatted awhile, and I felt a lot better. At least the stories were going to be good in this camp.

"The only way to get by with them, Tommy, is to stand up to them, talk back to them. They told me they were going to shoot me, and I told them where they could shove Hitler and their whole damned country. They'll actually think more of you if you stand up against them, instead of bowing down to them." He told me this as I waited to be assigned to a barrack. By this time I was actually looking forward to being in this camp with these famous fighter pilots.

But the next day they sent me right back to Frankfurt. No explanation.

Repatriation! They were going to repatriate me after all. That must be what it's all about. My mind raced through the possibilities as the train clattered on to Frankfurt.

I was treated completely differently this time. I was under constant guard and kept in isolation. They wouldn't tell me anything. Finally, they called me into a small room and told me bluntly that I was being sent to a different POW camp. Something had happened. They looked at me as if I was a real threat. I couldn't figure out what had gone wrong, but it was bad, they didn't make any secret of that. "You will be leaving the hospital immediately," the officer in charge of Allied prisoners said.

"Where are you sending me now?" I asked.

"You will be leaving the hospital immediately. You have been reassigned to a different POW camp," he said sharply.

SEVEN

KÜSTRIN

THE WEHRMACHT truck's engine kept dying in loud clanging shudders. It was mid-September, and the morning light covered everything with a thin blue cast that was hard and cold. The battery would just turn it over a few times and the motor would catch and blue smoke would billow out. The tires were bald, and the cord was visible on all four tires. The driver finally got it running and held his foot on the floor while he let the clutch out, which threw us all against the steel tailgate. There were about thirty of us. I recognized a few of the men from the hospital. They were the Polish soldiers. I was the only American.

"We all resisted the Germans. We've really given them trouble. Some of us tried escapes. Manuel has tried two escapes. We're troublemakers, and Küstrin is their way of getting back at us." The Polish soldier next to me was matter-of-fact in his explanation, but he lowered his voice and hesitated when he spoke the name.

"Küstrin is one camp you don't want to even hear about. Many, many men die there," a younger, very thin prisoner said. The other prisoners looked away when he said this.

"Why are they sending me up there?" I asked them, but they didn't know. When I told them I had been picked up by the Gestapo and sentenced to be shot, they thought this might have something to do with it.

"The Gestapo picked you up from the French Resistance, and the SS tried you—and they didn't shoot you? This is unusual for them. They shoot everyone. Especially now," Manuel said quietly as the truck lurched on through the bleak, endless marshlands.

THE SWAMPS around Küstrin stretched out for miles and miles. The wind blew constantly, flattening the tall, yellow grass. This was another melodramatic setting for a prison. Swamps. I remembered that in the Deep South they used to put prisons in swamp country, because it made escape almost impossible. The wind got colder and blew harder, flattening the high grass and my spirits.

The military camp at Küstrin was gigantic compared to the Stalag Luft camps. It looked like a feedlot back in Texas. The yard was about ten acres of dark, slippery mud that had been dust just a few days before. I had never seen so many men in one place before. There were two or three thousand men milling around, huddled in small groups. They wore several different kinds of faded uniforms, and many men had gray hair and tattered blankets.

"*Raus! Raus!* Move! Move!" The guards ran right up to the truck and shouted in our faces: I could smell the cigarette smoke on their breath. They were regular Wehrmacht troops, wounded and returned from the eastern front after three years of killing Russians. They were vicious, hardened men with razor-sharp combat skills. They covered each other as if they were in combat. I noticed the blueing on their submachine guns was worn off. This metal coating prevents a gun from rusting and normally would take many, many years to wear off. I thought again of the wear on the B-17s at Pyote and the wear on the men who trained us. War is an unimaginable corrosive—on steel and on people.

KÜSTRIN SMELLED like death and looked like death. The prisoners looked like walking dead men. Their faces said that they had given up on life. There was nothing behind their eyes at all.

The Germans treated these Russian and Polish prisoners like cockroaches. They never looked at them, they looked right through them. Every little gesture was loaded with animosity. The guards always shoved them—hard. They always rubbed it in, trying to get one of the prisoners to attack them so they could empty a magazine into the prisoners. The Russians took it stoically and kept their glowering hatred deep inside them. *"Pozhe. Pozhe,"* they would say under their breaths. Later. Later.

"Find a spot! Get out! Find a spot for yourselves!" The German guard shoved us out of the receiving building with his rifle. Manuel appeared out of the crowd and grabbed my arm. "Come with me," he said.

Manuel's shack was filled with Russian infantrymen and some Polish cavalrymen. The building itself was even worse than Stalag Luft 4. The boards had been slapped on the frame haphazardly, and there were many holes and large cracks in the walls. The wind whistled through these gaps and blew the warm stink of the prisoners into my face. Many of the men were sick, and there was constant coughing. There were at least thirty men in this shack alone who were too sick to get up. The smell was terrible. It was like the cattle car on the way to Stalag Luft 4. Vomit, diarrhea, filthy clothes, stale tobacco, and the visceral smell of fear was so thick you could almost see it. The smell was everywhere. In the air. In the shredded blankets. Smeared on the walls.

"This camp is not a POW camp, this camp is where the Germans kill people a little at a time. If we survive this camp, we will be very lucky," Manuel said to me as we walked around the yard. I couldn't believe it. *Why? Why had they sent me to die in this hellhole?*

The guards never hesitated to slam a rifle butt into the back of a prisoner, and they didn't stop with one blow. They were cruel, dangerous bastards. No one, but no one, looked at them. Never. Not for any reason.

One bit of lip to these guards was a death sentence, for anyone and everyone. Manuel was right: This wasn't a POW camp, it was a death camp. I learned what survival meant in this camp. Survival meant that nothing is more important than life, not dignity, not spitting in the face of evil, not anger, nothing. Survival was living, and nothing else.

THE FALL rains came early to Küstrin, and the cold wind that blew in off the Baltic and across the flat open country tore right through our shack, our blankets, and our clothes. The sick men started dying when the rains came. Their coughing would go on for hours at night, slowly getting softer, then ending. The same beat-up truck that brought us up here from Frankfurt came through the camp after count every morning for the bodies. The cold in that October wind killed these poor men. It was a special wind. It worked its way past your lips and hurt your teeth; it swirled around your ears and insulted your private parts. It stung, and it made elbows and knees ache all day. It finally soaked into your bones, until there was not a warm or dry place anywhere, no matter how you curled up or cupped your hands over your ears. That wind found you, and it hurt you.

There was plenty to do in this camp, though. Every day I worked from early dawn to way past dark, surviving. Trying to find food, news, a scrap of blanket, learning a little Polish here, a little Russian there. Anything that might help.

The hardest for me was the filth. There was one cold water tap and one sink for every 120 men—and no soap. The water would not take away the oil and grease, and most of all it would not take away the smell. My face itched from my ragged beard. When the rains came and the mornings were cold, very few of the men would even go to the sink to wash their faces. I did, every day. Just to remember what it was like to be clean.

The days at Küstrin seemed about a hundred hours long. A hand-cranked German air raid siren woke us at six-thirty. We pulled ourselves up from the wooden shelves and tried to shake off the stiffness and pain. The guards would walk around the shack and beat on the boards with sticks, yelling *"Raus, raus!"*

Each shack leader counted the men who could stand in the shack, closed the eyes of the men who had died during the night, and tried to help the sick men get up. I helped Manuel every morning with the sick men. If they stayed in their bunks more than a few days, they died.

THE DULL, heavy terror of Küstrin finally drove me to action after the second month. To accept this place was to accept death. I had to try something, anything. I marched into the commandant's building in early November and managed to get in to see his adjutant. "There must be some mistake. I am an American airman. I do not belong in this camp with these men," I said to the adjutant, a small, balding man with beady, dark eyes and skin so white I could see through it.

"And why not? You are an enemy of the Reich. You have killed many German people, and look! Look here, Mr. American airman! Your file orders you to this camp! The SS has insisted on this. You are lucky to be alive. They should have shot you! You *Luftgangsters* kill innocent German women and children day and night with your bombing. I would kill you myself. Now get out of here!" He ended every sentence with a slap on the desk.

"But, I don't—." The guard slammed the rifle butt into my lower back on some unseen command from the adjutant. The pain in my kidney felt like a big wooden stake had been driven into my side. I had just started to sit up when the guard hit me in the other kidney with the rifle and grabbed me by the back of my coat. I never touched the three wooden steps on my way to the mud in front of the administration building. The guard threw me that far.

The first streaks of blood in my urine were bright. Then they became dark, then the flow turned to mostly blood. Any small medical problem at Küstrin meant death. Any cold, any open wound, any infection. Death. My nightmare of dying in a muddy trench came back to me. The one thing I never wanted in life had happened to me. I was going to die in a dark, cold, muddy hellhole in a foreign country. *How could this happen to me? I tried so hard to fight and die as an American airman.* That night I passed out on the latrine and awoke to Manuel's urging. "Inside, Tommy. Come inside. I have some food for you. Tomorrow we will talk about getting out of here. Come."

Manuel was a wheeler-dealer without equal. Somehow he found extra food and made me tea from dandelions. "I need you, Tommy. I need you to live, to help me get out of here," I heard him say through the pain in my back. Somehow, hearing that someone needed me helped pull me out of my own pain and darkness. I could almost hear Jim Pilger talking to me in the hospital at Ridgewell. *We need you, Tommy, we need you.*

Manuel brought me dandelion tea twice a day for about ten days, and I drank all the boiled water I could. The blood in my urine slowly decreased. I had to lie on my stomach for two weeks because of the pain in my lower back. I had to hand it to the Germans, they knew how to hurt a man deep inside for weeks with one thrust of a rifle butt.

. . .

THE WEEKS passed in a blur of rainy days, mud, and death. The daily ritual of standing for the endless counting seemed like it took ten hours instead of two. There was rain every day now, mixed with sleet, and we got soaked every morning. Our new occupation was trying to dry our clothes over tiny fires in the shack stove. It sometimes took until two or three in the afternoon to get up to the stove, which was usually cold by then. The wetness sharpened the stench in the shack to an acrid level that hurt my nose after a few hours.

The only diversion we had was circulating little bits of information. There was no radio in this camp, so every scrap of news was passed along as it came in.

"The Russians have Budapest surrounded."

"The British have landed on Walcheren Island in Holland."

Little scraps of maps circulated that helped us figure out where the Russians and Allies were, but I had never heard of many of these places. We did find out where Aachen, Germany, was around the first week of November. The American First Army crossed into Germany for the first time there. A wiry young Russian soldier, one of those men no one can kill, with barely enough strength to stand and with green scabs on his forehead, hobbled over to me, gave me a little piece of cloth, and said in barking little coughs, "American in Germany. Hitler is kaput." Then he smiled a goofy, lost little smile and wandered off.

The coughing at night in the shack was so loud no one slept. We closed our eyes and tried to remember what a world of food and cleanliness was like. The little shreds of meat in the slop had disappeared completely. I asked Manuel about his escape plans, but he said nothing except, "When is ready, when is ready."

"They are not coming back, Tommy. The Russian work parties. They go out, but they don't come back," Manuel whispered this to

This photo was taken by the French for Tommy's pass. The discoloration from his frostbite wound is just visible between the cheek and ear.

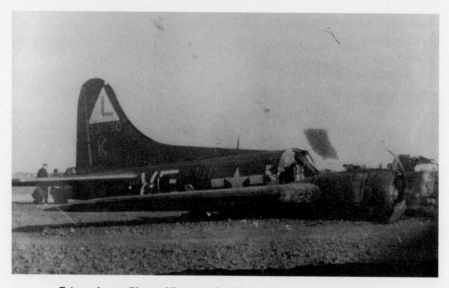

Extremely rare Photo of Tommy's B-17 taken the day after crash landing by the French. Approaching or photographing crashed aircraft was forbidden by German authorities. Resistance members salvaged ammunition, weapons, flares, etc. The L designates the 381st squadron, Eighth Air Force.

Tommy in the tail gunner's seat,
B-17 *Carol Alice* 1996. The night
this photo was taken Tommy
suffered a flashback of the
mission where he was wounded.

Tommy with New Mexico
Senator Peter Domenici.
Tommy attended veteran's
events frequently and
spoke on a
few occasions.

Tommy returned to Ridgewell in 1995, after what he called "a very long mission." He was deeply affected when he saw that the small building used for a morgue was untouched.

Tommy with Gilbert Marmuse at crash site in Carvin.

Tommy with
Medal of Honor winners
at banquet.

Tommy with B-17
Sentimental Journey.
This is a late model gun
mount, with optical
sighting.

GERMAN PLANE DOWN BACK IN THE WOODS.

THIS AREA IS WHERE OUR DECEASED WERE BURIED.

DOG HUT WHERE ENGLISH MAN WAS KILLED BY LIGHTING BETWEEN BARRACKS 2&3.

GERMAN KILLED WORKING ON THE ELECTRIC WORE.

LAGER C BARRACKS NOT FINISHED WITH WALLS MEN SLEEP ON FLOOR.

THIS LARGE HOLE THE GERMANS WERE DIGGING BEFORE WE WALKED OUT 1945 THEY SAID, "TO STORE POTATOES IN !"

100 ft X 30 ft X 8 ft.

R LAGER & RMAN BARRACKS

SPITAL

No File Door

BRITISH BARRACKS

THE BARRACKS IN ALL LAGERS B-C-D WERE BUILT 3 FT. OFF THE GROUND TOO PREVENT TUNNELING. A-LAGER WAS BUILT ON A CRAWL SPACE.

SHOWERS

RUSSIANS BARRACKS

STALAG LUFT IV

I HOPE THIS MAP OF STALAG LUFT IV WILL HELP YOU, IF YOU ARE HAVING TROUBLE REMEMBERING WHAT LAGER YOU WERE IN. THE DRAWING IS FROM BARBED BOREDOM BY CHARLES O. JANIS COPYRIGHT IN SEPT. 1950. AND ALSO THE INFO I HAVE RECIEVED FROM ALL YOU LUFT 4ERS OVER THE YEARS. AND ALL INFO IS 2 nd HAND. LEONARD E . ROSE

1W

Holiday Company, Bedford, VA 24

This line drawing of Stalag Luft IV has the interesting notation of a large and deep trench dug in 1945. There was tremendous fear that Hitler might order the extermination of allied POW's, particularly after the Dresden raid. Allied leaders signaled emphatically to German military leaders that any officers or enlisted men who engaged in atrocities against POW's would be tried and hanged after the war.

Tommy LaMore in 1996.

me as we stood in line for the morning count. They would march about five hundred of the Russian prisoners out of the camp every morning for work details. We noticed that the same officer went with the guards on these days, and they took a truck. These men didn't come back at night, and their barracks were reassigned the next day. "We must go soon, Tommy. Soon," Manuel said.

The daily rain turned to a driving sleet in late December. Several hundred new Russian prisoners brought news that Patton had broken through the Siegfried Line and was attacking the Saar Valley in a drive to the Ruhr. The Americans were bombing Japan with new B-29s, and the Russians had broken through German lines in Hungary. "The fascists will give up very soon now. They don't fight us much now, they just plant mines in the mud and run like rabbits," they said, laughing. "Like rabbits."

The news about the B-29s brought a wave of homesickness that made me cry like a baby. All I could think about was being back at Ridgewell and flying. At night I thought about each mission and tried to remember every detail of every day in the air, but my mind kept coming back to the mess hall at Ridgewell, to the food, and how it smelled and tasted.

There were several Polish men in my shack who were very sick and probably wouldn't live long. I tried to help them when I could. We made dandelion tea for them and tried to get them up. We got to talking about how Christmas was celebrated in our countries. I told them we would cut an evergreen tree and decorate it with bright glass bulbs and candles and popcorn. Soon, several men joined in and talked about their Christmas trees. We all felt better.

A few days later, I managed to scrounge three small limbs from the pine trees around the camp and tied them together with shoelaces into a little tree. I twisted some colored tin foil from cigarette packs into little bows and spent hours decorating our tree.

When I carried it into the barracks, the faces on the sick men beamed for the first time. I sang some carols, and we were just starting to sing some Polish carols when the door banged open. *"Vas ist los?"* the guards roared at us. They picked up the tree and tore it to shreds in front of our eyes. They laughed and crushed every little piece of that tree to smithereens and stomped out.

"We can have nothing. We can't even have a Christmas tree on this holy day. They have taken everything. We have no dignity. We have nothing left in our lives." Alex, one of the sickest men in the shack, said this so softly I barely heard him. He was an older Polish soldier from Manuel's outfit. He'd been a shoemaker once, and he helped the men fix their boots before he got sick. Now he was a gaunt scarecrow, and when the guards stomped our pitiful little tree, they crushed something vital in his tormented mind. Alex had uncontrollable dysentery. He rolled his head slowly from side to side as he muttered. Manuel and I warmed up some slop for him and tried to get it down his throat. It was impossible. I took him to the latrine and held onto his hand.

"Tommy, how can we live in a world with these people? How? They crush all light and goodness out. Forever. Crush it and crush it. Wherever they go. And they are so powerful. How can we live in a world with these people. How?" Alex drifted into a delirium I had seen over and over in Küstrin. I just held his hand. Suddenly he sat upright and looked at me and said, "Will you leave me now, please. I want to be alone now."

"Alex, this is Christmas. I want to stay here and help you," I said to him, but he wasn't listening anymore. I looked into his eyes. It seemed like he was a thousand miles away.

As I left, he said to me, "Merry Christmas, Tommy."

I looked at him and said, "Merry Christmas, Alex." He turned his head, and I suddenly felt alone in that freezing latrine.

I went back to get him about twenty minutes later. He was sitting on the latrine with his head back and his eyes wide open. He looked like a skeleton that had been covered with white skin. I looked at this man, tortured and degraded in death, and I broke down and sobbed uncontrollably until I couldn't even sit up. I lay on my side and cried in the rain.

I knew I would die in this place. Then I didn't want to feel anymore. I wore the same doomed look as the other men. I felt in my heart the black frozen terror that seemed to be a German specialty. *I can be defeated, I can be killed, I can be crushed, and it could happen here, and it could happen now.* I knelt and said a soft prayer. "God, don't let this happen to me. Help me to survive this hellish time."

When I got back to the barracks Manuel said to me, "What happened to Alex?"

"His life went down the toilet," I said.

Manuel looked away. Then in a half-whisper, he said, "Let's go. It will be very, very risky. Are you sure you want to try it?"

"I want to go. I don't care what happens. I don't care what the odds are, let's do it."

"We are going to take one other man, and you," Manuel whispered. "We go soon. We go." A tear spilled down his heavily lined face.

"We go," I said, closing my eyes.

FROM THAT moment on the despair that had attached itself to the bottom of my heart was displaced by a small factory, a factory that took everything in the world in, then found a way to use it in the manufacture of hope.

Each day was different now. I looked at the world only for what could help us escape. Manuel and I worked feverishly, trading cigarettes for small items, selling these items for more cigarettes. "Not yet enough. Not yet," Manuel would say every day, no matter how good the take was.

I loved to kid Manuel that he looked like Cagney. "You look like a movie star. You look like James Cagney," I said. He would put his thumbs in his lapels and strut around like Cagney and sing, "I'm a Yankee Doodle Dandy, born on the Fourth of July!" He still had a spark, in all that gloom and fear. He talked like Cagney, too, very fast and very direct. His eyes would flash from side to side when he was making a deal, and he would run his hands through his blond hair from front to back. He was the consummate operator, like many of Cagney's on-screen characters. And one of his specialties was goons.

"I've got the goods on some goons, and they've got to help me or they are going to go to the Russian front. Look at this," Manuel said. I couldn't believe my eyes. Two heavy wool coats. Dark colors, almost black, and in good shape. Bread wrapped in German newspaper. Manuel carefully pulled out a small tin can and pried off the lid. "This has taken a lot of time," he said with obvious pride. I thought it was gunpowder until I sniffed the can. He slipped the floorboard back in place silently.

Manuel worked feverishly every day getting contraband to the goons, sucking them in. He would talk to them quietly, explaining the horror of Russian flamethrowers and mentioning the names of the camp's German officers, as if they were his luncheon companions.

We worked so hard, the time flew by. January was a good month. The war news was good, too. We got a bunch of new Russian prisoners around the fifth. They had been captured in a big Russian offensive in southern Poland.

The rumor came from several sources at once. Poznan. The Red Army was in Poznan, only eighty miles east of us. There was a flurry of activity now in the camp. Several SS officers arrived in a small convoy of battered cars. They stayed only one afternoon, and I just caught a glimpse of them leaving. They walked quickly and looked extremely tense. They had about twenty SS troops with them who quickly inspected the gun towers. That night they quietly hauled up two more machine guns on each tower and stacked cans of ammo in the snow under the towers.

Cheese. I couldn't believe what I was seeing and smelling and tasting. Somehow, Manuel had obtained a large chunk of cheese from the goons, along with long underwear and heavy wool socks, Wehrmacht issue, very high quality and warm. "Tonight," he said, looking out at the gun towers where the guards were noisily pounding nails, reinforcing the new gun mounts. "Tonight."

Paul, the other man who was supposed to go, had opted out. He felt the escape was not going to work, but he helped us get ready. We waited a few hours after they locked us up, then we slipped through the floorboards and put on the heavy clothes and ate a few mouthfuls of bread and cheese. Manuel carefully pulled out a large object which I could hardly see. It was a roll of old threadbare carpet that spewed dust every time it was moved. He quietly handed this to me and took out an object rolled up in heavy oiled paper. He showed this to me in the reflected light of the searchlights that worked the perimeter of the shack relentlessly. Wire cutters. Almost new, still shiny. I looked at Manuel as he beamed. I made a gesture to say, *How the hell did you get these?* "Goons," he whispered, giggling. "Goons."

We quietly moved away from the center support of the barracks and took out the tin can. Manuel carefully sprinkled the dark powder in a circle around us and handed the can to me. I sprinkled another circle around that one. The smell of black pepper startled me for a moment, and I thought about the pepper steaks we served at the lunch counter back in Cisco. We sat back to back within the circle for three hours in the freezing dark. We waited silently and prayed. This new fear of being found in the darkness was different from the fear of fighting in the daylight. It was worse.

It's true what they say about dogs taking on the characteristics of their owners. The dogs the Germans used were big shepherds with long, shaggy coats that hung down below their bellies. They were vicious, high-strung dogs that would automatically snap at a prisoner if there was any slack in their leashes. They were loud. They knew that the sound wave of their bark weakened a man, made him bend his knees and hold out his hands. They loved blood, and they lived for the moment the guards would let the leash go slack. They bit hard, twisting their heads in a violent figure-eight motion, then bit again. Worst of all, they talked. They had a peculiar bark that meant they had found something, and they were never wrong.

The guards would set them loose under the barracks at odd times during the night to patrol the areas the searchlights couldn't reach. The guards listened to the dogs on some nights. But on some nights, if it was bitter cold, the guards would hurry their chores. They would stand together and smoke and talk, stamping their feet while the dogs ran under the barracks. Some nights they would forget to listen to the dogs.

The first guards came through the gate about eleven o'clock, slightly later than normal. We tensed when we heard the little metallic click of the leashes, then tensed again as the dogs tore off across the snow for the shacks, barking in a deep growling shout. Some of them had caught prisoners under the barracks and had been allowed to attack and bite until they killed, a special treat for them.

The snow flew up as a big shepherd dived under our shack and ran straight towards us, sniffing the ground rapidly in a side-to-side motion. He caught our scent, rushed towards us, sniffed again, then paused for a second. He tried to get off a high-pitched bark. The bark came out like an unfinished sentence. He started shaking his head violently and ran around in tight little circles, whimpering and sneezing and trying to shake the burn of the black pepper out of his nose. He finally ran out and sniffed at the snow for a few minutes, then ran on to the next shack. We listened intently to the guards talking. They were discussing *frauleins* and walking in tight circles to stay warm. They never heard the dog sneezing and yelping.

I hadn't laughed for so long I couldn't remember the sensation, and for a brief moment of blinding panic I thought the guards might hear our muffled giggling. The dog was still sneezing when the guards took him out.

THE GUARD was changed at midnight. This was the only time the searchlights stopped moving. The guards would clamber down from the towers and give the men coming on duty a short report. They blew a whistle, and the searchlights would begin moving up and down the wire again. When it was bitter cold, the procedure took an extra few minutes.

Finally, we heard the shout and the guards' boots clambering down the gun tower. Manuel looked me right in the eye and whispered, "Let's go." The words tightened my stomach into a hard knot.

We slipped out from under the barrack and looked around. We could just make out the shape of clouds in the dark sky. There was a steady, icy wind blowing the snow across the camp and through the two barbed wire fences. The first was barbed wire stretched out in big loops, about six feet high, and behind that was a barbed wire fence on concrete posts with a three-foot overhang at the top. We picked a dark spot on the wire. Manuel quickly unrolled the dusty carpet. Together we threw it up and over the rolled barbed wire. Manuel pulled himself up onto the carpet and over the fence. I quickly followed. Manuel slipped the carpet down and rolled it up quickly. We crawled to the second wire, Manuel began snipping with the cutters. The sound in the cold air was surprisingly loud.

My heart was pounding. I expected the searchlights to begin moving at any second. Manuel had worked out a way to cut the wire so it could be bent back to its original position by cutting it close to the posts. After we scrambled through the wire, he reached back and carefully bent back the strands.

"Do like me!" Manuel whispered. He began crawling on his stomach to a small low spot in the ground. "Breathe down into the snow when the searchlight comes over!" he said. Just then the searchlights snapped on and began moving. "Don't move now," Manuel said as he scooped up snow and threw it over us. The light ran up and down the wire, to the corner and back. The reflected light made the fresh snow sparkle in front of my eyes. We watched the light pass the point where we'd cut the wire, about three hundred feet from the tower. For an agonizing second the searchlight slowed, then it continued on. When the light started its swing away from us, Manuel tapped my leg.

"We go!"

We crawled at first, stopping when the light was working our side of the camp, then took off in a crouching run. It seemed like my breathing was way too loud, and the cloud of fog from my breath caught every ray of light from the camp.

"We have about five kilometers to go," Manuel whispered to me as we ran down the road. The snow was packed on the road.

We ran in the tire tracks to keep from making footprints. We ran in a kind of shuffle with the heavy coats. It had been so long since I'd run that I stumbled a lot. I remembered my years as a runner in Texas—another world, a world far away.

The pain began in my knees and spread to every joint in my body. It seemed as if my skeleton had come loose, and the muscle was tearing off my bones. The cold air was burning my lungs, and it seemed like I was running in slow motion. Every stride was agonizing. I began to stumble more, cursing myself for being so clumsy. I wondered if my feet would be under me when the weight of my body arrived. Each stumble was a jarring tangle of pain and cold. It took long, dreamlike moments to get up, to get my balance, and to run again. My mind began to wander. *You're a runner, Tommy. Remember that you are a runner, and you should be proud. . . .* Grandma LaBell's words came from somewhere. They helped somehow. I felt lighter, and the pain eased. Now it seemed the stumbles and falls were just an inconvenience. *I am a runner, and I am proud. I am a runner, and I am proud. . . .*

We had gone only about two kilometers when we heard it. The barking was loud, urgent. It was the dogs' alarm bark. The harsh noise seemed amplified from every tree. The fear grabbed my chest and squeezed hard. In the crisp night air, it seemed only a block away. If they let the dogs off the leashes, they could be on us in seconds.

We rounded a sharp bend in the road, and Manuel stopped suddenly and pointed. I could just make out the ripples on the dark open space in front of us. Water. I couldn't believe there was a body of water that wasn't frozen in this wrenching cold. We ran into the tree line and over a small hill and stopped at the water, completely out of breath. Manuel started grabbing at a pile of tree limbs in the dark and motioned for me to help. The first corner of a rectangular outline appeared quickly. A boat. Manuel gave me a *How do you like this one?* look. It was a small skiff, with two paddles. We jumped in it as fast as we could and pushed off. We paddled as quietly and quickly as we could. We could see a few hundred yards behind us. The dogs were going nuts. They yelped and barked and ran in circles. We could just hear the voices of the guards, shouting questions, running here and there, their flashlights stabbing into the treeline.

We paddled furiously for about two hours. Manuel tried to keep us headed straight by watching the night sky and the flashlights of the guards. We gulped down a mouthful of food and paddled on. Every stroke was like a heartbeat.

Finally there came a time when we couldn't hear the dogs or see the lights. We were out. The air smelled sweet. We were alive. We were free. Then the fear would return, and the paddle would seem heavier, the water darker.

The skiff grounded almost silently in high grass. We must have paddled about a mile. We pulled the boat up and covered it with branches in the darkness, then took off and ran through fields. Some parts of the fields were covered with water, which we carefully avoided. To get wet in this cold was certain death.

My mind started to wander, and I stumbled badly several times. My legs weren't doing what my mind thought they were, but there was never a second of hesitation in getting up. Every step was a step away from the death of Küstrin.

We had been running for about two hours when a sharp, screeching sound came from our right. A rooster. The sound was startling in the brittle silence.

"We have about one hour, no more, to run. Pick up the pace, Tommy!" Manuel needled me. We started encountering wooden fences now with an inch of frost and snow on them. There were more wooded areas now, which made us feel better. At least there was a little cover.

We saw the outline of a farmhouse in the distance and stopped for a few minutes. "We are too close to the camp to take a chance on this farmer here. The Germans pay them for information on escaped prisoners," Manuel said.

"We've got to get out of sight before dawn. I'm sure they'll have patrols looking for us." I was barely able to speak.

A bit farther on we found an abandoned shed that was half collapsed. We pulled some boards together to cover us in the shed and fell into a hard sleep.

It was late morning when I woke up. For a brief moment I thought my hearing was gone. There was no sound. Nothing. No wind, no birds, no sound of a road, nothing. Manuel was already up and looking through a crack in the wall. "We did it," I said. My voice sounded so loud it scared me.

"Yes, we got out. Now we have to see if we can find some people who won't kill us," he said, rolling a cigarette and watching the field outside.

EIGHT

THE ENEMY'S ENEMY

WE TRAVELED for three days by night. We walked fast and silently, through fields and occasionally on roads. We headed in as much of an easterly direction as we could. Our idea was to reach the Russian lines. The area was very sparsely populated with widely scattered farms. Most of the farms were abandoned. The mid-January cold was like a heavy glass that covered everything.

On the morning of the third day we saw a farmer working on something in a small shed on the edge of a large field. "We must now try. Our food is gone, and I think we are about thirty kilometers from the camp. I will go." Manuel took off his satchel and crossed the field to the farmer.

I watched from the cover of bushes about two hundred yards away while Manuel approached the old farmer. He was working on a small cultivating machine with a hammer and some kind of a clamp. They walked slowly to the small farmhouse, and after a long while Manuel came out carrying a bundle and a small round container.

Coffee. The smell. The taste. I carefully swished it behind my lips and caressed it with my mouth. The coffee ricocheted through my entire body in two seconds. It was dark, and hot, and beautiful.

"Here is some meat! He is a fine old man. He thinks the Russians are about forty kilometers east. He says the Germans have been here twice in the last three days, moving troops around and looking for places to retreat to. He thinks they will be back again, so we cannot stay with him. Too bad," Manuel said while chewing the boiled meat.

I could feel my body absorbing the strength from the meat and potatoes, and my headache slowly faded away.

"He thinks we should stay in this area and wait for the Russians. They should be here in about three days. He said the Wehrmacht is fighting north and south of this area," Manuel said later as we walked along. In a few minutes the clouds broke and the sun came out. Our spirits rose right away, although the harsh glare from the sun on the snow made it hard to see.

Later in the day we reached a rocky area that was perfect for us. We decided to stay there and wait for the fighting to reach us as we were very short of food and didn't want to leave the help of the friendly farmer too far behind. We piled rocks up to cover the entrance to a small cave. It was perfectly hidden.

We were also afraid that if we kept going we might run into retreating German units. This way we could wait until we knew we were behind the Russian lines and pick our friends, so to speak. At least the Russians were Allies. We walked around the area to make sure we were alone.

As we walked around that day, we began to hear a sound that was so distant the little scuffling noise of our walking would block it out. It would start suddenly and last for several minutes, then stop. At night we could feel the sound in the ground. The sound of distant artillery. The first rumbling blast hung for a moment, then other blasts followed, sometimes in a regular pattern, sometimes overlapping. The pauses were long, and sometimes there was a reply sound that was similar, but not quite as low-pitched. It was the sound of war approaching from far away. It was the sound of six million men slugging it out on a vast continent, and it was coming closer every day. To us, it was a wonderful sound. It was the sound of German soldiers dying, of Nazi Germany dying.

WE SPENT two days in the cave, resting and waiting and talking. "Do you have any horses for racing in Texas?" Manuel asked.

"I guess they've been racing horses in Texas since the day the Spanish lost the second one," I said.

"And there is, of course, wagering on these races of horses?" He looked at me quizzically.

"Oh, some of the boys like to try their luck now and then on horse betting, but the really big tracks are in California and on the East Coast. Those people out there have more money than they really need anyhow," I said.

"California? You have been to this place, where the films of Tom Mix are made?"

"Just to pick up a plane or two. California is a nice place." I tried to remember what it really looked like. The closest I could get was someplace warm, with sun and pretty girls.

We talked for hours in that cold cave. Manuel told me the story of the fight for Warsaw and about the thousands of brave young Poles who were killed by the Wehrmacht. "When the big guns began firing, the whole city shook. The trees lost their leaves, and many of the old people died when their hearts failed. You cannot believe the power of those guns. We could hear the shells coming through the air for a full minute. The sound was terrible, and people would get more and more tense, waiting for the shells to land." His eyes became hard when he talked about the war, and for both of us it was too much effort. The deep weariness I felt was in Manuel, too, but much more so. He looked like he could sleep for a hundred years and still be bone tired.

"Do they pay men much, to take care of the horses for racing in America?" he asked.

"I don't really know, but I know they pay the men a lot who ride them," I said.

"But these men must be small, like you, Tommy. You could be one of these horse racing men. We could be rich! I will take care of the horse, and you ride it!" As worn out as Manuel was, his spirit always lifted him along somehow. He was right back to his old operator self.

The questions came one after the other, hour after hour. "Do the rattling snakes bite the horses in Texas? Do they then die, or can you give them medicines? Do they have cabbages in Texas? Are they big ones? What are the foods of the Mexican people? Are there any Mexicans in Texas? What do the cows eat there?"

We talked a long time about Texas and horses and food. Manuel had been a chef before he became a veterinarian, and he talked for hours about Polish food, reciting recipes and carefully taking me through the cooking process. "And remember, Tommy, be very, very careful not to burn the butter when you are sauteing the onions. This is important." He rattled on, waving his arms around, while I drifted to sleep.

ON THE third day, we were out of food. When we got up, Manuel decided to make a scouting trip to try to find out where the fighting was and to get more food from the old farmer. Before he left, Manuel decided that we needed a recognition signal for when he returned. While we were in Küstrin, I had told Manuel the story of Jules and Henri giving me the invasion code phrase. We agreed that he would say "The peaches are green" when he returned. "Soon, Tommy, we will be out of this damn war. I'll be back in a few hours," he said as he left.

The afternoon light was beginning to fade rapidly. I had seen several planes in the air, including one German spotter plane that flew almost directly overhead. The artillery seemed much closer and hammered away all day. The hours dragged by. I decided not to walk outside the cave. German patrols or trigger-happy Russian advance units couldn't be far off now.

About four in the afternoon, I began to worry about Manuel. I'd figured he would be gone about three or four hours, not all day. I was just starting to plan my next move, to return to the farmer for more food, when I heard a noise at the cave entrance. The branches and rocks were being moved. Germans! It had to be Germans. Manuel would have called out to me, but these men were methodically moving the boulders away from the cave's mouth, and they were talking loudly. Manuel must have been captured and tortured. I thought, *If I walk out, they won't shoot me in the dark.* I was just starting out when I heard a familiar voice.

"Tommy! The peechess iss green!"

Manuel was standing next to the two Russian soldiers who were struggling with a large rock. He was swaying a little, and he started to sing a Polish song. Russians! I ran out to Manuel, who dropped the rock and bear-hugged me and started laughing. He was drunk. He smelled like a vodka bottling plant. The Russian troops stabbed the air with their fists and laughed heartily. "America! America! *Da! Da!* American! D-Day! D-Day! *Da! Da!*"

A bottle was thrust into my hands. The vodka burned through my entire alimentary canal in about one second. My head spun around eight times. We were free. We had made it to the Russian lines! We cheered and danced and gulped at the vodka bottle. My mind raced ahead. The Russians would turn me over to the British or the Americans, and I would be flown back to England. Good food. Clean clothes. Freedom!

"You're going to meet a really big Russian," Manuel beamed. "Their commander wants to meet you. He's never met an American before, and he wants to see you, and he is the biggest bastard you have ever seen."

The two Russian soldiers were so young, they still had acne, but there was a glint of hardness in their eyes, and they moved cautiously. They watched the ground constantly. They had us walk in a single file about ten paces apart. These men had plenty of experience with German minefields. The lines on their faces looked like they had been ironed on, but they were quick to laugh and very proud of the Red Army.

"*Hitler kaput,*" they said over and over. "*Goering kaput! Germany kaput! Fascists kaput!*" We stopped for a few minutes in a little grove of trees. The sky was particularly overcast, and the wind was steady and cold. Any little break from the wind was a relief. The Russians saw we were weak and stopped to give us a breather.

"These are good? Good guns?" I asked, pointing to one soldier's burp gun.

"*Da, da.*" He searched for a word in English. "Simply. Simply gun. Very good. Simply." He opened the bolt and held up four fingers to indicate the number of parts. The gun was a marvel of simplicity and rugged design, but the machining and blueing were so crude that I could see tool marks on the gun. "Many fascists, already, this simply gun. Many." He let the bolt slap back noisily. I didn't doubt him.

"American, good airplane. Good truck! Good movie!" they said, each offering a new recollection of America. They smoked and joked and kept asking me about America, but their eyes never stopped searching the treelines.

Soon we could hear vehicles on a dirt road. Heavy trucks and an occasional motorcycle. We came over the top of a hill and down to a narrow dirt road. Two big Red Army trucks thundered past, driving so fast they almost slid on the curve. The drivers never bothered to look at us.

WE REACHED a small farmhouse just as darkness fell and night's bitter cold began. The farmhouse looked like any small farmhouse in America, with a small porch and muddy boots by the door.

The Russian soldiers opened the door for us, and we stepped in. Seated at the head of a table was the biggest man I had ever seen. His head was so big it looked unnatural, like a circus freak's. He was wearing a big fur hat with the earflaps tied up. His face was stern and deeply lined. His hands, spread out over a map, looked as absurdly big as his head. Several Russians soldiers were conferring with him. He was quietly issuing orders to them, drawing arcs across the map with his long fingers. They were wearing the long warm coats of the Red Army, and they carried sidearms in brown holsters. I assumed they were officers. They didn't seem too interested in us—they probably thought we were local farmers. When they left the room a few minutes later, the big man stood up and looked at me. I thought I had seen some big bruisers in Texas, but this man was a full foot taller than any man I had ever seen.

He looked right at me and said something to Manuel in Russian. Manuel turned to me. "He says, 'Tell that man I am surprised at what I see! I expected to see a great big American airman from Texas coming in here!'"

Manuel replied in slurred Russian, "Tommy's not big, but he's a hell of a fighter!"

The big man roared out a laugh that actually shook the room; then he said, "Tell him I'll call him the Little Rooster then."

Everyone laughed, and I extended a hand which he carefully shook. That was the first and last time I have ever seen my entire hand disappear in another man's hand. "Ivan. I am Ivan," he said.

I stood by the fire in that farmhouse for hours, turning slowly. It had been so long since I had been warm, I'd forgotten what it felt like. When the cold settles in your bones, in the marrow, it percolates out slowly, in waves of pain. My knees burned, then loosened up so much I couldn't stand.

I watched the Russian commanders come and go. They all seemed charged up and happy. The Russians had just achieved another breakthrough in the German line. They kept careful notes of the units they had engaged, and they handed these to Ivan, who made quick pencil marks on the map.

Ivan said nothing to me. In between visits, he napped at the table, with his boots up on a chair. I tried to guess how tall he was. His legs covered three chairs.

One of the Russians showed me to a small room in the back of the farmhouse with a candle. There was a rectangular platform in the room. It took me a few seconds to realize it was a real bed. It even had blankets that didn't stink of death or vomit. I crawled under the covers and a deep, peaceful sleep washed over me like a black velvet wave.

I woke in a panic to the sound of trucks. For a long second I thought I was in the cave. Germans. Captured. Shot. Then I felt the bed under me and realized where I was.

The peculiar notion of looking forward to a day was exhilarating. I looked out the window and watched the big Studebaker trucks and American jeeps pull up in the farmyard, way too fast,

slamming on the brakes and jolting to a stop. When the troops got
out and began to mill around, I saw that they were very short and
dark skinned. They wore tattered, irregular uniforms of heavily
quilted material and dark green, Russian flap-eared fur hats. They
were a rough-looking bunch, even from a distance.

They squatted down in little circles and waited in the cold
morning. I had just noticed that they weren't carrying rifles when
Ivan's voice boomed through the house. "Come on, Little
Rooster! We'll get you some clothes!" He had an aide come in and
guess at my size.

The pants were baggy, but they were thick wool and warm.
My outfit came together a little at a time, and the Russians
laughed as I rolled up the pants and the heavy Russian shirt's
sleeves. They seemed to be impressed by the fact that we had
escaped from a German concentration camp.

"Escape from the fascists. Good, good! This not too many people can do. The fascists, they know how to kill people in camps.
Many, many people die in the fascists' camps," they said. They listened intently when I told them how bad the conditions were for
the Russian POWs, and they gathered around when I pointed
Küstrin out on the map. It was only about forty kilometers from
our position.

I looked at Ivan for a long minute. He slowly moved his pencil
north toward a notation that said Ninth SS Division. Ivan would
use Manuel as an interpreter, looking at me and talking to
Manuel.

"We have orders to move north from here; we are headed for
Stargard."

"I was in a Stalag Luft camp close to Stargard," I told him.

"This camp is gone. The Allied flyers were marched out a few
weeks ago. Now the SS is digging in there."

"Do you know where these men are?"

"No. But I know where the Ninth SS Division is. That is where we are going," he said flatly. I suddenly felt bad for the flyers, who were marching in this bitter cold. I briefly wondered if the Germans would kill them all. I asked Ivan.

"If they have been taken by the SS, they will be shot. If not, they will be marched south. We think the fascists will keep them alive for peace negotiation purposes with the West. The Russian and Polish POWs will die. There will be no negotiations with our side." He seemed bothered by the question.

I WALKED out onto the porch of the farmhouse to an odd sight. There were hundreds of small ponies lined up, tethered to a jump line. They were small and shaggy, and many of them were badly scarred. I hadn't seen a pony since I was a kid, and I just had to let it sink in for a minute. *What were ponies doing here, in the middle of this war?* I walked over and watched what looked to be Chinese troops saddle the ponies. The small saddles were different from anything I had ever seen. There was nothing to them at all, and the horn was very small and short. They must have been brutal to ride, but they were light. The Chinese soldiers looked at me and said nothing. I decided to go back into the house.

Ivan was listening to his lieutenants and issuing orders accompanied by concise hand gestures. He headed out the door with one man and covered the entire front farmyard in about four strides. He talked very briefly in a formal, wary manner with two of the horsemen, obviously the leaders. I started to walk over to him while he was talking with these men, but a stern glance from Ivan almost knocked me back to the farmhouse.

Manuel said in a low voice, while looking straight ahead, "These are Mongolian terror troops, Tommy. The Russians use them to keep the Germans off balance, to terrorize the population and spread panic. Stay away from these men. They kill everything. Everything."

These were the famous Mongol horsemen of Genghis Khan, who terrorized Europe for three hundred years, cutting through the best knights of Europe with ease. I could see why. They looked like warriors, like fearless, merciless killers, who loved every minute of war and killing.

"Where are their rifles?" I asked.

"They don't carry rifles. They use swords, pistols, and their smell," Manuel replied.

A group of four Mongolians worked their way over to us and stood staring at me rudely. I caught an aroma that was so acrid and sickening that my eyes began to water. These men smelled like a mop that had been dipped in sweat and urine and bacon grease. Their long black hair was oily, and their fingernails were jagged and black. It was hard to observe them, though, because their eyes held my glance. Each man was the same. They didn't blink. They held their eyes in one place and moved their heads while they talked. They had a way of getting close to you without seeming to move. Even their eyes were black and a little bleary. They were eyes that saw the entire world as one enemy. You could tell that only one thing was going through their minds. *How can I best kill this man?*

"Let's go inside, Tommy," Manuel said.

Ivan walked into the farmhouse. He told us, "We will be the first to meet the Allies, no matter what happens. I can use interpreters for these moments, and because of this you may come with us, or you may go to the rear areas where our political officers will make arrangements for you."

Manuel said to me quickly, "We do not want to be in the

hands of Russian officials. Let's go with these men. The war will be over in a few weeks, and we'll be turned over to the British or the Americans much sooner." That was fine with me. I didn't want to go into Russia. I figured that would be the long way home.

"We will be leaving in a day or two, and we are ordered north to reconnoiter the position of the Ninth SS Division," Ivan said; then he walked out to meet a Russian command car that had pulled up.

I stayed in the farmhouse most of that day and stood by the fire and ate. The food was a weird assortment of canned Russian fish, boiled turnips, a few potatoes, and strips of black cured meat, like jerky. Strange but delicious.

ON THE second morning, the weather cleared, and I was drawn outside. The Mongolians were gathered in front of the small barn. I stood watching them for a long time. I noticed they were carrying long-barreled automatic pistols in covered holsters. They were sitting around sharpening their short, heavy sabers and chattering in clipped sentences interrupted by hoarse grunts. I was surprised they didn't carry the Russian burp guns or captured German submachine guns. They had a few Russian carbines in flat leather saddle scabbards, that was all. They also carried several long-barreled revolvers that looked like Smith and Wessons. These men were real cavalry.

I walked back to the farmhouse, and Ivan started in on me the moment the door closed. Manuel translated as he lectured me. "These men are different from the Russian troops. They kill everything, everyone they find. The Germans are absolutely terrified of these men. You must stay away from these men. Stay with us, because when the fighting starts you might easily be confused with a German, and you would be dead in one second. Dead. Stay with me, in the jeep, and you might live." He looked directly at me.

I stayed in the house the rest of that day and only went out onto the porch. The next morning, I stood on the porch and watched the Mongolian unit leader call his men together and run through a short roll call. He read orders to them, and the platoon leaders turned to their men and shouted at them in short, quick commands. They quickly saddled up their horses.

There were about four hundred Mongolians altogether and about twenty Russians in our unit. Ivan's men packed up the maps, the radio, and a portable field kitchen in three jeeps and two trucks. I was flattered to be in the back seat of Ivan's jeep.

"Little Rooster, take this and keep it with you. It is a good one, and I'm sure you know how to use it," Ivan said, handing me a small, black automatic pistol. It looked almost new, with a full magazine. I started to thank him, but he waved his arm and the jeep lurched ahead.

I sat next to the radio operator. Manuel was in the jeep behind us. The horse troops had already headed out through the fields at full gallop.

We roared down a gravel road at top speed with the Mongolians galloping through the trees on both sides of the road. Ivan's eyes never stopped moving. He missed nothing. The radio operator would lean forward and shout something in his ear every few minutes, and he would usually reply with one or two words.

I never saw the deep gully in the road until I was about ten feet in the air watching the jeep drive away. Fortunately, I landed on my back and slid about thirty feet in the gravel and snow. "Now you are a flying rooster!" Ivan roared, as the radio operator helped me back into the jeep.

We tore along the road for about three hours, stopping every hour or so to check the position of the Mongolians who had left us. About two o'clock, I thought I heard the sound of small arms fire over the roar of the jeep. The radio lit up, and we slowed down for the first time that day.

The Mongolians on our left were taking sniper fire from a German unit. We jumped out of the jeep and ran to a small hill. Ivan watched the area with binoculars and directed the assault from there.

I could see gunsmoke coming from a treeline about three hundred yards away. The Mongolians had dismounted and were assaulting this position from several directions at once, running low to the ground. Suddenly about eight German soldiers burst out of the woods and started running for another stand of trees. They were throwing their helmets and packs off as fast as they could. They weren't very far from us, and I was surprised Ivan didn't open up on them. I looked at him quickly, but he just held up his finger.

The Mongolians rode through the trees so fast the small limbs blew off the trees. The first two reached the running soldiers so quickly I couldn't believe my eyes. They let out a blood-curdling scream you could hear for miles. *"Hiiiiyouuuu! Hiiiiyouuuu!"* They rode down on these men and drove their sabers through their necks and shoulders in a wide arc, then turned their horses around in one horse length, leaped to the ground and shot two Germans with their pistols. Two of the Germans made an effort to bring their weapons up, but they never made it. One of them tried to raise his hands to surrender just as he was caught by a saber slash to the shoulder. He went down and never moved again. The other Mongolians leaped off their horses while they were still running and descended on the dead and wounded Germans with a pistol in one hand and a saber in the other. I saw one wounded German hold his hand up. The Mongolian hit him just above the elbow and sent the arm flying. The arm was still in the air when he whirled the sword around and brought it down again on the German's neck.

They took packs, watches, and weapons in about thirty seconds, turning the bodies over as they worked. Then they thundered off back into the assault, German backpacks swinging wildly, watches glinting on their wrists, and yelling the whole time.

"If they weren't Germans, maybe it would be different," Ivan said as he turned toward the jeep. I had never seen horses ridden like that. I had never seen them turn so short and so fast, and I had never heard a yell anything like the Mongolians'. Now I knew why they called them terror troopers.

They loved photographs. For some reason the Mongolians would always take photographs from the dead soldiers, usually portraits of wives or sweethearts, and they would pass them around and comment on them. "Look at this girl! We killed this man. No sweetheart for her!" I could tell what they were saying. They loved killing. They loved souvenirs. They would take insignias off uniform lapels, anything like that. Watches were the best. They all had several shiny watches they kept in small bags. When they got drunk, they would wear them all, several on each arm, and dance until they fell down.

WE REACHED a small hamlet called Brzezno about six o'clock. Ivan surveyed the town for about an hour. He missed nothing. He sent men to search this house, then that house, always looking, always careful. He had obviously had a lot of experience with Wehrmacht snipers. He picked out a large house and barged in. An old Polish couple owned the house. They were about seventy or so. They looked bewildered, but they had decided to try to get along with the new conquerors. The old man wore a bright green wool shirt and smiled widely with the two teeth he still had.

Ivan began talking to him in Polish, asking about the Germans, especially if there had been any tanks moving through the village. To our surprise the old man reached into his pocket and carefully unfolded a small piece of paper. Ivan looked at it with great interest. The old man had carefully written down the units of the German troops, the number and type of vehicles, with dates. Ivan looked at this and shook the man's hand heartily. He circled one unit with pencil. It was an SS recon unit of the Ninth SS Division. The old man was smart. He had been in WWI and knew the value of troop movement information. His little favor went a long way with the Russians.

Ivan's lieutenants came in with large maps and set the radio up in a bedroom. There was something big going on, and they had a lot of coordinating to do. They had been moving fast for a long time, and a tactical mistake could easily mean death for everyone. The Wehrmacht was still very much alive and capable of division-level movements, which could easily trap small forward outfits.

That evening, after several hours of conferring with his men, Ivan stretched back on his chairs and said, "Now tell me about Texas!" He wanted to know all about Texas. It seemed that everyone I met in Europe had heard of Texas, and they wanted to know everything. He wanted to know about cowboys and Indians. Then came the big question:

"Do you know of Mr. Tom Mix?" he said, almost holding his breath.

"Why sure, I've seen all his movies, and I saw his horse once at the Texas State Fair," I replied. Tom Mix had been my favorite cowboy movie star when I was a kid.

"You saw the very horse of Tom Mix?"

"Yes, I did, and I got to pet him, too."

"You were allowed to pet the very horse of Tom Mix? This is unbelievable! On this we must drink. To the very horse of Mr. Tom Mix!" He shouted and threw down his little glass of vodka.

"Can you do those fancy rope tricks, like in the movies? Are you a cowboy? Are the rattlesnakes really big in Texas? How hot does it get? What are your horses like? What happened to the Indians, did you kill them all? What is your favorite gun? Is the Colt as good as they say? Do you have a Colt? Did you know that we Russians bought six hundred thousand pistols from Mr. Smith and Mr. Wesson? My father had one. Are there cattle of longhorns now?" The questions came all night until an urgent radio message tore him away.

I slept in a real bed that night, and before I fell asleep I began to feel lost again. All the talk about Texas made me homesick. I was among so many different foreign people, and I understood so little of what they were saying, that I really hungered for the day I would be with Americans or British again.

The radio operator knocked over a chair getting to his set, which woke me before dawn. I listened to him talking in Russian and thought for a while about the Russians and what this war was like for them. They had faced the full power of Hitler's army and turned them back with sheer courage and manpower. They had wiped out 150 German divisions. I tried to imagine the scale of that kind of fighting, but I just couldn't. It was the biggest war in history by far, and the shame of it all almost made me cry. I felt the weariness begin again.

I respected the Russians on a gut level. They were kind of like the roughnecks in the oil fields back home. They were a little short on manners, but they got the hard, dirty jobs done when no one else could. They had some good ideas about how to fight a war, too.

The Russian idea of using terror troopers was very effective.

Even elite SS units were afraid of these troops, and they pulled
out of areas we were headed for. The Mongolians were thought of
as not quite human, and I too came to feel this way about them.
They were different in every way. The way they talked, the way
they acted, and even the way they ate were bizarre to me. All they
ate were little cubes of white fat and dark bread. They drank
vodka out of bottles every night and danced around with watches
on both arms, whooping and hollering late into the night.

But in combat they were completely fearless, and they
swarmed to the fighting. They advanced relentlessly under fire
and never hesitated to attack. They charged bunkers and machine
gun nests like kids let out of school. They took terrible casualties
and never paused to bury their dead comrades. They just took the
dead man's weapons and booty and ran to the next firefight.

They looked as if they were born with weapons in their hands.
They moved in almost invisible, fluid movements close to the
ground. They had a natural balance on horseback that reminded
me of the Indians back home. They could leap off a horse at full
gallop, fire a pistol three or four times, and be within saber distance in one blink of an eye. They knew not to stand still in combat. They would weave and duck and zigzag when they attacked
German positions, holding their fire until they were within point-
blank range. They were consummate warriors.

A few of the Mongolians stood out, especially the one they
called the Devil.

Even the other Mongolians stayed away from him. He was a
little taller than the rest of them and very muscular. He had jet
black hair cut short, which was unusual because most of the other
Mongolians had long hair to their waists. He wore a black braided
leather band around his forehead. His eyes were black and bot-
tomless, and they darted around constantly.

"That man is special. He is a monster. The Germans have men

like him. Stay far away from him, Tommy," Manuel said one day when I asked him about the Devil.

I ROSE early on the third day. It was very cold and overcast. Outside the Mongolians were moving around, checking their ponies and trying to shake off last night's vodka. One of Ivan's men was starting a big fire in the fireplace and eating cheese.

"Comrade Rooster! Come, have some cheeses," Ivan said as I walked into the main room. I ate several big pieces and felt it slowly melt in my stomach. I could still feel the food rushing into me when I ate. It seemed like Küstrin had drained the marrow from my bones. The two days in the house had helped me gain strength and remember what warmth and comfort were.

I was able to heat water in a Russian ammo can, and I scrubbed every inch of the filth and death of Küstrin off my body with a bar of green Russian soap the size of a brick. I felt my self-respect and pride return as I watched the black, oily grime rinse off. Of all the humiliations the Germans put me through, forcing me to live in filth was the worst.

Ivan sat down at the table and pulled his boots on. He looked out the window for a long time, lost in thought. For a second I saw the weariness in him, too. He closed his eyes for a minute and just sat there. Ivan was a distant man to those around him. The other Russians quietly acknowledged him and gave him plenty of room. There was some problem with his rank. Ivan was a sergeant in the 2nd Shock Army attached to Zhukov's 65th Army group, but he ran the whole unit, and the lieutenants reported to him. I started to ask one of his lieutenants about this one day, but he rolled his eyes to the ceiling and said, "This matter is not for talking."

Ivan did an exceptional job of leading these difficult and dangerous men. His sergeants worked with the Mongolian platoon leaders in small groups; they spoke their language and knew how to get the most out of them. The Mongolians were very disciplined in a wild way and understood the importance of command in battle, but there were a few renegades. I saw Ivan deal with two of them that morning.

As we were getting ready to pull out, two Mongolians got into a fight over some booty, and when the platoon leader ordered them to stop, they didn't. The Russian sergeant left the jeep to stop the fighting, but Ivan, impatient to leave, strode off ahead of him. He walked over to the fracas and simply stood there until they saw him. They stopped fighting and stood up, one holding a necklace of some kind in his hand. Ivan waited a moment for the other one to stand up. When he did, Ivan took one stride, brought his arms around and casually grabbed both men by their necks and slammed their heads together so violently the sharp crack echoed off the house in the cold air. They dropped to the ground and stayed there in the dirt, bleeding from their ears and noses. Ivan turned to the platoon leader and said about three words in the Mongolian language and looked at the man for a long time. Then he said something in Russian to the sergeant, who blushed a bright red and slowly moved his head from side to side. The other Mongolians moved away, no longer interested.

One of Ivan's lieutenants brought over a medic who succeeded in reviving one of the men, though he died a moment later. The other man was dead. Both men were lying there when we left. I saw one of the Mongolians turn back, jump off his horse, and take the dirt-packed necklace from the dead man's hand. He didn't yell, though.

THE RUMBLE to the south of us seemed closer and louder than the night before. We moved slowly now, stopping every three or four hundred yards to watch and wait. The morning was quiet,

too quiet. Even the snipers had pulled out ahead of us. Ivan
looked worried. If the Germans wanted to, they could surround
our unit with a tank brigade and wipe us out at will, a specialty of
the SS tank corps.

We stopped about ten o'clock and waited for a mine-clearing
unit to check the road ahead. Ivan called for them on the radio.
They were operating just north of us. The Russians couldn't
believe the Germans would just hand them this sector without
snipers or mines to slow them down. They wondered if it was
some kind of a trap.

Ivan was lost in thought when the radio operator almost
jumped out of the jeep with excitement. He tapped Ivan's shoulder and yelled, "Zhukov! Zhukov will be there. Imagine that!
Zhukov! Stargard. They have eliminated all the German tanks at
Stargard!"

It seemed that the Ninth SS Tank Division we were hounding
had swung south to engage the main body of Zhukov's army, and
they had been chewed to pieces by the Russians.

Ivan grabbed the radio. *"Da! Da! Da!"* he bellowed, over and
over. "Zhukov!" When he handed the microphone back to the
operator, he leaned over in front of the little rear view mirror on
the jeep and looked at himself carefully.

Ivan spoke Zhukov's name with special reverence, as did all
the Russians. Zhukov was the tactical genius who had saved
Russia from the German onslaught in 1941. He was the father of
the Russian tank corps, like General Guderian was for the
Germans, and General Patton for the Americans. He had humiliated the Japanese in the thirties in the Sino–Soviet War, and he
had developed the crucial countertactics that stopped the
Wehrmacht in the suburbs of Moscow. He was a god to these
men, and they were sure they were going to see him at Stargard.

Suddenly the Russians began rummaging through their battered bags and talking excitedly in small groups. I caught a whiff of a strong aftershave lotion for the first time that morning on a young Russian sergeant. The odor was somewhere between a barber shop and a burning truck tire.

We had made it to the small town of Poznan, about fifteen miles south of Stargard, in a miserable drizzle that changed to sleet in the late afternoon. The town was only about three blocks long and mostly abandoned. There were a few old people sitting around looking up at us with blank looks. Ivan picked out the biggest house, but most of the roof was blown off, so we took a dreary yellow house next to it. Ivan warned everyone, over and over, to watch out for booby traps.

I took a small bedroom on the first floor, near the back door. Manuel was treating some of the wounded ponies and stayed near the horses. There was no mattress on the bedsprings in the room, so I laid a door from the water closet on them and threw some of the living room drapes over the door. But when I closed my eyes, I was too weary to sleep. I smelled the oily death of Küstrin and heard the shouting of the red-haired major in my ears. Sometimes I saw the face of Lauren in the Gestapo prison and heard the blasts from the Mausers. Sometimes I was back in my tail-gun position, waiting for the bright red tracers to hit the ship. It still took a while for me to remember where I was when I woke, and that scared me.

When I finally got to sleep, I began dreaming about Waco and selling ice cream. It was a hot day, and a dog was licking my face, licking the ice cream off with a big, sloppy tongue. "Get down, get down now," I said, laughing. I woke up with a start and panicked. Where was I? I felt my face. It was wet. A white, furry ball hopped on my chest. It was a little mutt of a puppy. I got up and opened the door to let the light from the radio operator's gasoline lantern shine in and looked at him. He was a short-legged, short-haired terrier of some kind, white with big, black spots and bright, black eyes. He was skinny and dirty, as if he had been running under houses, but he frisked all over the bed and even sat up, begging neatly.

"Comrade Rooster, what have you gotten there?" the radioman said standing at the door.

"I don't know what he is. Some kind of a terrier or schnauzer, but he sure looks hungry." I tore off a piece of bread for him.

"Well, we might have use of a dog like this. Maybe he is good at smelling snipers. Have some potato for him, so he'll get big and bite snipers." He dished out some potato and meat stew for the dog.

The dog attacked the tin plate and pushed it all over the dirty wooden floor to the delight of the Russians, who had crowded around the door to see the dog. "He is a fighter, this one. Yes, a fighter of fascists. Give him more!" they yelled.

"And what will you call this pup, Comrade Rooster? He must have a name," the radioman said.

"I don't rightly know just what to call him," I said. I slapped my knee loudly. "Come here, boy. Come to Tommy!" To my surprise he skittered across the floor and jumped into my lap. He looked at me with bright, black eyes as I tried to think of a name. I noticed he had very bushy eyebrows for such a small dog, and I had been looking at a Russian book earlier in the day which had a big picture of Stalin in the front.

"Stalin. I'll call him Stalin," I said, looking at the Russians. Their smiles disappeared, and they looked around at each other.

The radio operator broke the ice. "He is a fighter, like Comrade Stalin, yes, and he does look a bit like him so, perhaps, it is possible," he said guardedly. The Russians left the room quietly.

Stalin slept next to my head all night and gently licked my face when dawn arrived.

■ ■ ■

WHEN I woke, I knew there was something different, but I couldn't quite put my finger on it. I finally felt the floor with my hand trying to determine what was different. There was no deep rolling sound in the ground. The artillery was quiet. I heard groggy distant voices on the radio and a truck idling somewhere, but that was it.

"Maybe today will be a good day," I said to Stalin.

Ivan sat at the head of the large, wooden table in the kitchen and rubbed his face. "We must cover about thirty kilometers today. We are to sweep the area and see that the roads are not mined. I hope we will get into Stargard by nightfall. There should be no tanks. The 49th and 70th say they have liquidated the tanks," Ivan said to me as the radioman loaded the radio into the jeep. "And I hear you have located a fighting dog who smells fascist snipers! Well, where is this dog? Bring him along, we'll need all the help we can get."

I opened the door to my room. I didn't even want to ask him if the dog could go. Stalin burst out, ran around the room, and grabbed a green wool sock, shaking it violently.

"He is a fighter. Good, good," Ivan said to Manuel, who was barely awake.

"Do you have this kind of a dog in Texas?" Manuel asked.

"Oh, I guess so. We have all kinds," I replied petting Stalin while he shredded the wool sock.

"I thought perhaps the dogs of Texas would have long horns and eat the rattling snakes," he said.

"Well, long horns the Texas dogs don't have, and generally the dogs get the worst of it in a run-in with a rattler," I said, pulling Stalin around the room with the sock.

"If we had such snakes here, they would be working for the SS," Manuel said. "And they wouldn't have any rattles, because they would want to strike from hiding." He looked away. Manuel had changed dramatically in the last few days. He had become morose and distant, and his cocky grin was rarely seen. I knew he was thinking about going home and what that might mean. The weariness had overtaken him, too.

We left early, about seven o'clock, and moved very slowly. I wrapped Stalin in half a blanket and put him on the floor of the jeep. He stayed there for about two minutes, then hopped up on my lap and yapped loudly at the Mongolians, who didn't seem to like dogs. The radio operator said, "He does not like their smell either, your dog." None of the Russians were ready to call him Stalin yet.

The road was chewed up by tank tracks, and all the power and telephone poles had been chopped down. I looked at Ivan, who said, *"Essa es."* He spit this out and said it over and over. *Essa es.* What the SS had done to the Russian people I could only imagine.

I began to notice the weariness in people around me. I could feel it more than see it. It was a deep ache, and I could see the raw, exposed nerves just under the skin and right behind the eyes. These men looked at the world as little as possible and said as little as possible. They took deep breaths constantly and stretched their neck muscles from side to side. The tension from living in the shadow of death for years on end had exhausted them. When I lapsed back into it, I found myself reaching for the little dog. His yapping somehow chased it away.

The fighting we encountered was mostly small groups of snipers here and there, which the Mongolians loved. We saw a few Russian transport planes in the air in the early afternoon, and that caused a lot of excitement for the Russians. I heard the word Stargard every few minutes.

By now I could make out quite a few words of Russian. Ivan

would jabber intently into the microphone for a few minutes and signal over to his sergeants, who would pull in the Mongolian platoon leaders and give them directions. The Mongolians didn't need very much in the way of commands. All they needed was the general direction of the fighting. Once there, they knew what to do. Close the distance to the German units fast so they couldn't use their mortars, then kill them. Take their weapons and belongings and go and kill more. Fast.

The rain had just turned to sleet about four o'clock when the radio operator told Ivan that they were sending back a group of about fifty German soldiers who had surrendered. This was the first time I had even heard the word "prisoners." Ivan sent orders not to shoot these men if they had their hands on their heads. They staggered down the road slowly. Their uniforms were dirty and torn, their hair was covered in white dust and hanging in their faces. They never once looked at us. Many of them were wounded, with dried blood caked on their dirty uniforms. They looked completely exhausted. I didn't care. All I saw was the guards in Küstrin. I saw Alex dying on the latrine on Christmas Eve. I saw Lauren's face. I heard the dogs.

"These bastards are getting what they deserve," I said to Ivan.

"Isn't any possibility," he said, almost casually. "Isn't."

The prisoners wanted to stay by the jeep. They were deathly afraid of the Mongolians, and they kept close together. They looked around nervously whenever a Mongolian approached the jeep. The Mongolians looked at them the way a dog looks at a rabbit, hoping it will run.

For some reason, Stalin didn't bark at them. One of the Mongolian platoon leaders sidled up to the prisoners in the spooky way they have, leaned over, and let out his blood-curdling yell right in the ears of the Germans. They all jumped up in absolute terror, convinced they were going to die. The Mongolians all laughed in their weird, chortling grunts and rode off. The Germans shook their heads and looked down.

Ivan finished on the radio and walked over to the prisoners. He held his left arm in the air and looked at the men. They slowly began taking off their tunics and shirts. Ivan looked under each man's left armpit for the telltale blood-type tattoo required of all SS members. Three of the men stood apart and stalled. They had an arrogant look the other men didn't have. Finally, Ivan stepped over to them and looked at them. They slowly pulled off their shirts. Each one had a small blue tattoo with two letters under his armpit.

Ivan began to tremble slightly. He reached into the jeep and swung the burp gun around in a very slow, deliberate motion. I thought he was going to march them somewhere. He leaned into the weapon to control the muzzle climb and fired all fifty rounds into the three men. The bullets made a loud *whack whack whack* sound as they hit the men, who jerked backwards and finally fell in the dirt and broken glass. Stalin leaped for the floor of the jeep, and I waited a minute to pick the warm shell casings off my lap.

Ivan got in the jeep, and we drove off. He said nothing.

THEN WE were on the outskirts of Stargard. I thought I was seeing big piles of debris at first, but when we got closer, I could see they had been houses, houses that had been blown up by artillery, run over by tanks, and then shot to pieces by small arms. Every section of every stucco building was riddled with holes, gouges, and deep scratches.

We stopped for about an hour, and orders went out to the men to clean up and put on fresh uniforms. This was impossible for the

Mongolians. To them, dressing up was wiping the dark, greasy streaks off their faces.

The Russian officers and soldiers somehow appeared in perfectly clean and pressed dress uniforms with medals and decorations. Ivan was resplendent in a crisp dress uniform with several large medals and colored ribbons. He had one of the men cut his hair while he sat in the jeep. I had never seen him this excited. He was very exuberant, and he cut a fine figure. His eyes glittered, and for a brief second he almost smiled.

Stalin jumped into his lap, and he said, "The fighting dog of the Little Rooster! And what is your name now?" The scissors stopped, and the radio operator slid his earphones off his ears. Ivan looked at me.

"Stalin. His name is Stalin." I pointed to his eyebrows.

Ivan looked at the dog in his lap for a long moment, stroking his eyebrows, and said, "*Comrade* Stalin."

"Comrade Stalin," I said. The scissors started again.

STARGARD WAS heavily damaged, but there were still many buildings standing. We attracted a lot of attention, even from the regular Russian troops. They looked at the Mongolians warily.

The roads were jammed with heavy trucks and tanks on trailers. I had never seen a Russian tank before, and as we passed, Ivan commented, "Very good, T-54, very good for snow. We have many, many of thousands T-54s." I noticed how little paint was left on the tank. There were many round rust splotches where bullets had chipped off the paint. Stalin barked at them as they lurched and ground gears.

We were directed to a large abandoned commercial building by a traffic officer with flags and a broad smile.

In the center of Stargard was a large square befitting its status as a district center in northern Poland. There were green military cars with red flags and flashing red lights racing around the streets. The Russian brass always wore their big hats in the cars and stared straight ahead.

We settled into our quarters in the abandoned warehouse building and tried to nap amid the sounds of truck traffic and celebrations. My back was bothering me, and I just wanted to sleep. But the noise and hellraising continued all night, with an occasional pistol shot or a burst of submachine gun fire.

The next morning when I walked out into the assembly area, it looked like a barber college. All the Russians were shaving and helping each other with their uniforms. They each had a small, brown case for their medals, and they carefully polished each one before pinning them on.

"Stalingrad, this one. I was there when we overran the Romanians. We killed them like chickens. Stinking goddamned Romanians. It was stupid of the fascists to trust them to hold such a big part of the front. And this one from Paulus! Ha, we all got this medal when the Sixth Army of Paulus surrendered to us. They are pretty sorry bastards now, the men of Paulus. This one, Kursk. Such a battle was Kursk. You could walk for miles on the burned fascist tanks!" The radio operator gushed on, explaining his medals. The weariness came over me when I thought about the years of fighting these men had been through. Stalin made a lunge to chew on one of the ribbons.

"You'll get one, boy. Calm down now," I said, as I pulled him back.

"He'll be a good help in finding snipers. Then he will get his own medals, but he can't have my medals, not on this very special day," the radioman said, straightening his uniform.

When we got into the jeep, I almost passed out from the after-shave. It smelled like a perfume truck hit a vodka plant during a toothbrush shortage. Stalin whimpered and looked out the back of the jeep, trying to get some clean air.

"He's in that group over there. Right over there!" one of Ivan's men almost shouted in my ear. "Zhukov! Think of it, Comrade Rooster!" I watched as Ivan and a lieutenant walked ceremoniously over to the group and shook hands with the great man. Zhukov stood in the middle of about forty men in long military coats and dress hats. Booming laughter erupted every few minutes, and they slammed each other on the back like someone serving a tennis ball. Ivan stood at least a full head and then some above the biggest man in the group. He was beaming. The lieutenant hurried over to me. "Come on, Little Rooster, Ivan has told Marshal Zhukov he has an American flyer with him. You're going to meet Zhukov. It is unbelievable! Come! Come!" I handed Stalin to the man next to me and hurried over.

Manuel came with us, and we walked over to Zhukov. His uniform was immaculate, and he had that same sparkle of fame I had first seen with Bonnie and Clyde. His eyes were the first thing I noticed. They looked like two twinkling Christmas lights. He had a very broad face with black, bushy eyebrows and a dimpled chin that would shame Cary Grant. When he looked at me, I broke into a big, stupid grin and shook his hand.

The Russians never really shook your hand, they crushed it in an up-and-down motion. Zhukov was poised on the brink of one of the greatest military achievements in history, and I felt the thrill of greatness in my numb hand. We looked at each other for a long time.

Looking at me, he said to Manuel, "So you're the American flyer who decided to join the Russian Army."

"No, I'm just hitchhiking with the Russian Army, I'm trying to get home," I said.

His eyes sparkled. "Do you have any complaints?" he asked.

I was kind of surprised, and I said without thinking, "Yeah, the food is lousy!"

He looked at me for a second, and time stopped. No one breathed. Then he laughed heartily. "Next time you visit us, we'll have better food for you!" he shot back. Ivan looked at me, still holding his breath. Then everyone started laughing. Zhukov hustled off with his large entourage. They looked like a moving wall of green wool and flapping arms.

As we headed back to the jeep, Ivan told Manuel to tell me that no one ever said things like that to Zhukov—but he had seemed to enjoy it. I felt very honored, and the story of my complaining to Zhukov about the food was retold many times.

Manuel would never let me forget it. "I don't believe you said that to this man! He is Field Marshal Zhukov, the commander of millions upon millions of men!" He would shake his head and laugh. "The food *is* lousy, but to say such a thing to Zhukov? Perhaps there are no men of Field Marshals in Texas?"

NINE

THE LAST MILES

TO MY surprise, the radio operator woke everyone up the next morning around four A.M.—or rather, tried to wake every one up. I heard him walk from room to room and then back again, loudly trying to penetrate the heavy curtain of vodka. I heard Ivan's voice boom out, "All right, all right!"

Ivan pored over the big military maps with his staff for about an hour, loudly talking and looking at the radio operator's notes. There seemed to be some lively discussion about which units would take which tracks. He finally gathered us together and told us we were going west from Stargard, toward Stettin, right away. There had been some information that the Germans had pulled back farther than expected, so we had to hurry up to capture the area before the Wehrmacht changed their minds. Zhukov had decided to keep the pressure up, and we were to be in the lead as usual. We would cover the northern route, with the overall objective being Rostock, in northern Germany.

Germany. We were going to cross over the German border in a

few days. The news had a strange effect on the Russians. Though they were excited to be approaching the German border at last, everyone knew the Germans would dig in and fight for every meter from here on out. There was some muted talk about hidden Panzer divisions, poison gas, and secret weapons, but the bottom-line sentiment was the same. *Let's get this thing over with.* Stettin was only 20 miles away, but Rostock was 130 miles away. There were a lot of guns between here and Rostock.

We rolled out in a great flurry of jeeps, horses, chattering Mongolians, blaring radios, and most of the Russian officers still wearing their tossed-salad dress uniforms. I paused for a moment to take it all in, and I really had to smile. What a strange world we lived in. Here was the "subhuman" (Hitler's words) Slavic horde with a medieval horse cavalry roaring out to fight the invincible German super race. And winning. The worm had turned.

Zhukov was right. The Germans had retreated far west of the Oder River. The area between Stargard and the Oder was wide open for the taking. We drove at full speed and encountered only scattered sniper fire. The Mongolians were disappointed at the light resistance and almost ran into each other to get to what little fighting there was.

We reached the Oder about two o'clock. The rain stayed in the dark, overcast sky, but the wind was cold and relentless with the sharp bite of the Baltic.

The pontoon bridges over the Oder were weaving in the strong current. The Germans had blown the bridges just upstream and chunks of crossbeams were still floating down and damaging the pontoon bridges. Trucks, jeeps, cars, troops, and horses were crossing in a hurried, uninterrupted stream. The exhausted Russian engineers were sleeping under trucks and standing around in little groups, their arms hanging limply at their sides.

These men had done a hell of a job. This was their first break in days of frantic effort, and they were beat. I saw one man leaning against a small caterpillar tractor, sound asleep with a lit cigarette in his mouth.

We advanced rapidly on Pasewalk, a fairly large town in northern Brandenburg province. When one of Ivan's lieutenants told me we were only seventy-five miles north of Berlin, I was shocked. The end of the war had to come any day now. The Germans would surely surrender.

We turned north, away from most of the traffic, and arrived at the outskirts of Pasewalk about five o'clock. Ivan didn't like what he saw through the huge German binoculars he used, and we slowed way down.

A miserable drizzle started about the same time the sniper fire intensified. It sounded like a slow motion string of firecrackers all around us. I saw two muzzle flashes in a house on a small hill ahead of us. The Mongolians saw it at the same time and swung around to the side of the house and dismounted. A few minutes later the house burst into flame, and they tore off on their horses, booty bags slapping wildly. The Mongolians were fast and highly skilled at attack, but ten of them were killed right away. I could tell how many men they had lost by how many ponies were being led away without riders.

We were getting close to some large Wehrmacht units, and they had positioned their snipers to hold up our advance, but there was something different. The sniper fire was extremely accurate. I watched two Mongolians stop to light cigarettes, with their backs to the wind, about two hundred yards away. Suddenly they both jerked and fell off their horses. Then I heard a distant *crack crack*, the sounds almost on top of each other. Somehow the German snipers were scoring kills from a hell of a distance.

There was another flurry of fire, and I saw several horses running without their riders. The Mongolians reacted immediately.
They swarmed with even more fury than normal and surrounded
the area from which the fire had come, a little group of trees on a
hill about half a mile away. They passed us a few hours later with
several new German backpacks swinging from their saddles, passing around photographs while they rode. Two of them had new
Mausers with long telescopic sights slung over their backs. I pointed this out to Ivan, who nodded silently.

I expected some kind of ceremony or celebration from the
Russians when we passed into Germany, but instead they became
more quiet and morose. I finally realized why. These men had
been fighting the world's finest military machine for almost five
years. They had pushed the Wehrmacht back a thousand miles,
one mile at a time, sometimes one mile a month, and they had
paid for every yard with the lives of their friends. The thought of
more bitter fighting ahead snuffed out the jubilation of crossing
into Germany.

The countryside changed noticeably. Some of the roads were
still in good shape, and they were very well built, with neat curb-
stones. The houses were larger than the houses in Poland, and
they were very handsome. Many of them had big windows and
large, covered porches that wrapped all around the house.

Some of the street signs were still in place. We were sitting at
an intersection about a mile from the town waiting for a radio
message when Ivan reached down and picked up his burp gun. He
looked right at me, winked, stood up in the jeep and fired the gun
at a street sign until the drum magazine was empty. The bright
brass shell casings landed in my lap and bounced off my face. The
sign disintegrated into little pieces of white wood. Even the post
was shredded by the .30 Mauser round the Russians liked so

much. The fire rate and hitting power of the PPSH burp gun was unbelievable.

The Russians called it the Pee Pee Shah, and it was one hell of a killing machine. Ivan said something to Manuel and walked off. Manuel interpreted. "The fascists put up such street signs in Russia, so we will be needing to put up some Russian signs here, and these must go." Stalin had his head buried in my armpit. The depth of hatred the Russians had for the Germans was unimaginable.

Pasewalk was a nice-looking town with well-kept forests and fields surrounding the town. There was a large town square with several two-story government buildings in the center. The word was that from here on out we were going to be fighting large units of the Wehrmacht. We commandeered a large two-story building for a headquarters and settled in. The rain started at twilight and pounded the windows all night. The Russian squad leaders who handled the Mongolians said the German snipers were the most deadly they had seen. I noticed that there were many horses without riders in the corral.

The radio chatter kept up all night, with the operators standing watches and carefully laying out their notes on a large table. There was a low-key urgency to the messages that kept the operators sitting upright and holding the earphones tightly.

We left very early and in a great hurry. Ivan didn't want the retreating Germans to have too much time to dig in. We piled into the jeep and roared off in the half-light of dawn. The rain had settled into a steady drizzle that soaked everything. The pace was furious now. We grabbed every kilometer we could as fast as we could. Stalin stayed under my poncho and poked his head out only to bark at the motorcycles that blasted past us.

Anklam was about twenty-five miles due north of us, a large

crossroads town just west of the Kachiner Sea. We were hurtling down the road that morning with the Mongolians on both sides of us. I felt kind of useless, but Ivan had made it very clear that I was to stay out of the fighting. He told me several times how quickly the Mongolians would kill me if they mistook me for a German civilian.

There were only small pockets of fighting that morning. Suddenly I heard a strange noise, a high-pitched whistling sound. A second later, explosions bracketed both sides of the road, close enough to scare the hell out of me. Artillery. They were trying to get the range on us. Ivan slammed the jeep to a halt and directed the Mongolians to sweep around a hill in front of us. We crept ahead slowly and waited. The rounds came in pairs now, closer each time. Suddenly it stopped. The radio operator yelled something in Ivan's ear, and we roared off at top speed.

The big 88-mm cannons were still intact when we got there. The Mongolians had overrun the position with their usual frenzy. There were three Germans still alive, two of them wounded and sitting on the ground in a little circle. The other one had his hands on his helmet. He couldn't have been more than sixteen. There were six or seven dead artillery men scattered around the guns. The Mongolians were still working over the dead soldiers when two of them leaped up and let out a long, ear-splitting squeal. They had a big photograph they were fighting over. Ivan motioned to one of his sergeants to break it up. He grabbed the picture and brought it over to Ivan. It was a picture of a big naked German woman with two men doing something I thought impossible. Ivan laughed and gave it back to the Mongolians, who tore off on their ponies, yelling and whooping. "The fascists cannot even do a decadent thing without looking ridiculous," he said to Manuel.

I walked up and looked at the 88s. The guns were a lot bigger than I thought, and they were beautifully designed. I'd always wondered what they looked like when my plane was flying through flak. I told Ivan that I had been shot at a lot in the air by these guns.

He laughed. "These two won't be shooting at us anymore. Tomorrow they will be shooting at Germans."

Two Russian soldiers jumped out of a truck and quickly checked the guns over. They looked carefully for booby traps in the barrels and got them ready to tow. The Russians manufactured ammunition for the 88s and greatly respected their accuracy.

We pulled into Anklam slowly and carefully. The Mongolians jumped off their horses and started the house-to-house search. Ivan pulled the jeep around the back of a concrete wall and looked over the town with binoculars. Anklam was the first town we had found where most of the civilians had stayed. Civilians in a small town trying to go about their normal business in the middle of a war was a bizarre sight. Ivan was very suspicious, but there was no sniper fire. We drove down the main street slowly in the jeep, about a hundred yards behind the Mongolians.

The residents had pulled most of the war debris out of the roads, and there was even a small bakery that was open. I asked Ivan if I could go in, and he reluctantly let me go. The civilians made him nervous. I got the feeling he might order them out of the town.

I went into the small bakery with a Russian soldier. He flipped the safety off his burp gun and stood in the door, covering me. The Germans tried not to look at us, and the older woman at the counter was working very hard at being cheerful. She made up a big sack of fresh rolls and handed them to me. I told her I was an

American flyer, and she smiled. I noticed most of the people had holes in their shoes, with cardboard sticking out. I hadn't seen that since the depression.

I walked back to the jeep quickly with the warm rolls. Ivan looked at me as if I had come from the moon. Stalin nailed the first roll just as it cleared the bag.

"Looks like you made a friend. Was she young and pretty?" Ivan asked slyly.

"No, no, just a bakery maid. Here, have one." We passed the rolls around. Ivan ate several while his eyes raked the town, every window, every rooftop.

"Okay. These are okay," Ivan said as we roared off. He had picked up this word from me and used it all the time. Soon I heard the Mongolians saying "Okay."

IVAN DECIDED that we needed a few days to regroup, so we stayed in a small village fairly close to Greifswald. The horses were exhausted, and the tires on the jeep were completely worn out. We could hear continual artillery firing south of us, where the main battles were taking place.

The towns were getting bigger now and, surprisingly for us, there wasn't much resistance. We kept expecting to run into large German units, but they had apparently moved out ahead of us, probably headed south to meet the main Russian thrust.

We left early on the third day. The weather cleared, and the sun came out. Finally, in the first week of March, there was warmth in the sun. Feeling the heat on my face was like standing in front of the fire at the farmhouse. It slowly, slowly drew the harsh winter cold out and lifted my spirits. There were flowers blooming, and I began to feel like I was going to live and get back home.

We advanced more slowly now. The small towns were closer together, and the looting took a lot of time. The Germans left all the doors open in the houses they had abandoned. The Mongolians would tear through a house in a flurry, looking first for mines and booby traps, then for women, then for booty, then for liquor, then for food. They tore through everything. Every dresser drawer, every closet, every shelf and basement. They piled the booty outside the house, and big Studebaker trucks would roll up and load it up. They missed nothing. They took lace curtains, wall clocks, silverware, everything. The few women they found they took to basements or small buildings behind the houses and raped. Usually the women went with them quietly, trembling and looking over their shoulders, hoping they would live.

We encountered German liquor for the first time. They found several large wine cellars with hundreds of small bottles of schnapps. The Mongolians went crazy over the schnapps. Twice Ivan caught them drinking during the day, and once he knocked a Mongolian down and made him walk to the rear. The Russians had one hard and fast rule. No drinking during the day. That Mongolian glared at him for days after that.

Ivan struck absolute terror into the German townspeople. He was so big and fierce-looking that they scattered out of his path, lowering their eyes instinctively. He always carried an automatic pistol and a saber. That seemed odd to me, as it was awkward for him to get into the jeep with the saber, but he was never without it. He showed me his Tokarev TT33 pistol while we waited for orders. It was smaller than a .45 but looked a lot like one of Browning's designs. It fired the .30 round that the broom-handled Mauser pistols of WWI used. I thought the barrel was too long and the gun a little front heavy. I asked Ivan if it was accurate.

"Accurate? The pistol of Tokarev? I think accurate." He got out of the jeep and leveled the gun at a shop front about seventy-five feet away. He fired very carefully, shooting out six small windows on the second floor, one after the other. He missed the last one.

"I guess that's accurate enough for me," I said.

The radio operator motioned Ivan over and began pointing down the road. Manuel told me there was a slave labor camp ahead of us, near Damgarten. I thought of Küstrin, and the smell of the camp came back to me. Manuel also heard that there was a large group of German soldiers preparing a defense of Damgarten. Probably at least two companies, about four hundred men, with heavy weapons. We held up here for about a week, waiting for orders. I slept and ate, ate and slept, trying to put on some weight and to somehow wash the weariness from my soul.

The countryside had opened up now. It was flat, open country with straight treelines and large farms, mostly abandoned. As we approached Damgarten from the north, mortar fire opened up all around us. Ivan got on the radio and directed the attack. It sounded like the end of the world to me. The Germans must have had ten or twenty heavy mortars zeroed in on the approach to the town. We quickly pulled back out of range, about two miles.

Ivan spent several hours collecting reports from the squad leaders, then requested artillery support. We camped right off the road and set up a perimeter. It was a tense, long night, with sporadic rifle and machine gun fire.

I saw Manuel talking to Ivan. Then he walked over to me and said, "This is a big one. Headquarters thinks the Ninth SS Division has moved back into this area, perhaps with tanks. I don't like it." I noticed for the first time that Manuel's hands were beginning to shake very slightly.

"The artillery is on its way," Ivan said to Manuel proudly. "This town will not exist in twelve hours." When the first big artillery pieces rumbled past us, I believed him. The Russian guns were huge, and they kept coming all afternoon. I had heard a lot about the Russian artillery capability, but seeing it was really something. They opened up about four in the afternoon and hammered away for hours and hours with no letup. You could hear the heavy rounds going right over us, *zoosh, zoosh*, and tearing into the ground and the buildings. The smoke gradually grew into one large black cloud over Damgarten. I still ducked my head every time a shell thundered over, which made Ivan laugh.

"You are not tall enough for the gunners to hit you, Little Rooster!" he said.

Manuel was in bad shape. My friend had seen so much fighting and killing, he was completely worn out. His grip was beginning to go. "I don't like this place. This battle is bad, Tommy. Maybe it will be the last." He sounded very old and distant.

"Maybe so, Manuel. Maybe this will be the last. Maybe the Germans will see the handwriting on the wall and give up," I said, hoping to cheer him up a little. He walked away and sat on the road with his back to a truck tire and held his hands over his ears. I walked over and sat down. We talked at length for the first time in a long while.

"I am tired, deep inside, Tommy. My mind is very tired," Manuel said, almost sobbing. When he looked at me, the weariness flooded out from his soul in dark waves. "When, when will these monsters give up?" He stared at the ground and shook his head.

"It can't be long now, Manuel. It just can't be. We'll be up to the British lines in a few days, and this whole damn thing will be over. You can come to Texas, and we'll get a race horse." I tried to cheer him up, but the artillery fire started again, and we could feel the heavy rounds hitting the ground like a pile driver.

"Before Texas I must go home, to find my sweetheart and my family. Then I can come to Texas, and we'll get a race horse. But now, the Russians are the masters of Poland, and there will be trouble," he said, rubbing his temples with his thumbs. "There will be trouble."

TEN

DAMGARTEN

DAYLIGHT DAWNED slowly. The colors of the trees and grass emerged from the gloom so gradually it seemed as if the trees were still gray shapes after the sun was up.

Usually when I got up early, I was alone, but this day almost everyone was up. Waiting. Hoping. Hoping the day would go by quickly. We left much earlier than usual, about six-thirty, creeping along the road in the jeep with the Mongolians spread out in the fields on both sides. It was quiet.

We were about five kilometers from Damgarten when firing broke out on our left flank. We screeched to a stop. We found out that there were about 250 German soldiers dug in around a warehouse complex, and they cut the Mongolians up badly. The fearlessness of the Mongolians worked against them as they rushed prepared defenses with patterned gunfire and minefields.

I lay under the jeep with Manuel and listened to the intensity of the fighting. I taught Manuel how to cross his fingers, which confused him a little at first. The Germans killed about fifty Mongolians in the first two hours, but the horsemen broke through around noon and decimated the Germans. I didn't see any German prisoners, just a truck full of backpacks. They looked new.

We rolled into the outskirts of Damgarten about two o'clock. The artillery had taken huge chunks out of the town, and fires were burning everywhere. There was no gunfire. Ivan stopped and waited until the Mongolians cleared each block. There were several sandbagged machine gun nests that still had little camp stoves and food cans in them, but no guns or Germans.

We rounded a turn in the road and saw a camp ahead of us, with towers and barbed wire fences. The camp was on the outskirts of the town, in an industrial area. It was about a square block in size.

Ivan stopped and checked the camp towers with binoculars. They were empty. We rolled up to the gates of the camp. A huge crowd of people suddenly appeared and jammed up behind the wire gate. They were all women, and they were all young. There were hundreds of them, and many of them were very pretty.

We jumped out of the jeeps and swung open the barbed wire gates. The girls swarmed around us, cheering and jumping up and down, squealing with delight. We were completely flabbergasted. I noticed that even these young faces were deeply lined, and they had a hunted-animal look in their eyes. Many of them were holding back, ready to run back into the camp, wondering what liberation by the Red Army would mean. Fortunately, the Mongolians were kept several blocks behind us by the rest of Ivan's men.

Manuel was talking rapidly in Polish with one of the girls, and they were both pointing at me. She was a lovely girl with a strong, striking face and blonde hair down to her shoulders. She was wearing a man's blue shirt and baggy wool pants. Manuel was smiling and laughing, and I walked over to kid him that he had already picked out the prettiest girl.

"Your friend told me you are an American flyer," the young woman said in slow, deliberate English while she looked at me with beautiful hazel eyes. As we looked at each other, I felt a wave of warmth wash over me. The noise around us faded away. I felt a strange, exhilarating electricity from her eyes. I never heard the clatter of hooves that scattered the crowd around us. Rosa, for that was her name, did, and she darted behind me, pressing against me and holding tightly to the jeep.

The Mongolians arrived and went completely crazy. Women. Young, good-looking women! They leaped off their horses, ran past the gate and into the small courtyard. *Heeyyiiii! Heeyyiiii!* They screamed their war cries and rushed at the women, knocking each other down in their haste.

"Nyet! Nyet!" Ivan boomed out his command, and the Mongolians stopped. He walked over to the platoon leader and ordered the Mongolians out of the camp. They stood there in disbelief, staring at Ivan and the Russians for a long silent minute. Several of them started walking toward the women. Ivan motioned to his sergeant, who slowly started walking towards the Mongolians, his burp gun lowered slightly.

Rosa's hand closed on my arm as the Mongolian platoon leader talked to Ivan. He started to argue, but Ivan cut him off and swept his arm around to point to the camp gate. The Mongolians were stunned, but they didn't move. Why couldn't they have these women? Were the Russians saving them for themselves?

Ivan could cover thirty feet in just a few strides. He strode quickly, forcefully toward the Mongolians. They shot nervous glances at each other, then turned and started for the gate before he reached the first group. It was then I noticed Ivan was still wearing his dress uniform, with all his medals.

I smelled the Devil before I saw him. He had worked his way around the side of the jeep and was standing there staring at Rosa hungrily. He thought he was the best soldier in the world. He resented taking any kind of orders.

"Out! Take your men and get out of the camp." Ivan pointed at him, but he stared at Rosa. Her hand in mine suddenly went cold. The Devil stayed his ground until Ivan started to move. He looked at me with an expression that said one thing: *I'll be back.* Then he walked out of the camp.

"Commandant! Take me to the camp commandant!" Ivan roared to the women. They quickly led us to the main building in the camp. Rosa and I walked along and glanced at each other. We were still holding hands, which surprised us both.

The commandant's house was a large, squat yellow building with concrete stairs. Two girls holding crude clubs stood at the door. There were two more girls standing at the rear door. They said they had arrested the commandant, who was inside. Ivan motioned to two of his men. They readied their burp guns and went in, then signaled us inside.

The commandant emerged from a back room in a flurry. She was built like a wrestler—big round shoulders, strong arms, and a thick neck with short-cropped brown hair. She was wearing a light tan uniform with a starched skirt. On her collars she had a small insignia which indicated some kind of high rank. The first time I got a close look at her face, a bolt of fear shot through me. Her eyes were close set and very deep, and she had bushy eyebrows that were too big for her face and almost concealed her darting black eyes. She had an intensity about her that affected all of us, except Ivan.

She was very nervous. She realized Ivan was the ranking officer and began right away. "Oh, I am so glad to see you! I have been trying to save these women's lives. I have been trying to get them food."

"Liar! Murderer! Liar! Murderer, filthy killer!" The girls shouted her down every time she tried to plead with Ivan.

Manuel and I looked at Ivan, who listened, stone-faced. "Why are there no men in this camp?" Manuel asked her in German.

"This is a special camp," she struggled to explain. Ivan looked at her in silence as she squirmed under the questioning.

"Look! Look at this. This is what they have done to me!" one of the girls burst out, as she pulled her shirt open to reveal a crude flower tattooed above her left breast. "They owned us and abused us. The guard who owned me is locked up over there!" she screamed, pointing to a locked room. The commandant looked at the floor.

"Go, go in the back!" one of the girls screamed, motioning to the room behind the desk. "You'll see what beasts they are!"

We slowly moved to the back rooms. Ivan flipped open his holster and rested his hand on his pistol. The rooms were small storage areas, like big closets. Items were scattered everywhere. Ivan began to look at some large black-and-white photographs. He handed one to me silently and leafed through the stack. It was a picture of the commandant, naked, holding a young prisoner, also naked, and kissing her on the mouth. You could tell the young girl was struggling. Her eyes were wide open with fear.

Rosa was holding my hand now. She whispered in Manuel's ear and pointed to the door of another room. I thought for a terrifying second that there was someone in that room with a weapon. I touched Ivan's shoulder and motioned to the door. His pistol came out of the holster in one silent move as he motioned to his sergeant, who gave the door a kick. Rosa looked at me with a faraway look, then looked at the floor.

Ivan had to duck to get into the room. I went in behind him. It was a small, dimly lit room with shelves along one wall and one small, dirty window. On the shelves were five or six small brass lamps, with strange shades. We took a few of them out and held them up to the little window. We could just see the small dark nipples on the breasts and make out the tattoos. They were the same crude flowers we had just seen on the girl. The air in the room smelled of chemicals. It was very quiet.

Ivan slowly looked at every lamp and gently put them back on the shelves, then walked outside. The commandant was sitting at her desk with her hands folded in front of her, ready with a new explanation.

Ivan stood looking at her for a long time. He slowly walked behind her, bent over, grabbed her under her armpits and quickly stood up, slamming her head into the ceiling. He held her there for a moment, and then drove her head into the ceiling several more times. Then he held her at arm's length, looked at her for a long moment, and dropped her to the floor with a shock that rattled everything, the doors, the windows, the small things in cupboards. The girls gathered around and spit on her as she struggled back to consciousness.

"She was selling these horrible things to foul men who would come to the camp. She was selling them. Selling them!" the girls cried, kicking at her and spitting on her. She sat there in a daze with blood from her nose dripping off her chin.

"Ivan, this is important. We have to gather these materials and files so the families of these women will know what happened here," I said, overwhelmed by the evil I had seen. He agreed and detailed two men to start boxing up the files and photographs. They spilled out everywhere. Photos of young women splayed out on beds, forced into every imaginable degradation. The faces of these young women, desperately afraid for their lives, jumped out of the photographs. There were hundreds of them. Rosa told

Manuel that many of the girls had been murdered during these sessions. Suddenly I could hardly breathe, and I stepped outside.

It took the sun longer to warm my face. I felt like I had been kicked in the stomach. The questions started to wheel through my mind. How could anyone torture and kill and butcher innocent young women? If that could happen, then anything could, and nothing was safe. I looked at Rosa. I felt everything at once. A tidal wave of affection, overwhelming sympathy, and an avalanche of desire to hold her and protect her and keep her from all the evil in the world washed over me.

We walked slowly out of the camp. There was a large crowd of women standing around the open doors of a garage-like area. They were cheering and throwing rocks into the building. One of the female guards was hanging by her neck from a beam. Still kicking and gasping, she struggled to reach the rope around her neck. Three others hung limply, their tan uniforms torn to shreds. The women were screaming at the corpses, spitting at them, their faces twisted in rage, their eyes glittering with hatred and vengeance. The broken handles of brooms were just visible between their bloodied legs. One of the girls ran in and jumped up to push a broom with both hands. Rosa looked away. Ivan slowly shook his head, and we walked on.

Ivan ordered all the Mongolian platoon leaders to keep their men out of the camp. He told the women to close the gates and stay in the camp for the time being. He put a Russian guard at the entrance to the camp and sent food in.

"We've got a big, big problem here, Little Rooster. Handling two thousand women is not going to be easy." Ivan seemed genuinely worried.

"Handling one is not going to be easy," I said, looking at Rosa. Ivan laughed.

We walked down the street away from the camp. "Take this house. I'll put guards on both doors for you." Ivan pointed to the small house next to the larger one he was using. It was a blue stucco two-story house, and Rosa and I took the upstairs. We could see the street and the town square from the window, and we felt safe there. Manuel had brought one of the girls from the camp and took the room next to us. Her name was Francile. She was a slender girl with black hair and deep, brown eyes.

Rosa and I sat down on a badly torn lavender couch in a back bedroom and held hands. Her skin was beautifully translucent. I just looked at her hand in mine for a long time. The events of the day whirled through my mind as I tried to settle down. We would glance at each other every so often to see if the exhilaration was still there. I had never really been head over heels in love before, and the feeling I got when I looked into her eyes was almost frightening.

Slowly, Rosa began to talk in clear and deliberate English. She wanted me to know why she was in that camp and what they had done.

She had been a German prisoner for four years. "They took all the young girls from my town. My sister and I, too. I was fourteen years old. My parents thought it would be best if we went to school that day. The Germans came with trucks to my school and took us all. They beat us and held us in a dairy farm outside of the city for several weeks. They told our families nothing. Then they sent us to a camp to make parts for some kind of an airplane. We worked sixteen hours a day with old machines. Then they moved me to another camp, where we did farm work for some time. Many of the girls escaped or were raped and killed during this time, so they moved the camp to this place. A year ago, this com-mandant came, and all the men guards were replaced by her friends." She talked softly, but there was a deep, burning ferocity in her. "This woman and her friends killed about two hundred of the girls. They killed several every night." The sentence hung in the air for a long time.

I couldn't think of anything to say. Stalin licked my hand and jumped into my lap. He seemed to know when the weariness came for me.

We both dozed off sitting on that beat-up old couch. When I opened my eyes, it was dark, which startled me. Rosa was sleeping with her head on my chest. Her hair was wonderfully soft to touch. I started to wonder if I was dreaming, but Stalin sat up and licked my face. My anxiety eased, and Rosa woke up. "I am so sleepy," she said softly.

We quietly ate some cheese and bread, gazing at each other from time to time and looking away when the brilliance became too much. It was quiet outside.

We stayed there holding each other and trying to rest for a long while. I had just dozed off again when a strange sound began to drift through the room. It was the bizarre, discordant concertina music of the celebrating Mongolians. Soon I could hear shouts, smashing bottles, and pistol shots.

I was stroking Rosa's shoulder, thinking about home, when the noise at the door started. It was about ten o'clock, and the voices were loud. One was a Mongolian saying, "Ivan, Ivan," over and over. I walked halfway down the stairs. It was the Devil, standing in the doorway trying to convince the Russian guard that Ivan had said he was to relieve the guard. The other guard at the back of the house came around and decided to go find Ivan.

The Devil was roaring drunk. He had a new German P-38 pistol on his hip, and he bore down on the Russian guard with everything he had. It was clear he was telling the Russian to leave.

The young Russian looked rattled but stood his ground. The Devil turned to walk away, then lowered his shoulder and slipped under the guard's arm in one fluid motion. He spotted me on the stairs, and a weird smile broke out on his grease-smeared face. He started up the stairs and flung his arm into the air. "Out of my way!" he screamed at me, slurring the words.

I had just turned to grab my pistol when the top hinge of the front door exploded. Ivan crossed the room in two steps and took the Devil by the shoulder with one hand, tore his holster off with the other, and slammed him into the wall. He grabbed him by the throat and held him in the air while he carried him to the door. Ivan rocked back and threw the Devil about fifteen feet into the street, where he landed on his side with a loud crunch. Two of the Devil's men helped him up and quickly carried him toward the Mongolians' rope stable. Ivan closed the door quietly.

Soon the noise from the street increased dramatically. The Mongolians were smashing the windows of houses and throwing furniture out and burning it in a large bonfire. I saw one drunken Mongolian with a leather valise of some kind. He was sitting against a wall, and every few minutes a group of Mongolians would stagger up and throw down some money. He would carefully open the valise, then snap it shut suddenly. I found my binoculars and finally figured out what he was doing. He had the pornographic picture from the dead German artillery man and was charging the other Mongolians to look at it.

The memory of the photographs in the camp came back to me as I looked at Rosa's beautiful face. Somehow nothing happened, no revulsion, or anger, or sickness. I just stopped feeling.

Ivan tapped on the door softly and came in. He looked at Rosa for a long time and finally sat down. He took a small canvas bag out of his tunic, pulled a pistol from it, and handed it to Rosa.

Rosa looked at the small black pistol intently. She worked the slide carefully and ran her thumb over the safety lever several times. "Just point it and pull the trigger," Ivan said in Polish as he handed her a small bag of ammunition. "The Little Rooster will take care of you. This is for the time when he is not near you," he said as he touched her shoulder. He looked at her, nodded, then left.

We sat together on the couch trying to talk. She flinched every time a rifle or pistol was fired. We tried to ignore the noise, but all of a sudden there was a crescendo of yelling and screaming coming from the direction of the camp. She looked up at me and hugged me, then started beating her head against my shoulder. It was then I realized that she couldn't cry. She just moved her head side to side and listened to the screams and firing from the street. I held her head to my chest.

The Russian guard at the camp was relieved at midnight. Unfortunately, his relief was a Mongolian soldier.

About one-thirty we heard a new commotion in the street and went to the window to look. There was a large crowd of drunken Mongolians dragging a woman by her hair down the street past the light of the bonfires. It was the camp commandant. The Mongolians were howling drunk, yelling at the top of their lungs, and pulling a hay cart of some kind. They stopped right across the street from our window and threw the woman on the cart and tore her clothes off. It took several Mongolians to finally strip her. She fought savagely and nearly choked one of the Mongolians to death.

I expected Rosa to turn away and cry, but she didn't. She said, "This is God's punishment for her. God's special punishment."

The Mongolians raped the commandant all night, turning her over from time to time. Rosa watched it all. She watched them hold the woman's ankles for the men in line, then they found some rope and tied her legs to the cart. Then they turned her over and tied a thick rope around her waist so they could hold on to her heavy body.

Toward the end, I tried to pull Rosa away from the window. She wouldn't move. Finally six or seven of them threw the commandant into the street, knocked her down with a piece of concrete, then urinated on her. They kicked her and jumped on her with their boots as they sang some strange Mongolian song.

"She deserves it. They should kill her now. She deserves it. I hope they cut her throat. Kill her. Kill her now," Rosa chanted over and over. The look in her eyes was molten hatred. She rubbed her left breast in a circular motion.

I started to pull her away from the horror in the street, but I couldn't. The weariness hit me, worse now than before, and I had to sit on the couch. Stalin jumped into my lap, and I petted him for a long time.

Then I felt Rosa's hands in mine, pulling me up from the couch and towards the bed. We lay down. It was dark and quiet. We slept in short stretches.

You don't really wake up when you don't sleep, you just open your eyes and it's not dark anymore. A gun keeps you from really sleeping. I awoke looking at our guns, almost side by side in our hands. Dark, cold, and heavy. Rosa would twitch almost imperceptibly every few minutes, and her thumb would pass over the safety lever, and then she would squeeze my hand.

"How did you sleep?" I asked.

"Better than I have slept in years, because I felt someone was there to protect me," she said softly. She kissed me in a long, flowing motion. "I am going to have this taken off when I get home," she said, running her finger over the crude rose tattoo on her left breast.

The commandant's bruised and bloody body was lying in the street. The last thing the Mongolians had done was smash vodka bottles over her head and drive the broken necks into her face. Tiny rivers of blood and urine ran away from her body to the gutter. Rosa looked down at her for a long time.

IVAN KNOCKED softly and came into the room with Manuel behind him. He looked like he hadn't slept for a week. He sat down on the couch and began to speak as Manuel translated. Rosa seemed to understand Russian.

"We've got trouble, real trouble with the Devil. He is stirring up the Mongolians about these women you and Manuel have." Ivan looked at me.

My heart stopped. *Will I have to leave her?* Ivan looked very serious. I searched frantically for a solution, then it came to me.

"I can cut her hair, put her in a uniform, put a hat on her, and take her as a man. I'll move over and give her my seat in the jeep," I tried to say, as evenly and quietly as I could. Ivan stood up and walked to the door. My heart was in my throat.

"Come over here, Little Rooster." He put his arm around me and looked at me. "Do you know the danger of this? These Mongolians are going to find out sooner or later, and we might have *real* trouble. Are you up to that?" He looked right at me.

"Yes. If you'll let me do it, I'm up to it," I said, pulling myself straight up.

He was quiet for a minute; he just looked at Rosa and me. Then he said, "You talk to her, get her ready. Tell her it is dangerous." He walked out.

I don't know where the Russian uniform came from, but it looked fine on Rosa. Two of Rosa's friends from the camp cut her hair. One was Francile, Manuel's friend. She was beautiful, half French and half Polish. She had the most beautiful brown eyes I had ever seen. Francile cut Rosa's hair very carefully and very close. How these women kept their good looks in that evil place was a mystery to me.

Francile told Rosa that she was going back to Poland that day with a group of girls who had arranged transport. Rosa tried desperately to talk her out of it, but she left anyway. Manuel tried, too, but he just didn't seem to have much strength.

"Texas? Real cowboys? Real Indians?" Rosa wanted to know everything about Texas.

"You're going to make a good cowgirl," I told her, which was a mistake.

"What is a cowgirl? How can there be cowgirls? What do they do? Do they ride horses? What kind of horses? Are there many of them? Must they ride far? Is it dusty among the cows?" She gave me less than a second to respond to each question. I would humor her, and she would play along. Her smile was wonderful, and her curiosity boundless. I felt for the first time in a long time that I had someone who really meant something to me, and I meant something to her.

We stayed in that little town all that day, and Rosa and I rested and talked. Later, a Russian guard and I found a store that had been abandoned. We dug around and found some tins of corned beef and other small foodstuffs. Rosa was elated. Beef!

That night we sat down to a small meal in our room. "God bless this food we are about to receive. . . ." I began a blessing at the exact same moment she did. It was one of those magic moments. We held hands while we finished the blessing, and the world was a warm and happy place again. The Russian guard had given us a bottle of German beer, and we toasted our good fortune at finding one another and surviving the evil and death all around us.

The magic continued when we quietly undressed and went to bed. She had an indomitable spirit that allowed her to rise above what had happened to her. She wanted to become herself again, a vivacious young woman full of life and love. I was worried she would withdraw at some point, but she didn't. Afterwards she looked at me, her face flushed and a bright sparkle in her eyes, and told me it was the first time she had been with a man because she wanted to.

We talked all night about the hate inside her. Sex had always been a vulgar, unpleasant act forced on her by dangerous people. She talked on and on. Then she said something that I'll never forget. She said, "I feel like I belong to the world." She wanted to be free, and travel, and be a part of the larger world. She knew instinctively that she had to move on, to deny the poison inside.

I decided that night to bring Rosa back to the States and marry her.

ELEVEN

THE WAY BACK

PRIVATE ROSA looked good. Her hair was cut very close, and she was wearing a man's sweatshirt, with a Russian army shirt over that. Her pants were baggy and too long, but that was fairly common. We were trying to hide some of her contours, and we were mostly successful.

We stayed in the room for the next three days and rested. Rosa ate everything I could find for her, and her face began to fill out. We had boiled cabbage and canned Russian fish, some tinned beef, and a very small piece of cheese. We cooked in the room with a small Russian field stove. She made a delicious cabbage stew that Ivan loved.

Most of the Mongolians had forgotten about her by now, after several days of vodka stupor and round-the-clock mayhem. I kept Rosa away from the window, but I knew the Devil would never forget, and he wouldn't miss an opportunity to make trouble. I wondered briefly if Ivan could have him transferred, but I knew it was impossible.

The Polish girls, including Francile, had left Damgarten and joined the streams of Polish refugees headed home. Manuel had tried to talk her out of it, because there was still so much danger on the roads from mines and more than a few German stragglers, but she just wanted to go home. I was relieved. Taking Rosa with us was a real strain on Ivan's patience, and taking another woman would have been tough. When Francile left, Manuel became very sullen and wouldn't talk at all. He was having stomach problems, and I saw him double up several times in pain.

The radio operator told me that the scuttlebutt was that there was going to be one last big battle. Large remnants of the Wehrmacht, including several SS units, and a few Panzer armored units were supposed to be between us and Rostock. I noticed that Ivan always took particular note of reports of SS units on the radio. Maybe that was why he kept the Devil around. I had learned that Ivan's entire family was killed by SS units outside of Vertyuzhany during the Stalingrad battle. He knew which units were involved and kept an eye out for them.

The next morning, as we were getting ready to leave, I showed Rosa the seat belt I had made for her. Rosa looked at the rope seat belt with a certain amount of trepidation.

"This is for when Ivan drives," I said loudly.

Ivan looked back. "Yes, yes, you'll need that!" he boomed in Russian, and we roared off down the road to Rostock from Damgarten. The weather had cleared, and it was almost warm. Rosa held my hand on the floor of the jeep while Stalin barked at just about everything that moved.

The Germans had sent millions of people from the occupied countries to Germany for forced labor, and they were now walking home. They lined all the roads headed east, and they all had the same look on their faces. Fear. For them the war might not be over. None of them knew what to expect when they got home. These poor people had their belongings in children's wagons, baby buggies, and all kinds of pushcarts with little iron wheels that squeaked as they pulled them along. Some of the Russian soldiers would stop them and go through their pathetic belongings looking for loot. This really upset me, but there was nothing I could do. Ivan said nothing.

For a while it seemed as if we were on a joyride through the country in springtime. The radio was quiet, and the Mongolians were subdued. They rode lazily in the fields on both sides of the road, and the sun was bright and warm. Except for a few sniper incidents, it was a lovely trip to Ribnitz.

RIBNITZ WAS a quiet little resort town on the Saaler Bodden, a small inlet on the Baltic. The Germans had retreated farther than we thought, and Ribnitz was almost completely intact. After the usual reconnoitering trip through town, we pulled up in front of the large house that was the Burgermeister's residence. The Burgermeister's wife was tall and stately, with white hair perfectly combed and pinned up. She was in her seventies, and she was terrified, but she was doing a good job of pretending everything was normal. She was very thin and looked like she had been sick recently. She led us into a large dining room with a long banquet table. There were several places on the wall where pictures had recently been removed. Ivan acted as if he had seen it all before. He began to tap loudly on the table, waiting for the Burgermeister. There was a beautiful crystal chandelier hanging over the table. You could tell it was the family's pride and joy. It was almost too big for the room.

The Burgermeister was quite large, with a balding head, huge, bushy eyebrows, and small, round glasses. His gray mustache quivered as he formulated his answers to Ivan's questions. Ivan looked straight at him, as he did with everyone he addressed. He immediately established that he was in command. He wanted to know how long ago the German troops had departed and how many there were. He wanted to know if there were tanks and what units they were attached to. The Burgermeister's eyes shifted, and he was slow to answer. I watched Ivan closely for a reaction, but there was only a slight indication that he was very tired of being lied to by Germans.

Standing in the doorway was a young girl, about sixteen. She was very pretty, and I was shocked they didn't have her hidden. Rosa looked at her nervously and tried to signal to the older woman to get her out of sight.

"I am going to leave a soldier here, and I want you to prepare food for us when we return," Ivan told the Burgermeister through the interpreter.

We drove back into town to search an abandoned arsenal. Ivan scoured this building from top to bottom, but the dust was too much for Rosa and me. We waited in the jeep. All they found was some old rifle ammunition.

About an hour later, we returned to the house and walked into the dining room with the chandelier. We were covered in whitish dust, and the old man's wife stiffened when we sat down. The table was set for eight places. There were beautiful silver soup tureens and several large, covered dishes. Ivan stood there and looked at the table for a few moments.

"Eat out of each bowl—now!" Ivan ordered the Burgermeister, who blanched. "Eat out of each bowl—now!"

The Burgermeister shot a glance at his wife and looked down at the floor. Ivan looked at him for about two seconds. Then, in one motion, he drew his saber and cut the cord holding the chandelier. It crashed to the table and smashed the dishes in an explosion of glass, food, and hot soup. The Burgermeister tried to hold his hands up, but he never made it. Ivan thrust the saber through his chest and drove him into the wall. I jumped about six feet. The women screamed loudly. Ivan stood back and watched the Burgermeister as he died, stuck to the wall by the saber. Then he pulled the saber out. The Burgermeister slid slowly to the floor, a startled look on his face. The pool of dark blood spread quickly. Rosa grabbed my arm and turned toward the door.

"Give these women to the Mongolians," Ivan ordered a Russian soldier. "And send the young one to my quarters!" Ivan wiped his saber clean on the white tablecloth and walked out.

Rosa and I were given a small room in a house next to Ivan's. We stayed awake all night wondering what was happening to the young girl. I braced myself, waiting for the screams and the sobbing from Ivan's quarters, but thankfully there were none.

Rosa and I talked all night about the war and what it had done to people. "Even though she is a German, I feel bad for her, bad that she is going through what I have gone through," Rosa said, her head buried in my shoulder.

"I'm so glad you're here, here for me to talk to at times like this," I told her. She squeezed my hand and fell asleep. I lay there for a long time, wondering about the great forces swirling around us. I felt like a man in a small boat in a large ocean.

We left late the next morning after hearing a lot of artillery fire east of us. We were held up for a while, waiting to hear of battlefield developments. Ivan was very disturbed about the wait, and he got on the radio himself several times to argue. He was in no mood for humor or small talk. About eleven o'clock, we pulled out. I never saw the young German girl, and no one mentioned her.

. . .

WHEN I'D left Clyde, Texas, I didn't think I would ever see such destruction again. I didn't think I would see trees shredded, houses gutted, bodies everywhere, and black smoke all around me, or groups of terrified people huddling together, crying.

I saw that now. Schwarzenpfost was a small town just off the main road to Rostock from Ribnitz. The Germans had tried to hold the town, and the fighting must have been savage. The artillery had chewed up every square yard of the town, like some giant rooting animal. There were corpses everywhere, and a few wounded German soldiers were propped up against buildings. The dead German soldiers hadn't been looted yet, which was a mystery to me. The Mongolians descended on them like locusts, yelling and fighting over watches and pictures.

We stopped for a while so Ivan could gather up his troops and issue orders on the radio. Rosa was dozing in the jeep, with Stalin in her lap, so I took a short walk. I saw a dead German soldier a couple of hundred feet away from the road with some red showing on his uniform lapels. I looked around, then walked a little closer. He was a major or a colonel, and he still had his Walther P-38 pistol on him, which I wanted. His hand was draped over his side, and a gold watch glinted in the sun. I looked back at the jeep. Ivan was shouting into the radio, and Stalin was sitting up on the back of the jeep looking at me. I figured I could get the pistol and get back quickly.

I was about twenty feet from the body when I heard Stalin barking. Damn! I looked back, but Ivan was still on the radio, so I started to run the last few feet to the body. Stalin jumped out of the jeep and tore after me, barking loudly. He must have alerted Ivan. Just as I reached for the holster Ivan yelled, "Stop now! Don't move!" Caught. Damm it. I really wanted a P-38, everyone did. The small pistol Ivan had given me was not much of a weapon, and I was pretty sure we had some more fighting ahead of us. I backed up a few feet.

Behind me I heard the rapid *clippity-clop* of Mongolian ponies. Three Mongolians rode up in a tremendous hurry, leaped off their horses, and shoved each other in their rush to the dead German officer. The first one there grabbed the German's arm and slid the watch off.

The explosion sounded like a 500-pound bomb. The blast knocked me back about ten feet and threw me flat on my back. Dirt and debris stung my face. A wood splinter had been driven into my face, and I couldn't pull it out. Stalin started licking my face as I tried to get my eyes open.

The Mongolians were heaving, gurgling, bleeding lumps when I got to them. Only one had a face, and he died as I tried to prop him up. I could just hear Rosa screaming through the buzzing in my ears. Ivan had told me not to do anything on my own, and this would have been my first departure from that order. I should have known the body was booby-trapped when I saw the watch exposed. Ivan was shouting at me, but I couldn't hear him.

A blinding headache started in the back of my head and forced me to close my eyes. Rosa helped me back to the jeep, and we left in a cloud of dirt and gravel.

When I opened my eyes, I saw Stalin licking my pants leg and Rosa wiping my coat off with a wet towel. There were chunks of flesh and black hair all over me. I just closed my eyes and held on. Ivan seemed to hit every pothole in that damned road.

We pulled up at a crossroads and stopped. Ivan was involved in a big dispute on the radio and was fuming mad.

I slowly came around and sat with my face in my hands for about an hour. We were only about seven miles from the town of Rostock, and we were expecting the worst. We moved very slowly through battlefields that were still smoking and littered with glass and thousands of spent rifle casings.

A small Russian military van came flying down the road toward us, flashed its lights, and stopped. A big, red-faced Russian officer leaned out of the window and told Ivan that the Wehrmacht was in full retreat. The fighting in Rostock was almost over. The SS had pulled back to Weismar, about thirty-five miles east of Rostock.

Ivan nodded slowly when he heard this. We couldn't believe it. No fighting at Rostock! We were so glad, so excited, so relieved. The end of the war had to come soon.

We tore down the road to Rostock, passing burning vehicles, German trucks, a few cars, and one German half-track that had taken a direct hit. There were large pieces of bodies lying in the road. Ivan drove right over them. The buildings were torn to hell, and there were smoking shell holes everywhere.

I thought the ground was plowed around us, but when I got out, I could see that tank tracks had turned up the ground to reveal the dark soil. There were two burned-out German tanks sitting very close to us, smoldering and occasionally popping loudly. The smoke smelled like burning rubber, hot steel, and something like a Texas barbecue.

We stayed in an abandoned dairy farm that night. There was a lot of excitement on the radio. The Germans were reeling in full retreat, and there wasn't much farther for them to go. This war was really going to end.

Rosa and I fabricated a bed from some debris and made a little shelter in the far corner of the building. Ivan was very busy with his radio operators. The pace was picking up noticeably. To think that this war might really be over, and to think of what life would be like afterwards, was an impossible, intoxicating dream.

"Here is something for the young lovers. To celebrate the end of this hateful war," Manuel said as he set down the two small mud-smeared bottles and staggered out. Manuel had been drinking constantly since we had found the booze in Germany, and he hardly spoke at all. All the years of war and prison camps seemed to be catching up to him, sapping his vitality.

I could just make out the word "schnapps" on the torn label. Maybe the Germans hadn't given the world much, but they did give the world schnapps. Rosa and I started with small sips as we worked on my Polish. The small sips got a little bigger, and we managed to get tipsy together. Getting carried away with the woman you love, in a war, in a blown-up dairy farm, is great fun. We laughed and kidded each other and got so mawkish we joked about it. It was one of the great moments of my life.

We tried to sing "Lili Marlene" in Polish, which was a mixed success. I told her how we were going to name our first B-17 "Pistol Packin' Mama," and that completely confused her.

"What is a pistol packing mama? What is packing? How does a mama pack? Why does she pack this pistol and not carry it?" I just mumbled a little while the questions zinged past me.

I finally tried to sing the words to "Pistol Packing Mama" to her:

> *Drinking beer in a cabaret, and was I having fun!*
> *Till one night, she caught me right,*
> *She put me on the run!*
> *Lay that pistol down, babe, hey, lay that pistol down!*
> *Pistol packing mama, lay that pistol down*

No response. I decided to try a polka.

There's a garden, what a garden,
And only happy faces bloom there
There's never any room there
For a worry or a care there

She had heard this one, and off we went. What a duet. Ivan even wandered in and joined in the singing.

"The Rose of San Antone" was a crowd-pleaser.

Deep within my heart lies a melody
A song of old San Antone,
Where in dreams I live with the memories
Of old San Antone . . .

Then I made up a song for Rosa, complete with lyrics and melody. I had been working on it for days.

I'm lost in a blue cloud,
A cloud drifting away
My heart is like this cloud,
Hoping you'll return someday.
I'm lost in a blue cloud,
Wondering where you can be,
Thinking of you always,
Hoping you think of me.
You know and I know we're not being smart,
You might fool your friends,
But you can't fool your heart.
I'm lost in a blue cloud,
Blown by winds afar,
Searching here and there
Wondering where you are . . .

I sang for all I was worth and looked at her smiling face. I sang it again, and Ivan excused himself graciously. We felt like we owned the world, and the worst was behind us. I remember looking at her and marveling that she had thrown off the darkness so completely. What a girl. I couldn't wait to get her to Texas.

After the schnapps ran out, we turned to one another. It was different that night. The deep touching and careful exploring were gone. We rushed together in a frenzy, over and over. It was like a dam breaking. A great passion rushed from deep inside us. There was so much that had been bottled up and held back. Every wave of exhilaration was followed by another wave. "Tommy . . . Tommy. . . ."

THE ACTIVITY the next morning started earlier than usual, and every little sound seemed terribly loud. Weismar. Everyone who walked by said the word. Weismar. We were going to Weismar. Everyone was excited and moving quickly. Weismar meant the end of the war. The British Army was on the other side of Weismar.

I was suffering. I tried to pull on my second set of socks, but they just squirmed away from my fingers. Rosa looked at me and tilted her head. "Did I do that to you? You can hardly move today!" she said, laughing and tossing her head from side to side. She loved to needle me.

So did Ivan. All that day he leaned over to me and said, "Tommy . . . Tommy . . ." in my ear and laughed hysterically. It was a long day.

The counterattack came without warning. The heavy mortar shells landed in the corral area just as the Mongolians were saddling up. There were about ten men killed outright, and several horses were wounded or blown apart. We spent the rest of the day helping the wounded Mongolians and listening to the fighting. The Mongolians caught up with the German mortar units and overran them about four o'clock. They came back with the usual backpacks and watches, but they didn't celebrate much.

Ivan put Rosa and me in a small concrete building for the night and put Manuel in the building next to us. The fighting flared up again at around dusk. Ivan took off in the jeep to direct the Mongolians when the word came over the radio that it was an SS unit. We could hear torrents of heavy machine-gun fire and occasional blasts from mortars or field guns.

We had just begun to settle in for the evening when I heard our sentry arguing loudly with someone. I pulled back the door slightly and saw the Devil with three of his men. He was shouting at the guard to leave, that they would take over. He was roaring drunk and really wound up.

"Oh, my God. Ivan is gone," Rosa said, looking nervously over my shoulder. "If he gets in here, get out of the way and let me handle it." She quickly dressed and slipped her pistol into her pants. I tried to argue with her, but it was no use. She was determined to handle this situation.

The Devil kicked in the door with one blow and was in the center of the room in a flash, waving his Walther P-38. He screamed in a drunken rage. "Give the Polish woman to me! I am to take her away!" He said in Russian, then crossed to her and grabbed her arm. He looked at me and jerked his head toward the door, letting me know his men would kill me if I moved. He pulled back the door to the bedroom, threw her in, and slammed the door with his boot.

The next few moments passed like hours, and the sounds knotted my stomach. I heard clothes tearing, grunts, and then the bed squeaking. The other three Mongolians walked off.

The two shots came very quickly together. I ran over and ripped open the door. Rosa was just getting up from the bed. The Devil was on his back with a big hole in his chest and another one in his neck spurting blood.

"Is he dead?" I said, holding my gun on him.

"I don't know, but this pig of a man got what he deserved. I hope he dies." Rosa's eyes were smoldering. All the hate and malice had flooded back into her. She put the black gun down on the dresser and started to change her torn shirt.

Ivan's sentry burst into the room with his burp gun ready. "What has happened here? What was that firing?" he said.

Rosa pulled open the door, and the sentry looked at the dead man. "This will be a big problem for Ivan," he said, shaking his head as he closed the door.

Moments later Ivan pulled open the door so violently a dust cloud flew up. He looked at the Devil, covered in blood with his greasy pants pulled down to his boots. "He had it coming, this animal. He has been trouble for us for months. I should have killed him myself. But we can't let his men know what happened here, they don't understand these things," he said quietly. He put his arms around Rosa and told her he would have done the same thing. That meant a lot to her.

The Russian soldiers brought in a tarp, rolled him up in it, and dragged him off. Ivan posted two sentries at the building and left us.

"I felt like he was going to kill me, and I had to do it. I had to do it. It is still a life, though, even if he was a pig of a man," Rosa said. I held her for a long time until the trembling stopped.

I tried to tell her that it was almost over, that soon all this danger and death would be behind us forever, but then I just held her and stroked her arms and rubbed her temples.

The morning light seemed unnatural, cold and bluish, and it illuminated the blood stains on the floor. I looked at the floor for a long time in the weak light. The weariness came for me again, and it seemed like I was floating in a world where it was too much work to understand reality. All feelings were dead. Stalin licked my fingers from under the bed until the weariness passed.

Rosa finally woke and held me for a long time. We wanted a few minutes to walk around and wake up, but there was very little time for waking up. The radio operator was already packing the receiver in the jeep, and the Mongolians were already leaving when we came down. We were tired that morning, tired of the war and the killing and the endlessness of it all. We wanted to be far away from that place, forever.

No one, not even the Mongolians, ever mentioned the Devil again.

WE ROLLED toward Weismar from what was left of Rostock. The weather was clear and warmer. The town of Kröpelin was about fourteen miles west of Rostock. There had been reports of resistance here, and we heard firing as we approached. We stopped for a while while Ivan checked in with the scouts and the Mongolian units. The area was hilly, with groves of trees on the tops of the hills.

We proceeded slowly for an hour until Rosa told Ivan she needed to stop. We lurched to a halt. She got out and headed off behind us while Ivan stayed up with the radio traffic. We moved forward a couple of hundred yards past some big shell holes covered with tree limbs and other debris. Ivan was looking through the binoculars when we heard a yell behind us and the sharp crack of a pistol shot. Stalin started barking and jumped out of the jeep and ran toward Rosa. I could see Rosa standing next to a large shell hole holding her arm straight out with the little pistol in her hand. There was a commotion, and she fired twice more, carefully, deliberately.

We wheeled the jeep around and roared back to her. There were two German soldiers laying dead in the debris-covered crater. One of them held a sniper rifle with a scope. The rifle was pointed up the road toward where our jeep had been.

"They appeared out of the tree limbs like rats. They didn't see me because I had walked past their hole. I shot the man with the rifle first. The other one was trying to swing his rifle around to shoot me," Rosa said, quivering slightly.

Ivan was mortified. He quickly jumped into the crater and took the weapons from the Germans, then shook his head for a long time. He carefully examined the scope on the sniper rifle. It was a new Leitz design, bigger and more powerful than we had seen before. He walked over to Rosa and gave her a big hug. The radio operator emptied the burp gun into the snipers in a long burst that showered us all with shell casings. Ivan quickly searched the men for papers and pulled up their shirts, looking under the left armpits for the SS tattoos. There were none. These men were regular Wehrmacht.

"She is a lucky charm. Rosa is a lucky charm for us," Ivan said softly, walking back to the jeep. Stalin was tearing at the dead Germans, trying to rip the lapels off their heavy winter coats.

We all felt lucky to be alive. The Germans had learned the importance of a good sniper corps in World War I, and their snipers were deadly. Ivan kept the rifle in the jeep for several days, looking at it in a detached way once in a while. I wondered if his grip on reality slipped sometimes, like mine.

Rosa just held my hand and looked down all day. She had killed three men in two days. Her hand was cold, and she would shake her head from side to side for a long time with her eyes closed. Stalin would jump up and lick her face when she did this, which helped bring her back.

NEUBUKOW WAS only about three miles down the road. We regrouped and waited for the Mongolians. Ivan told us that they were expecting a stand from several SS units, and we were to await orders in this town. They were bringing up several large Russian infantry units from the south, from Schwerin.

The artillery opened up about three in the afternoon. It was different this time, much louder than before, and it crashed on for hours without a single pause. The return fire was constant and intense. The Wehrmacht were out there this time. There wasn't going to be any retreat. I was afraid. It sounded like this was going to be the big one, and I desperately wanted to live. I wanted Rosa to live. I wanted Ivan to live, and I wanted Manuel to live.

The SS units were bad news. They were extremely clever in planting booby traps. They fought and killed with a cruelty and efficiency that impressed even the Mongolians. I found myself praying deep inside that this battle would not happen.

We stayed in our clothes that night, trying to get a little sleep under a tarp next to the jeep. We had to be ready to move at a moment's notice. The artillery never stopped all night. I watched Rosa's face in the pale yellow light of the artillery flashes as she rocked back and forth.

Early the next morning Rosa and I were standing next to the radio operator when he jumped up and yelled, "They are retreating! The SS are retreating at full speed!" Ivan ran up and grabbed the mike to talk with one of the Russian commanders.

Then he turned to us. "They are pulling out. The war is over," he said.

The firing stopped almost completely. The radio was going constantly now. I heard the Russian words for "pulling out" over and over.

Everybody, even the Mongolians, were thrilled about the victory at Weismar. Ivan told the Russian unit leaders, "Tell your men that Weismar has been taken." The celebration started right away. There was no drinking, as it was daylight, but the dancing and whooping and gaiety continued all day.

My prayers were being answered. Rosa and I held each other by the jeep and swayed back and forth for a long time.

We left about three o'clock for Weismar. The fighting had been slightly south of us, so most of our sector was pretty much intact. The flat countryside was dotted with small, low buildings. Weismar was a port town, and we stayed in the outskirts in a commercial area.

Weismar itself was badly damaged. The shells had torn massive holes in the blocks of the city, and there were several places where the buildings were still burning. There were Russian military vehicles everywhere, with troops waving red flags and singing with all they had.

In the middle of the town there was a dull yellow two-story government building. A large Nazi flag was waving from the flagpole of this building, which surprised me. I thought the Russians would have torn it down by now. But there were still bursts of small arms fire going on around the city, which kept the Russian troops occupied. The looting was very good as well, and that came way before enemy flags in importance. I asked Ivan if I could go up and get the flag, and he reluctantly consented.

I had to go out on a small landing and shinny up to a second landing to get to the flagpole, but when I reeled it down a big cheer went up in the street. I held it upside down for a few minutes to more cheering and folded it up. I finally had my big souvenir.

"Cease fire! Cease fire! The war is over!" The Russian words came over the radio in a gush of yelling and turmoil. I thought for the briefest of moments that I saw Ivan smile. "It is time—time for a very big party!" Ivan boomed, and he threw up his hands.

We took over a big warehouse right in the center of the town. The war was really over now. The radio was reporting the surrender of German units all up and down the front. We figured the formal surrender would be announced the next day.

The Russians quickly organized a street celebration. They pulled two large carts together in the town square to make a stage, and it quickly filled with Russian soldiers playing concertinas. The crowd materialized in a matter of minutes. Everyone was dancing and eating and drinking vodka and schnapps. Ivan took over the stage and even brought up several of the Mongolian leaders and loudly announced that they were all going to be decorated.

Someone found two German accordion players who gladly took the stage and played as loudly as they could. They played several Polish folk songs, which was all the Russians needed to start their crossed-arm dances. It was a crazy scene. The Mongolians were playing their concertinas and dancing all over the place. Everyone was happy, even the German civilians.

Rosa and I were swept out into the dancing and held each other in a free-style dance. We hugged and drank from a bottle of schnapps and looked at each other. We could have each other now, we could have life and peace and children and food and clean beds and quiet days. We hugged and kissed and let the music and the happiness pour over us.

Rosa was bubbling over. She had been given a beautiful red

dress by one of the German women, the first dress I had seen her in, and she looked ravishing. She was the most beautiful girl at the party in a walk, and it was a real pleasure to be with her, to be graced by her light and her love. Then she sang on the stage. Manuel knew she could sing and encouraged her to join the accordion players. She sang so clearly and beautifully that the crowd became quiet and stood looking at her. I was startled to feel tears running down my face.

She had just finished a beautiful Polish song when I was lifted four feet high in the air. "Here is someone special I want to introduce to you all!" It was Ivan, completely smashed. "This is the Little Rooster here! He and I have won the war!" There was a burst of applause as Ivan reached up and picked Rosa off the stage and swirled out on the dance floor. The crowd opened up for them, and they spun and danced in huge circles. "I must now give the Little Rooster his lovely hen!" Ivan laughed and reeled out into the crowd, ricocheting between groups of his officers, who patted him on the back so hard he stumbled forward.

LATE THAT night, the radio operator told me the British Second Army was only about three miles away, and that they were reinforced by some Canadian paratroopers. I was worried about the regular Red Army units that were showing up in Weismar. Ivan had told me that he was supposed to have sent any POWs back into Russia, but he had heard that this was not so good for American POWs.

I decided that I wanted to get to the British lines right away. I was afraid of being picked up by Russian Army units and sent to another camp somewhere. I just couldn't do that. Rosa and I had talked about this several times, and when I heard that we were going to stay in Weismar, I figured it was time to make my move.

Manuel agreed, and we quietly started getting ready to go.

Stalin wagged his tail while he watched me pack up my little satchel. There wasn't much I could do. Taking a beautiful young Polish woman and a Polish soldier across no-man's-land was one thing, but a dog could bark at the wrong time and make some real trouble. I knew I could never get him much farther than England anyway, if I got him that far. I took him out for a little walk and tried to figure out what to do with him. He knew something was up. That dog was the smartest dog I've ever seen. He knew when the weariness came for me, and he knew when Rosa was hurting. I hated to leave him, but I knew I didn't want to end up in any more stinking, muddy camps.

I saw an old woman sitting on a stoop just rocking back and forth. She was all alone. Stalin ran up to her and licked her face and hopped around her little yard, and she began smiling with the few teeth she had. *"Gut, gut,"* she said. I motioned to her that she could have the little dog, and she started crying. *"Gut, gut."* Stalin was in her lap when I left, wagging his tail and licking her face. I walked away quickly and didn't look back.

I didn't want to tell Ivan of my plans, because I wasn't sure how he would react. But I did want to thank him. I found him and told him how much he had helped Rosa and me, but he was knee-walking drunk. I patted his shoulder and squeezed his huge hand. He was holding a small green canvas bag in his hand. He finally looked at me and opened the bag in a tearing motion, dumping the contents out on the table. There were about two hundred SS lapel insignias in the bag, which he carefully arranged in little rows. "These SS, these SS did not get away," he said. Then he passed out.

THE THREE of us started walking at first light. The refugees struggled past us in an endless stream, the little iron wheels on the carts squeaking loudly in the crisp dawn air. There were old people, children, and women with bright scarves and big hips walking in worn-out Wehrmacht boots. They were tired, hungry, and dusty, but they were alive and they were headed home, and so were we.

The checkpoint was manned by Russian troops with clean, pressed uniforms. I hadn't seen a pressed shirt for so long I stared at them. Manuel walked up to the officer in charge and told him that I was an American and we needed to get to the British lines. He told Manuel that the British paratroops were about two miles away, but there were pockets of resistance and lots of mines and booby traps.

We avoided the areas with trees and brush and tried to stay in the open. We heard some voices in the distance and jumped into a large ravine. Finally, a voice rang out. "I say, who goes there!"

English! My heart leaped a thousand feet into the air. "I'm an American flyer, and I have people with me who have escaped from the Germans!" I hollered as loud as I could.

"Where are you from?"

"Texas," I yelled. "Texas!"

"Step out and be recognized!"

We stood up and walked over to two British soldiers who lowered their Sten guns and greeted us.

"How was the Nazi hospitality?" they asked.

"Marvelous, the food especially," I said. They gave us some chocolate and some real American cigarettes. I don't think a cigarette ever tasted so good. They put us in a jeep and drove us to a group of tents at a road intersection about three miles west of Weismar.

The British major looked at me very oddly while he twirled his gray mustache. "What do you mean you have a problem? You've just been freed."

"I've got a girl with me, and I'm trying to get her back to the U.S. with me, but I have to get her to Paris to the Polish Consul first." I tried to sound like it was no big deal.

"A girl! With you, here, in this bloody combat zone? You Americans! You're all such tomcats after the ladies, war or no war! Now I've truly seen it all. Hmmm. . . . We'll see what we can do about the girl, but you've got a real problem now, mate," he said, in a sudden note of seriousness.

My heart sank.

"Delousing," the major said. "You'll all have to go through. No exceptions. Sorry about that."

Rosa was waiting nervously, wondering what was going to happen to us. "It's okay, Rosa, we're going to Paris," I said. The major hadn't really said he was going to let her go, but I was hopeful. We soldiered through the powder delousing and took hot showers. They gave us some clean clothes, and Rosa got a British uniform that fit fairly well. Manuel looked great. He was much happier than I had seen him in a long time.

When we finished, it was time to see the major again.

"Can they be small and not seen?" The major looked right at me.

"Yes sir, they can be very small," I said.

"All right then, I'll make out a manifest for you and your invisible friends here, and you'll fly tomorrow to Le Havre. We've set up a center there for the POWs, and they'll set you right there. Cheerio."

Rosa was ecstatic. We were going to Paris. Paris! She was so thrilled she kept turning in little circles, holding her hands tightly to her chest.

■ ■ ■

THE AIRFIELD outside of Hamburg had been a Luftwaffe base and was surrounded by barbed wire that had been torn out in big sections. There were a few pieces of German fighters sitting on the grass next to the strip. I hopped over the short fence and walked over to the forward section of a burned-out FW-190. It was a very small plane, even up close. I noticed how much wear there was on the rudder pedals and the throttle handles.

The British loadmaster looked kind of rough, but I noticed he made jokes with everyone. He was responsible for loading the planes that were warming up on the strip. I waited for a lull in the activity and said quietly, "I spoke with the major yesterday, and he said that if these two Poles were small we might get them on this plane."

"I think I can handle that," he said, looking at Rosa, who smiled at him. Rosa was a knockout. She had found some lipstick and rouge, and everyone thought she was a USO singer. "Yeah, airman, we can work that right in," he said, looking at me. "War is hell, huh?"

"Awful," I said. "Just awful."

Rosa, Manuel, and I took off from Hamburg at about nine o'clock the next morning on a C-47 that rattled like an old Ford. I hadn't been in the air for so long I forgot the thrill of it. The memories flooded back to me in a rush. Rosa was timidly looking out of the small window, and she seemed a little frightened at the noise and vibration. This was her first flight. "Hold my hand, Tommy. This is exciting," Rosa said quietly, trying to remain low-key.

Hearing the British voices and hearing those big Pratt and Whitney engines on the C-47 was like music to me. When you haven't heard your own language for months at a time, it feels like walking through the door of your own home after a long trip.

The British were great to us. They wanted to know all about the Russians and about how I was shot down. The questions never stopped.

"They're a bloody tough bunch, the Russkies, aren't they? I don't suppose they minded their manners much with the Jerries, did they? Genghis Khan's boys, as well? Bet they bloody well scared the Jerries stiff! Do they really have women in the Russian army? Do they shoot guns as well?" I did my best to answer, but it all seemed like a blur. I was just glad to be alive and glad my friends had lived. It was on that flight to Le Havre that we all finally, truly, knew what life was worth. We felt suddenly rich.

TWELVE

HOMEWARD BOUND

"WE'RE REALLY free now, Rosa. We're going to make it," I whispered to Rosa as the plane lined up to land on the runway at Le Havre. She looked at me, smiled, and closed her eyes tight.

It was all over. No more war, no more missions, no more death and punishment. I could just see Rosa in Texas, charming all the locals with her beauty and good nature. I knew we would have a rough time with the official part, but after what we had been through, dealing with red tape and bureaucrats didn't seem too tough. Still, I was worried. Would they send her back? What would I have to do to keep Rosa with me?

Camp Lucky Strike was another spelling of mayhem. The POWs were coming in on trucks, planes, cars, and bicycles. No one knew what the hell was going on. There were signs everywhere telling us where to eat and where to find all the services—medical help, paymaster, etc.—but everyone seemed very confused. "How do I get back to my unit? Where's my unit? Where's the food? How can I get a telegram out?" Men would bump into each other and trade what little information they had.

The Army had really put a lot of effort into the camp. There was a big medical tent with twenty or thirty doctors checking the men as they came in. Many of the POWs were in bad shape. Some of them were limping, some were on crutches, and many were walking skeletons, but every single one of those shattered men had a lopsided grin on his face. It was over, and we had won—we had lived.

The receiving officer at Le Havre looked like a nice guy. I quickly heard that POWs were supposed to get some special treatment. I had my fingers crossed. "I've got a problem here. I have two Polish nationals with me, and I need to get them to the Polish Consul in Paris," I told him. He looked at Rosa and Manuel incredulously, smiled, and directed me to the major's office.

Rosa and Manuel waited in an outer office while I went in to talk to the major. I was optimistic. If there was ever a time in history when the entire world was in a good mood, it was those days right after the war.

I told the major our story as quickly as I could. I told him that I had helped liberate Rosa from a slave labor camp and she had saved my life by killing German snipers. I quickly told him how Manuel had helped me escape from the death camp at Küstrin. The word Küstrin caused him to look straight at me, and he held up his finger for a minute to look something up in a thick file.

"Did you say Küstrin, airman?"

"Yes, sir, I was in a big military death camp in Küstrin, the worst hellhole you could imagine. Thousands and thousands of Russian and Polish prisoners," I said, hoping for a little additional sympathy.

He started to say something, then stopped.

"We're completely jammed up now, sergeant," he said. "We're sending everyone home by ship now, and there's going to be about a five-day wait here, so I'll give you a three-day pass, and you can sign here for some of your back pay. You can take your friends into Paris and get them settled. How does that sound? I'll call the motor pool and get you some transportation."

I stood up and shook his hand. "Three days in Paris sounds mighty good right about now, sir!"

Rosa was walking in tight little circles when I got back. She looked at me with a scared look in her eyes. "Well?" she and Manuel said at the same time.

I held up the pass and a fistful of fresh francs. "We're off to Paris! I've got a three-day pass and plenty of money!"

Rosa's eyes widened, and she hugged me. I spun her around.

"The francs, they are the same as before the war," Manuel said, looking intently at the crisp bills.

"As long as they spend, I don't care what they look like," I said.

"I could help you very much with that," Rosa said, laughing. "I could help the poor American airman with spending this lovely money very, very much!"

We all leaped into the air at the same time. Everything was going to be better than fine, it was going to be great. We were like three little kids who had won a big spelling bee, jumping up and down. We passed the funny-looking bills around and tried to remember how money worked.

About an hour later, our transportation arrived. We rode in a big, cushy American car into Paris. It was a GI car with a big white star on the side. It was so quiet and comfortable after the weeks in the jeep, it seemed like the car was riding on a cloud. "This is Eisenhower's car, but they wanted me to have it," I said, kidding Rosa.

"The very car of Eisenhower is our car?" she said, wide-eyed again.

"Yes, Tommy here knows Ike well, and just one word from Tommy and we have the General's car," Manuel chimed in.

"Tommy, you beast. This is not possible! The very car of Eisenhower!" Rosa said.

The driver wanted to know all about Rosa and Manuel and the Russians. I found to my surprise that I didn't want to talk about it. I didn't want to wake up from this dream, riding in this big, wonderful car with my friends who were alive.

Manuel was looking out of the car window, lost in thought. He knew that he had to begin the task of finding out what had happened to his family. These things just come first. He tried to be happy and enjoy our day, but he was already on his way back to Poland.

I tried for a minute to think about what it would be like if my entire family in Texas had been trucked off to a place like Küstrin. I couldn't do much until I had gone home.

Rosa was the same. She couldn't really let go. Her family was out there somewhere, maybe alive, maybe dead. I watched her looking out of the window and knew what she must be thinking: *What happened to my sister, my father, and my mother?*

The road flashed past. There were even normal cars with normal people in them, on normal errands, with odd little things sticking out all over. Pieces of lumber, flowers, and even children. We saw a car with several children and a family, and my grip on reality started to slip again. Somehow it seemed out of place, and I half expected to see a Russian military truck covered with mud, smoking badly, full of bleary-eyed soldiers with rifles. I expected to see burning tanks and bloated horses lying on the roadside.

The driver stopped on the outskirts of Paris at the Polish embassy. Manuel went in by himself and came back shortly.

"There is a group leaving for Poland this afternoon. I can go. I can go to home!" he said.

Rosa seemed startled, but she was happy for him. We said our goodbyes with hugs, tears, and promises to meet up again. I looked at Manuel for several moments. This man had saved my life. We had been through hell together. He was a good man and a good friend. I knew I would miss him, and I regretted not spending more time in the last weeks talking with him.

I squeezed his hand, and Rosa touched him on the shoulder. He ran up the stairs two at a time and was gone.

ABOUT AN hour later, we jumped out of the car in the Montmartre area. The driver pointed out a motor pool pickup area and told me I could get a ride back to Lucky Strike there around noon each day.

Paris was full. Full of living, happy people. There were people everywhere. The sun was out, and people were smiling and talking rapidly and laughing. The cabs were furiously picking up and dropping off passengers.

Rosa was marvelous. She glowed in her red dress. She inhaled everything about Paris. We looked at people and clothes, and we darted into every shop we passed. It was wonderful because there was no war damage, no ugly pockmarks, no gaping holes in buildings. It was still the City of Light—the most beautiful city on earth. There were flowers everywhere—and noise, the delightful noise of peace. People were yelling, cars were honking brightly, children were laughing, waiters were taking orders at sidewalk cafes. It was like oxygen to us. Every sound, every sight of normal life in peacetime seemed infinitely precious.

In the window of a small, bustling cafe we saw a handwritten note. The notice said there was a small cottage for rent a few blocks away. We asked for directions and went looking for the cottage.

The cottage was small and completely covered with ivy. Rosa gently knocked, and a lovely middle-aged woman came to the door. She was tall, with a very distinguished face and soft blue eyes. She was dressed very neatly, with a white blouse and a light blue blazer jacket. She spoke very good English and took an immediate liking to Rosa. Rosa spoke some French, and they started chatting right away. I was finally able to tell the woman that Rosa had been in a German camp in Poland and that I had helped liberate her.

"You have saved this beautiful creature from *le Boche*. Then you are a grand hero! *Viva Monsieur Hero!*" she said, clapping her hands and kissing me on each cheek. I felt a little stupid. "Come with me. I have just the room for you sweethearts," she said, then led us to a bedroom in the back of the house. The room was large, bright, and beautiful. When her husband was alive, it had been their bedroom. Her name was Annette. Her husband had been in the resistance during the war and had not survived. This room had known a lot of happiness.

"My dear, is that all you have for clothes?" Annette looked carefully at Rosa. "I'll take you shopping in the Montmartre. I know just the places. The brave airman will give you plenty of money, and we will go." Rosa's eyes lit up like a Christmas tree. I reached into my pocket and grabbed a big wad of francs and put them in her hand. Rosa looked at me for a long moment, until I reached into the other pocket and gave her the rest.

Rosa and Annette began working on a list of shops with a stub of a pencil and some lavender paper. I finally realized I was just in the way and tried to disappear to get a little rest.

"But you must come, Tommy. You must! I must know what you think." I suspected that my opinion was not going to be a huge part of the equation, but I wanted to go, to see Rosa in some new clothes.

We hurried off to the Montmartre, where Annette made a

beeline to one particular shop. The shop was operated by two older ladies who surrounded Rosa with affectionate clucking. They held up one beautiful dress that seemed a little small to me.

Holding her ample breasts, Rosa said, "But these won't fit in there!"

The old women screamed with laughter.

They rushed over with dress after dress, and Rosa would dive into a changing room and emerge in a blur of little adjustments. They fluttered around her and adjusted each dress, pulling here and there. Finally Rosa would say, "Tommy! What do you think?" This being my first run as a boyfriend in a dress shop, I actually thought she was waiting for my opinion. I began to tell her that I thought the skirt was a little too long when she scurried off to look at another dress. "I'm glad you like it, Tommy. So do I!" she said as she dived into the changing room again. We finally left the shop with a dress.

We tore through several more wonderful shops with Annette, and when I couldn't carry any more parcels, we headed back to the cottage.

There was fruit for sale on the street. Lovely bright oranges from Tunisia, and crisp red apples from Italy. I thought about the German girl on the train who had given me—a filthy enemy POW—an orange. It seemed like years and years ago. We clumsily bit into the fruit and let the juice drip down our faces. Flowers were everywhere. It seemed like everyone wanted flowers, everyone wanted color and fragrance again. I stumbled along with the brightly wrapped packages, trying not to drop the flowers and trying to eat my orange and watching Rosa's hips sway under her red dress as she and Annette bustled along at top speed.

Dinner was wonderful. Annette cooked us a lovely dinner of cognac beef and trimmings. We toasted the great victory of D-Day with brandy. Rosa shimmered in a new daffodil yellow dress—the one I didn't pick. Annette had loaned her some makeup. She was suddenly not just vivacious, but strikingly beautiful. Her hair was beginning to grow out a little, and her hazel eyes twinkled with every word.

Annette left us after the third round of brandy with a wink. In the bedroom, we melted into one another in wave after wave of warmth and love. Afterward, we fell into a deep sleep.

WHEN I realized it was morning and I hadn't been awakened by nightmares or artillery blasts or rifle fire, I couldn't quite believe it. To sleep an entire night without waking seemed so strange. I felt like I could sleep for months. For the first time, I realized the depth of the weariness in me. My mind wanted hundreds and hundreds of days of rest and peace.

There was a knock at the door, and Annette brought in a small tray with coffee and brandy. I held each small sip in my mouth until it was completely absorbed. The brandy made me feel warm right away. We drank another toast to the end of the war, and Annette slyly asked us how well we'd slept. "We didn't have much sleeping," Rosa said, yawning. Annette laughed and shot me a knowing glance.

Annette told us about her husband, who was betrayed by a collaborator and shot. She felt that all the collaborators should be shot, but there were too many of them. "They were everywhere, all over the country," she said, with a stridency that was out of character for her. "Tell me about yourself and your experiences with the Nazis," she said to Rosa.

Rosa told her how they came to her school and took her and her sister away to several harsh labor camps. She spoke very quickly, talking in a near whisper. Her eyes became glassy, and she halted several times. It was the first time she had really told anyone else besides me, and it was clearly a painful experience for her.

Annette looked at the crude tattoo on Rosa's left breast and began to cry. "At least they could have done a better job," she said after a long pause. I looked at the tattoo with her, and the revulsion began to well up inside me again. It was so jagged and sloppily done. The red spilled outside of the dark blue lines, and the short stem was crooked. I imagined what it must have felt like, to be owned by a Nazi, fondled and abused and threatened for months. Suddenly the room began to spin, and I felt nauseous. I saw the tattoos on the lampshades at Damgarten, and that strange chemical smell came back to me.

The deep trust Rosa had in Annette not only made it bearable for her to talk about the camp, but also gave Rosa her first chance to hear herself talking about it to another woman. It poured out, first in halting sentences, then in a rush of blurted words that changed in pitch until she had to stop because she was shaking with anger. She buried her head in my shoulder and sobbed quietly. Annette looked out the window and cried softly, too.

Later, we went for a long walk. We walked for the entire morning with a speed that told me Rosa was walking away the bad feelings. We found a lovely little restaurant for lunch and ate outdoors on the sidewalk. The sun poured down, and we exulted in every taste, every bite of the food, and every minute of sunshine.

As I dissolved two little brown sugar cubes in my mouth, I remembered the feeling of absorbing the atoms of the dandelion soup in Stalag Luft 4. I looked down at our hands in the sun and thanked God for every second of the life I was living, and I thanked Him that Rosa was living, too.

When we returned, Annette carefully cut and styled Rosa's

hair. She clucked her disapproval of the way we had cut her hair. "My goodness, these people who cut your hair! They were savages. Look at this. It is like a hedge!" Rosa smiled quietly. When she was done, Rosa was absolutely striking. They asked me what I thought about the hairstyle, then rushed into the other room to pick out a dress while I worked on my answer. They picked the daffodil yellow dress per my expert recommendation.

I borrowed one of Annette's husband's shirts, and we went out to enjoy the famous Montmartre night life. All the cafes and bistros were overflowing. People were standing in large groups at the entrances to the clubs and restaurants with drinks, laughing and talking loudly.

The good food and drink had just begun to arrive back in Paris. We drifted from place to place, watching people and enjoying snacks and champagne.

By ten we were ready for a full meal. We drifted into a large bistro with a piano and an accordion player. Rosa suddenly leaped up into the air. "I know that song! It's a Polish song. They must be Polish," she said, and she rushed up to the musicians. They jabbered away in Polish and threw up their hands and hugged her excitedly. They shared some little joke and laughed so loud it was embarrassing. Then the piano player tried out a few bars of a song, and the accordion player joined in, and suddenly Rosa squealed and did several little hops. Her eyes were glittering with joy as the fond memories of the song and her home washed over her.

She began to sing, and the entire restaurant became dead quiet. Her voice was like a pure golden light from another world, filled with boundless love and empathy. She soared away, and everyone in that bistro flew with her. People began to cry as she sang the sad parts, and tears flowed freely down our heavily lined faces. We shouted when the song reached a crescendo, then bowed our heads for long moments when the music ended. I thought my heart would beat its way out of my chest with pride and love when I looked at her.

Rosa had a voice like an angel, soft and smooth, but strong and very powerful. She could have sung anywhere in the world. She was better than the singers I'd heard on the radio before the war at the Laguna Hotel. Everyone was amazed and wanted to know who this girl was. Was she famous? Where did she come from? She will record right away, won't she? The people in the bistro asked me these questions all night, as Rosa's voice filled the room.

The night flew by. By midnight Rosa was exhausted. The thunderous applause brought her back, over and over, but she finally looked weak and pale, and she stepped down. The waiter rushed over with a magnum of champagne and the club owner right behind him.

"Your evening is on us! Here, take this champagne with you," he said, as he grabbed our check. "She will return tomorrow night? Yes? Yes?" he shouted in my ear.

Tomorrow night was a hundred years away. "Yes, yes, we'll be back tomorrow night," I shouted, suddenly realizing that tomorrow night was our last night in Paris. We slowly strolled back to the cottage, carrying the big bottle. Rosa was hoarse and dripping with sweat. She held me tightly and laid her head on my chest as we walked.

We fell into a deep sleep, holding each other all night. We woke up in exactly the same position we'd fallen asleep in. I looked at her face for a long time in the weak light that peeked around the window shade. I saw years and years of fun and wonderful times. I saw her with children, I saw her cooking and setting a dazzling table. I saw her running through the hills of Texas and awkwardly riding a horse. I thought about all the wonderful things we could do: build a house, raise a family, grow old to-gether. With a woman like Rosa, life would be one long, sunny day.

As we woke up, we took time for every one of the little moves that are part of awakening. She stroked my back for a long time and hummed a little song. We talked a little, but didn't really say much. We just talked to hear our voices and to draw in the air around us.

When we finally got dressed, we helped Annette cut flowers in the garden, then struggled to find another vase. The house was full of flowers, light, and love.

The thought that fear and despair might come again kept nag-ging me, and finally angered me. I just wanted to be left alone with this woman. Left alone to live.

We took a boat ride on the Seine in the early afternoon. Everyone on the boat was boisterous and laughing and kissing in the bright sunshine. We must have stood out because we were so quiet.

I knew it was coming.

I knew she had made up her mind to go back, to find her fam-ily and help them if they were still alive. I admired her for this, but I couldn't help trying to talk her out of it, hoping she would come back to Texas with me and go to Poland later. But Rosa loved her family, and she was the youngest child. There wasn't much I could do. The Air Corps would never allow me to go to Poland with her. There was already nervous talk about what the Russians were going to do with their half of Europe.

We spent a quiet night in the cottage. Every move seemed to remind us that she would be leaving. Talk was too painful. We just held each other and slept in fits of touching and stillness. The world seemed big again—and dangerous.

After a while, the frustration knotted my stomach and welled up inside me until I had to go outside. I missed Stalin then. He would always know when the confusion and the weariness came for me, and he would lick my face. I sat in the garden and cried. I didn't want to lose her. The tears dropped on the brick path in big dark circles.

The next day was a blur. I could hardly pay attention to the little details of getting dressed, helping Rosa with her packing, and finding our way to the Polish Consulate.

The secretary at the Polish Consulate was a small, balding man who squared himself up by moving his shoulders from side to side before he began talking. He seemed genuinely interested in our problems. He had seen the same look on many faces before, the longing that only a trip home would cure. He told us that a group of refugees would be leaving early the next afternoon, and Rosa could go if she wanted. Rosa signed the list, and we left. Seeing her sign the long book was like watching something precious drop out of my hand.

We drifted into a small cafe featuring a guitar player. Rosa sang some beautiful Polish songs with him, but they seemed to be sad ballads, and she cried during the last one. I hardly heard her sing or noticed her crying. I felt so far away. I couldn't look at her any longer. I didn't have the strength.

We walked slowly back to Annette's, holding each other and trying to fight the emotions welling up inside us. We lay awake all night, trying to talk, but not really succeeding. Finally, we just held hands, wondering what the great forces swirling around us would do.

Annette had cooked us a nice breakfast with toasted baguettes. The moments ticked by. We slowly walked back to the room and talked. I gave her every address I had—my aunt's in Waco, everything I could think of. She said she'd write me right away and tell me what she'd found in Poland. I planned to get out of the service and travel back to Paris, then Poland, to get her. She said she would send an address as soon as she could. We agreed to use the American embassy in Warsaw as a last resort.

Annette came in to tell us it was time to go, and she broke down and cried with Rosa. They held each other, sobbing. I was devastated. She was really going to go. I hoped for a second that Annette would talk her out of going, but she seemed to understand that Rosa had to go home.

We walked past the busy shops in a daze. I found myself looking in one shop window for a long time until I realized that it was a jewelry shop. We walked in and looked at the small collection of rings. The jeweler could tell we were sad. He was an old man who had been a jeweler his entire life. We picked out two matching gold rings, and two gold chains to hang them around our necks. We planned to use them as wedding rings, and we didn't want to wear them until we were married. I slipped her ring over her head and she slipped my ring over my head. We looked at each other and fell together in a kiss. We stood there in that shop for what seemed like hours in that kiss. I kissed her ring, and she kissed mine. In that moment our souls were bound together forever.

The walk to the Polish Consulate passed quickly, even though our steps were short. I wanted to stop, to delay, to plead, to grab her and tell her that she couldn't go, that it was still dangerous now, that I was not letting her go, but I couldn't. I tried to realize what it must be like to have your entire family swept away in a dark cloud. I thought of the sobbing groups of people in Clyde after the tornado, and I remembered how their first instinct was to find their families.

The big yellow building stood in front of us. It was time. She started up the steps, then turned and threw herself into my arms and cried so loudly everyone around us turned away. "I can't go. I can't leave you. I can't, I can't!" she sobbed. I could barely hold her, she was shaking so much.

She wasn't going. *We can turn around now. We can go now!* I held her as tight as I could and picked her up off the step, then slowly rocked her back and forth. Her face was white as a sheet, but when she looked up at me, I could tell she was already far away.

Then I walked with her up the stairs and into the office. The consul was in a great hurry. He told us the train was leaving and that Rosa would just make it. The train was to go through Frankfurt an der Oder and on to Warsaw. I held her one last time and kissed her deeply. I told her that I would always pray for her safety, then with a deep breath and all the strength I had in my body, I turned and walked away.

At the cottage I burst out crying. Later, I couldn't seem to get into the truck at the pick-up point. The guys finally dragged me in, thinking I was drunk. The trip back to Camp Lucky Strike was a blur.

THIRTEEN

THE WEARINESS

"THE MAJOR wants to see you right away!" The sergeant seemed to be shouting, but he was talking in a normal tone. I was afraid I had violated my pass. I didn't want any trouble. I just wanted to go home. I noticed that I was the only one around who was not exuberant. I felt so weak I could hardly walk. I felt lost, confused, and alone.

The major was very busy and asked me to sit down. He didn't seem angry, which was a relief. "There are some people here who need to talk to you, Sergeant," he said. I was puzzled. The door opened and three men wearing white shirts and slacks with Red Cross emblems came in. "Sergeant, these are members of the International Red Cross. They've read your report about which camps you were in, and our authorities have cut orders for you to go back to the camp at Küstrin."

"What?" I gasped.

"Shortly after your escape, there was a mass breakout by the prisoners in Küstrin. The Germans killed the entire camp population. Over thirteen thousand men. We think about eight hundred escaped. We have reports that there were some Americans in this camp, and you have orders to go to this camp with the Red Cross and see if you can identify anyone," he said curtly.

"I never saw any other Americans there. I can't help at all. I can't, I just can't," I pleaded. But the orders were cut, and the Red Cross men were waiting.

"You'll leave at 0800 hours tomorrow with these men, Sergeant. You're the only American we have who was in that camp, and we owe it to the families of our men who were held there to do all we can to identify them. That is all."

Küstrin. I never wanted to see that hellhole again in my life, ever. I worried now, really worried that there wasn't much left. The weariness came suddenly, and my knees felt weak. The room blurred, and my words didn't make it out of my throat. I just shook my head and stared at the floor.

WE LEFT early the next day. The weather had closed in, and there were banks of thunderclouds hanging in the western sky. We flew to Frankfurt, to Leipzig, and then to Frankfurt an der Oder. It seemed strange to me, to have nothing to do in a plane. I watched the pilots joking and eating sandwiches. I half expected an Me-109 to come tearing out of the clouds and start firing, but we just droned on.

The Red Cross men had been working with POWs for a while, and they seemed to understand I didn't have much to say. They were weary, too. They had been working in death camps for several months, and I sensed that they were close to the limit as well.

We landed at Frankfurt in a cold drizzle. The wind still had that vicious sharp edge from the Baltic. A couple of jeeps and a big Chevrolet pulled up, but they were waiting for someone else.

After about an hour, a large American army truck pulled up. I don't think the Red Cross men noticed how much it affected me. I had to work to fight the panic. When I looked out of the back of the truck and saw the wet roads, the wind blowing over the grass, I could hear the Polish prisoners talking. I could see the faces of the guards at Küstrin, their pink scars and the twitching in their eyes. The tricks your mind can play. . . . *What if time had slipped and somehow I wasn't really where I was, when I was there? What if it had all been a dream, and I had never really left Küstrin?*

I was rubbing my forehead when the truck stopped. The driver dropped the tailgate and everyone got out. "This won't take long, Sergeant, then you'll be on your way home," a Red Cross man said softly.

I took a deep breath before I looked at the camp. I pulled myself up and rolled my head around, trying to loosen up my neck. The tension didn't go away, it just receded a little from time to time. The rain was starting to run down the back of my neck as I turned and looked at the camp.

At first I thought they had taken the clothes from the prisoners and spread them out in the yard. Thousands of them. Shirts and pants and the heavy wool trench coats of the Polish and Russian soldiers. By the wire the clothes were piled up about four feet high. There were pieces of cloth fluttering in the cold wind all along the wire, and the water was standing in big puddles between the piles of clothing.

"This won't take long, Sergeant, this won't take long." The Red Cross man handed me a cotton surgical mask. The big wooden gates had been run over by tank treads and lay on each side of the entrance. The main administration building had been partially burned, and all the windows had been smashed out. I looked in as we walked by. There were two big gray rats sitting in the middle of the big room where prisoners were processed. They just looked right at me.

The only sound was the raindrops plopping into the puddles on the gray linoleum floor. I stood there for a few minutes trying to place another sound. It was so faint I could hardly hear it, but I had heard it before. Finally, the wind picked up, and so did the sound. It was a high-pitched keening. The relentless Baltic wind blowing through the double barbed wire fences made a maddening, forlorn sound. The song of Küstrin.

I was back.

I could still hear the guards screaming, still see the lost faces of the Russians and the Poles, still smell the raw fear and the filth and the death. The smell reached me now, slowly closing around me like a greasy fog. The smell of death was everywhere, in every fencepost, in every board, in every inch of earth.

The prisoners had charged the wire en masse in their escape attempt in mid-February. The Germans had opened up with every machine gun from every tower. I had watched them hoist the old water-cooled machine guns up the towers just before Manuel and I escaped. They had four machine guns in each tower. Now I could see the shell casings piled up under the burned towers. They still shined brightly in the flat light. The rusting German ammo cans stuck up out of the grass around the towers.

I slowly walked out into the yard. Nothing had been touched since the day of that final escape. The piles of clothing were corpses. They were lying everywhere, piled up two, three, four deep. They were dark, silent shapes covered in gray and khaki overcoats and shirts. They had sunk into the mud, and the rats moved under the clothing in little jerking motions. The faces of the men were shriveled and black with jagged round holes and purple blotches. Every second of their last moments was there to see—the panic, the screaming, the gunfire, the fear, and the agony. There were thousands and thousands of black and purple faces. I leaned against a shack and tried to steady myself. I held my face up to the rain and prayed. I prayed to God for strength, strength to fight the weariness that engulfed me.

"We'd like you to look at some bodies in this barracks over here, Sergeant," the Red Cross man said softly. The bodies were laid out on the floor of one of the shacks. They all had some kind of GI clothing, a hat or a shirt but no dog tags. I started to get angry, to tell them I had never seen any Americans in Küstrin, but it was too late. I walked between the bodies and dutifully looked at each face. There were about sixty bodies in the shack.

"No, sir, I don't recognize any of these men," I said, holding on to the corner post of a bunk.

"Thank you, Sergeant. Now please come with me. There are more in the next shack. I know this is hard for you, but we are trying to do everything we can for the families of these men." I thought for a moment about the families of the dead men, how they would live out their lives wondering what had happened to their loved ones, lying awake at night, year after year, wondering. Maybe that is the cruelest anguish of war.

They took me from barrack to barrack, and I tried to remember if I had seen any of these men, but I didn't recognize any of them. Soon I was vomiting, and the smell was so overwhelming I couldn't breathe. We were wearing makeshift masks from cloth, but they didn't help much. The death began to cover my skin, it began to sink into my pores, and I felt dirty and greasy again. It soaked into my clothes and burned my nose. It got under my fingernails and into my hair.

About three o'clock, they took me out to a small group of tents in a field upwind from the camp and brought some food. I was shown to a cot in a large tent. I sat down on the cot and listened to the wind. I was starting to black out with my eyes open. I wasn't lost in thought or preoccupied, my mind just quit working for a little while. Normally it would have worried me, but the weariness was with me all the time now, and somehow it didn't matter.

I held my plate for a long time, then set it down in the mud. The rats watched me while they ate my dinner, probably happy to have something warm for a change.

The rain became a steady downpour, and the north wind picked up and got colder as it grew dark. It was blowing hard now, in long brutal gusts that bent the trees over. I lay on my cot in the tent, trying to gather some strength and trying not to think anymore. I missed Stalin. I wanted to pet him and feel his warm, sloppy tongue on my face.

"They're bringing up a bulldozer tomorrow to bury these men, Sergeant, so we'll have to have you look at about three hundred bodies in the morning." The Red Cross man held the tent flap against the wind. "Why don't you come down to the tent later and have a little whiskey?" He waited a long time for me to answer. "Sergeant! Did you hear me?"

It seemed like he was hundreds of miles away. "Yes, sir. Yes, sir," I said. The effort was excruciating. It was like trying to talk with a splitting headache.

I crawled into the GI sleeping bag and buttoned up my field jacket. The gasoline lantern didn't work, and I didn't want to be around people, so I tried to sleep. The blackout spells alternated with sudden vivid recollections of the last few months. I would see Lieutenant Bowen and our crew bowed down for prayer before takeoff, then see the face of the Devil as he dragged Rosa into the bedroom. I woke up sweating about ten o'clock when one of the truck drivers pulled the tent flap back.

"The guys down below sent this up to you, Sergeant. Might help you sleep." He set down a big glass of whiskey. I looked at it for a long time.

The weariness had slipped over me now like a wet coat. I just wanted it all to stop. I needed some time to absorb what had happened to me, but the thoughts kept coming. *What will happen to Rosa? Why did I let her go? What will it be like for me when I go home? Where is Manuel now? What happened to my crew? Did Henri and Jules live? Will I see Rosa again? Why did I let her go? How could I possibly be back at Küstrin?*

I desperately needed something to stop the thinking. The thoughts began to rush together and accelerate into a knot of panic. Somewhere deep inside me it started. Just a crazy little saying I heard somewhere.

Come one, come all, this rock shall fly, from its firm base, and so shall I . . . Come one, come all, this rock shall fly, from its firm base, and so shall I . . .

I drank the glass of whiskey in two long gulps and sat on the cot. The burning and coughing were welcome, because it was a different kind of pain.

The wind and rain built up slowly. I lay on the cot and hoped the whiskey would help me sleep, but my stomach began to turn, and I felt like throwing up.

I put on a poncho and walked outside. As cold as the wind and rain were, it felt good to be outside. I stood looking at the dark camp when the first lightning strike tore through the sky. It was very close, about a quarter of a mile away. The sharp crack was followed by a loud hiss. I walked down to the wire and looked at the camp. The Germans had put the camp at the bottom of two small hills, which ensured that the water would run into the camp and stay there.

I was thinking about trying to find the spot where Manuel and I had cut the wire when a huge lightning bolt lit up the sky. I was under one of the gun towers when it happened. The hard blue light was frozen in the air for a long moment. I looked at the sea of bodies. They were all looking at me, and they started to move. They started to get up and walk towards me. Then it was dark again, and the thunderclap exploded above me.

A new terror I had never felt before began welling up in me. I held the support of the gun tower for a long time with both hands, totally terrified. I finally opened my eyes. The bodies were still. I touched my face and asked God for help.

I tried to find some dry clothes in the tent, but my bag had been left in the mud and everything was wet. I crawled into the sleeping bag and pulled my coat around me. The whiskey had worked its way through me now, and I had terrible cramps and a pounding headache. I prayed for sleep and tried to think about Stalin, and Rosa, and the flowers in Paris.

I fell for hours into a deep, silent blackness, to a place where there was no light, no form, no sound, only the one terror. My death came from behind me and almost touched me before I knew it was there. I turned just in time to see the death. It was just a darker part of the blackness. It lunged for me, and I jumped up and ran, as fast as I could. It was right behind me. I ran and ran, feeling the cold presence of my death behind me.

Suddenly I was in the camp, inside the wire. The dead men in the camp got up slowly and came to me. "Help us. Help us get out, Tommy! Please help us!" They came past me and through me, thousands of them, talking to me as they walked by me. Alex walked right up to me and said, "Merry Christmas, Tommy.

Merry Christmas." Lauren, the young Frenchman executed in Brussels, stood right next to me, smiling. "The peaches are green, Tommy! The peaches are green! *Viva* Tommy LaMore!" He looked at me and suddenly pointed behind me.

I knew the death was close, but where? I spun around and started running. I was overwhelmed and thrown down into the cold wet mud with a sickening crunch. The terror tore through me like a jolt of electricity. The scream came from the deepest part of my soul and obliterated everything. I screamed again as the death wrestled me down and pulled me into the dark underworld of the dead. I screamed again, but no sound emerged. I fell backwards into the darkness, falling and falling and falling.

The blackness slowly gave way to a dark green. I tried to move, but the death had tied me down. I felt pain again in my body, which seemed odd for someone who was dead.

"Sergeant, as soon as you feel better, they're gonna take you to the airport. You're going home. It's okay now. It's all over, buddy. Try some of this coffee, it's pretty good. I made it myself. I'll take these off you now." The voice was soft and kind, but very far away. The rain tapped ever so quietly on the tent where I had died. I didn't know what came next, and I didn't really care. I had never died before.

The morphine wrapped me in a warm, fuzzy blanket, and I thought of nothing. I slept all that day and night without moving. Nothing happened when I woke up. On the morning of the next day, a doctor helped me dress and brought me some warm porridge. They helped me into the car that would take me to Frankfurt an der Oder. I had a wool blanket to cover my legs.

The big green Army bulldozer was just finishing a long slit trench next to the camp, and some laborers had arrived in blue work clothes to begin the work of burying the bodies. The workers had loaded two trucks with the black and purple rag-covered bodies and were taking a smoke break when we drove past. It felt good to have a blanket. It was warm and clean.

The rain began to pound on the roof of the car, and the vacuum-operated wipers barely cleared the windshield. Every minute of travel made me feel better. I wanted the driver to drive faster. I wanted him to drive a hundred miles an hour all day. I wanted to get in the fastest plane in the world and fly ten thousand miles away. I kept looking out the rear window, grateful for every foot of road behind us.

The weather worsened, with long insolent gusts of wind and drenching rain. We waited for three hours at the airport at Frankfurt an der Oder for a break in the weather so we could take off. I stayed in the car while the driver checked the flight status. He returned about three o'clock and said, "We're gonna send you back to Berlin on a train, Sergeant. You'll pick up a plane there for Le Havre. I'll drive you down there. How are you feeling?"

"Tired," I said. "I'm tired."

I didn't want to ride on a German train again, but at least it was traveling away from Küstrin. I was afraid some German would say one wrong thing, anything. One little word. I didn't want to kill a German civilian. I never wanted to kill anyone. Not until today.

THE TRAIN station at Frankfurt an der Oder was very crowded that afternoon. The Germans were subdued and very businesslike. They seemed obsessed with keeping occupied. They would turn their newspapers over and over, reading the same stories. They were embarrassed to have holes in their shoes, and they seemed to rub their hands a lot and look down. There wasn't much said between the Germans and anyone else. They were a shunned people, and each carried a world of feelings that no one wanted to hear.

I started down the long divided ramp to my train. This last ordeal was finally over. I was so exhausted I could hardly walk, but each step was a step away from Küstrin, away from the death. I could still smell the death in my clothes, but it was faint now. I turned to wave goodbye to the driver who had helped me all afternoon. He was a nice kid from Detroit. The effort to turn and wave was difficult for me, but he'd let me keep the blanket, and I wanted to thank him.

A small group of people were coming up the ramp as I turned back. I didn't want to look at anyone, but in the middle of the group I caught a glimpse of bright blonde hair. She was between two men and two women, walking toward me on the other side of the low partition. We were about fifty feet apart. For a terrifying moment I thought my mind had gone again, I thought my eyes were seeing what my mind wanted them to see, but it was her. It was Rosa.

She looked at me, and our eyes met. I stopped breathing. She looked straight at me, and her hand flew to the ring around her neck. She brought the ring to her lips and kissed it. I did the same with mine. We stood there and looked at each other for a long time, until I began to feel weak. I started to wobble, and the driver came up behind me and grabbed me. "Come on, Sergeant, you're gonna be okay now. Let's just get you on the train."

I felt dizzy. When I looked up, she was gone.

On the train I sat by the window and carefully tucked the blanket around my legs. As we pulled out of the station, I heard a sob and a choked cry on the platform.

"Tommy, Tommy. . . ."

I didn't look back. I held the blanket to my face and tried to breathe.

CODA

TOMMY LAMORE returned to the United States in June of 1945 and was hospitalized in West Palm Beach, Florida, for treatment of his broken jaw, dislocated shoulder, and severe malnutrition.

After his discharge in September of 1945, Tommy grappled with another difficult problem, a hurried wartime marriage just prior to going overseas. This marriage caused him considerable distress and ended in an acrimonious divorce in 1947, a very common outcome in the postwar years as returning GIs struggled to cope with civilian life.

Tommy made desperate attempts to reach Rosa throughout the late 1940s, but the Iron Curtain had descended rapidly, and travel to Poland for Americans was impossible. He never received a single letter from her. About 1955, he learned from a Polish friend of Manuel's who lived in South America that Rosa had joined an anticommunist guerrilla movement in Poland shortly after the war. She was hanged by the communists in 1949. The only detail he knew of her death was that she told the communists nothing in five months of interrogation.

Manuel was executed by the communists in the same year.

. . .

TOMMY EXPERIENCED a difficult readjustment to civilian life that was, sadly, quite common among war veterans. He suffered frequent nightmares, sudden anxiety attacks, and terrifying flashbacks, one of which he described.

"I was in a diner in west Texas one night in 1947. There was a big spring thunderstorm going through. I went out to my car to get something. There was a dead dog in the bushes next to the car. Just as I opened the door, a bolt of lightning lit up the sky, and I smelled the wet death smell that was Küstrin. Suddenly, the whole parking lot was filled with the dead men from that place, all slowly walking towards me, asking me to save them. I ran into a wooden fence and blacked out. The police thought I was drunk, but I had my Army Air Corps uniform in the car. In those years, things like this were not uncommon. I sat in that diner and drank coffee for two days."

TOMMY WORKED at a variety of jobs, including stints as a traveling salesman and a used car salesman. Later he entered business in Idaho, running a resort that was frequented by Ernest Hemingway. He taught himself gourmet cooking as a way to deal with his compulsion to hoard food. In his later years, he operated a series of Southwest Indian art galleries and made several important contributions to the Heard museum in Phoenix.

HE WAS able to enjoy two long-term marriages in later life and raised two children.

Tommy ultimately regained his health and ran marathons until his seventy-sixth year. He was a warmly welcomed speaker at veterans events and was able to travel back to Carvin, France, in 1995 for a reunion with Gilbert Marmuse, the French farmer who hid him from the Nazis in 1944. He also returned to Ridgewell, his B-17 base in England, after what he described as "a really long mission."

He wore the ring that he and Rosa had bought in Paris around his neck until his death, November 5, 1997, at age 78.

TOMMY'S DECORATIONS

European Campaign Medal
American Campaign Medal
American Defense Medal
The Air Medal, with two Oak Leaf Clusters
WWII Victory Medal
Purple Heart, with two Clusters